A HOUSE DIVIDED

THE AMERICAN MOMENT
Stanley I. Kutler, Consulting Editor

The Twentieth-Century American City
Jon C. Teaford

American Workers, American Unions, 1920–1985
Robert H. Zieger

A House Divided: Sectionalism and Civil War, 1848–1865
Richard H. Sewell

A House Divided

SECTIONALISM AND CIVIL WAR, 1848–1865

Richard H. Sewell

THE JOHNS HOPKINS UNIVERSITY PRESS
Baltimore and London

© 1988 The Johns Hopkins University Press
All rights reserved
Printed in the United States of America

The Johns Hopkins University Press
701 West 40th Street
Baltimore, Maryland 21211
The Johns Hopkins Press Ltd., London

LIBRARY OF CONGRESS CATALOGING-IN-PUBLICATION DATA
Sewell, Richard H.
  A house divided.

  (The American moment)
  Bibliography: p.
  Includes index.
  1. Sectionalism (United States) 2. United States
— History — 1849–1877. I. Title. II. Series.
E415.7.S525   1988   973.7   87-14305
ISBN 0-8018-3531-3
       0-8018-3532-1 (pbk.)

∞

*The paper used in this publication meets the minimum
requirements of American National Standard for Information
Sciences — Permanence of Paper for Printed Library Materials,
ANSI Z39.48-1984.*

For Alan, Deborah, and Rebecca

Contents

Editor's Foreword

The Civil War and Reconstruction era is the "dark and bloody ground" of American history. It often is said that American historians have spilled more ink on the subject than the blood lost by contemporaries. And still, the period compels our attention as perhaps no other in our history. The polarization over political, economic, and moral issues was the most extreme in our history, and resulted in the extreme consequence of fratricidal war. The Civil War truly is unique for it reflects the nation's most notable constitutional failure, a failure that stemmed from a system rendered morally deficient and politically paralyzed by slavery. But it also uniquely offered the nation an opportunity to rededicate itself to the ideals that Abraham Lincoln so eloquently described in the Gettysburg Address and to truly "a more perfect union." The period is a pivotal one, linking and separating the America that had emerged from its colonial and revolutionary past, and the one that reflected the realities of a continental nation, with vast new stocks of people, vital and alive with economic and industrial energy. To understand modern America requires an understanding of the trauma and drama that freed the nation from the shackles of its past.

Richard Sewell has eloquently described and analyzed the issues and emotions that characterized the conflict and division of the nineteenth century. His synthesis of familiar events is fresh, imaginative, and sensitive to their effect and impact on the lives of ordinary Americans. He has tracked the profound political, social, and economic forces that swirled so divergently, and sometimes so aimlessly, in American life. He has done so keenly aware of both the political and moral imperatives that dominated the period. Sewell's narrative and analysis of the Civil War era thus gives us an enhanced understanding of that special moment that re-forged and renewed the American sense of nation.

THE AMERICAN MOMENT is designed to offer a series of narrative and analytical discussions on a variety of topics in American history. Books in the series are both topical and chronological. Some volumes survey familiar subjects—such as Puritanism, the American Revolution, the Civil War, the New Deal, and the Cold War—and blend necessary factual background with thoughtful, provocative interpretations. Other volumes—such as those on women and reform movements, urban affairs, ethnicity, sports, and popular culture—chart new or less familiar terrain. All provide narrative and interpretation to open significant new dimensions and perspectives on the American past.

Stanley I. Kutler

UNIVERSITY OF WISCONSIN
MADISON, WISCONSIN

Preface and Acknowledgments

This short history of what Abraham Lincoln called the American Union's "fiery trial" seeks to refocus attention on slavery as the taproot of sectional discord and civil war. It represents, that is, a modest challenge to those historians who see slavery as a largely artificial or symbolic issue and who emphasize instead the role of such "ethno-cultural" concerns as temperance and nativism in shaping public events at mid-century. Of course, slavery was not the only item on the political agenda in the troubled 1850s, but it was, I think, the most important. The North and South may not have *been* distinct cultures, but by mid-century each section *thought* of itself as possessing a distinct and superior way of life, one shaped most profoundly by the absence or presence of human bondage. The debate over slavery's right to expand not only aroused feelings of jealousy, honor, and regional pride, but raised fundamental questions about the future direction of American society. Unable to find common ground with such vital issues at stake, the Union broke asunder.

The course of the war that followed, I believe, was also powerfully influenced by Northern and Southern attitudes toward slavery. While the Union government came rapidly to accept emancipation as an effective war measure and by 1862 was enlisting former slaves in its armies, the Confederacy confronted both subtle subversion from its black labor force and self-serving obstruction from many slaveowners. So, too, growing complaints among slaveless Southern whites that they were being asked to carry a disproportionate share of the war's burden, that a "rich man's war" had become "a poor man's fight," sapped morale and contributed to Confederate defeat.

My greatest debt in the writing of this book goes to my good friend, esteemed colleague, and solicitous editor, Stanley I. Kutler. It was his idea that I undertake this project — seeing much sooner than I the rewards of doing so — and it was his unfailing encouragement and wise counsel that kept me cheerfully at my task. Both he and Bertram Wyatt-Brown gave my entire manuscript a careful reading and offered numerous helpful suggestions for its improvement. I sensibly accepted most of their advice, but have rejected enough of it to let them off the hook. For the mistakes and shortcomings that remain, I accept all blame.

I am also deeply grateful to a whole generation of students at the University of Wisconsin–Madison for sustaining my interest in the Civil War and for helping me to think clearly about it; to Onno Brouwer, David DiBiase, and the staff of the University's Cartography Laboratory for preparing the maps in this book; and to Karen Delwiche who skillfully punched the first draft of my manuscript into her word processor and taught me to enter revisions on my own. A generous grant from the Research Committee of the University of Wisconsin Graduate School gave me time in which to think and write.

Adrienne Mayor of The Johns Hopkins University Press, a superb copyeditor who combed many a burr from my final draft, has earned both my gratitude and respect.

As always, family and friends have bolstered and nurtured me throughout this enterprise. My thanks to them all, especially to my wife Natalie and the three free spirits to whom this book is dedicated.

A HOUSE DIVIDED

The American People at Mid-Century

Americans in 1848 stood poised between two worlds—the placid, basically agrarian world of the early republic and the urban, industrial, increasingly atomistic world of modern America. Behind them, though well within memory, lay the heroic struggle for independence, the elaboration and legitimization of republican institutions (including political parties), the first stirrings of industrial capitalism, breathtaking territorial expansion, and the development of a vigorous sense of American nationalism tested—at times threatened—by countercurrents of sectionalism. Ahead lay the cataclysmic upheaval of civil war, emancipation of a long-enslaved race, rapid urban and industrial development, and the slow but steady emergence of the United States as a world power. It was a time of bewilderment and anxiety, but also of confidence, pride, and great expectations.

I

In many ways, the most modern element in American life at mid-century was politics. In structure and style, the political system of 1848 more closely resembled that of our own day than that of the Founding Fathers. For at least a decade Whigs and Democrats had competed on nearly equal terms in all parts of the nation. Only recently had sectional identification become more important than party preference as a determinant of voting behavior, and the major parties, symbolically pairing Northerners with Southerners on their national tickets, remained strong bonds of the Union. An earlier belief that political parties were essentially evil agencies of divisiveness, corruption, and special interest had long since evaporated. Party competition, most now agreed, was both legitimate and beneficial. "Organized parties," observed Governor Enos Throop of New York in 1829, "watch and scan each other's doings, the public mind is instructed by ample discussions of public measures, and acts of violence are restrained by the convictions of the people, that the prevailing measures are the results of enlightened reason." Accordingly, both major parties had developed into elaborately organized, well-oiled electoral machines, and for men like Martin Van Buren and Thurlow Weed politics became a reputable (if not universally esteemed) vocation.

The style, no less than the structure, of politics was strikingly modern by mid-century. The deferential politics of colonial days (marked by such practices as ranked seating at New England town meetings and gentry control of local government in the South) had undergone a steady erosion during and after the Revolution, all but disappearing in the rough-and-tumble, "hickory pole and hard cider" voter-oriented campaigns of the Jacksonian era. After 1851, when Virginia swung into line, adult white males could vote in every state in the Union. More important, those entitled to the ballot used it. Politics, not baseball, was the great national pastime—a game, remarked an Ohio journalist, possessing "all the fanaticism of religion and all the fascination of gambling." Parades, banners, and bonfires; torch-lit rallies and stump-speeches; glee clubs and brass bands; political barbecues and picnics; and an intensely partisan press, offered stimulation as well as entertainment to an alert citizenry. In North and South alike, then, voter participation in both presidential and off-year elections was impressively high. Turnouts of 70 percent were common, and at moments of special excitement the total rose to levels higher than at any other time in the nation's history. Fully 78 percent of the eligible electorate cast ballots in the "log cabin–hard cider" campaign of 1840; 82 percent of Northern voters and nearly 70 percent of Southern voters would do so in the momentous election of 1860. Intensifying voter interest was the fact that by mid-century most state and local offices had been made elective, instead of appointive. Not only governors and presidential electors (often chosen by state legislatures in Thomas Jefferson's day) but here and there even judges and militia officers were popularly chosen.

Those who went to the polls displayed increasing independence as the nineteenth century advanced. Party attachments once formed were not easily set aside, yet officeholders who failed to keep step with their constituents or who put on airs soon found themselves private citizens. Not only did politicians pay noisy homage to "the sovereignty of the people," but many, often the most successful, went to great lengths to appear as common men themselves. "I have always dressed chiefly in *Home spun* when among the people," Congressman James Graham of North Carolina confided to his brother. "If a Candidate be dressed Farmerlike he is well received and kindly remembered by the inmates of the Log Cabin, and there is no sensation among the children or the *chickens.*" Similarly in 1840, the "god-like," Harvard-educated Daniel Webster, darling of the Boston Brahmins, publicly apologized for not having been born in a log cabin.

Officeholding itself had become in good measure democratized, as once-formidable property-holding requirements were swept away and the tasks of government routinized so that all "men of intelligence," as Andrew Jackson put it, might "readily qualify themselves for their performance." Especially among Democrats, "rotation in office" was viewed not merely as a way to reward the party faithful but as "a leading principle in the republican creed," a way to enlarge the ranks of public servants and scotch the notion that office was a form of property best held by a trained elite. Thus even south of the Potomac, where big planters continued to claim a disproportionate share of public offices, small farmers and middle-class shopkeepers found their way into government in substantial numbers once the constitutional reforms of the Jackson years had taken hold. Although in 1850 slaveholders were a majority in the legislatures of all but four Southern states, only in aristocratic South Carolina were planters (that is, owners of twenty or more slaves) numerically dominant. In two states of the Deep South, Louisiana and Texas, nearly two-thirds of the state representatives owned no slaves at all. Well over 40 percent of all Southern county offices belonged to nonslaveholders.

This is not to say that some men did not count for more than others. Then, as now, money, family, and education often counted for a good deal. Compared to the deferential style of politics practiced in colonial America and into the early decades of the nineteenth century, however, politics was a distinctly democratic—and demagogical—art by the time Andrew Jackson passed from the scene in 1845.

In one way only was politics at mid-century distinctly premodern. Government was both small and predominantly local. A widespread distrust of "consolidation" kept federal government tiny by present standards. Counting every minor customs official and land office clerk, every crossroads postmaster, the federal establishment in 1850 numbered a mere 20,000 employees. In addition, the U.S. Army kept some 10,000 soldiers under arms after the Mexican War, while the navy, with forty-six ships in commission, claimed roughly 8,800 seamen. Washington bureaucrats were fewer still. The Treasury Department, easily the largest of federal agencies, boasted a staff of 400 to 500 comptrollers, auditors, customs officers, and the like. The State Department, on the other hand, conducted all its business with a secretary, assistant secretary, translator, financial officer, librarian, and a dozen clerks. In 1849 Congress added the Department of the Interior to the six executive agencies established during George Washington's presidency, but although farming remained the nation's chief economic enterprise its needs were consigned to the Treasury Department's Patent Office. Total federal expenditures on agricultural activities between 1789 and 1851 came to $29,000. Such frugality netted the U.S. Treasury a *surplus* of over $4 million in 1850.

Understandably, such small-scale government rarely, and for the most part indirectly, intruded upon the lives of most antebellum Americans. To men like Henry David Thoreau, town meetings and county courts seemed vastly more familiar, responsive — even legitimate — than did federal or state authority. "I meet this American government, or its representative the State government, directly, and face to face, once a year, no more, in the person of its tax-gatherer," Thoreau remarked in his celebrated essay "On the Duty of Civil Disobedience" (1848). And even then, he noted, it was his "civil neighbor," not some faceless bureaucrat, who embodied the power of the state. Thoreau overlooked one other federal officer — Concord's postmaster — but his point about the political provincialism of his generation was altogether apt.

It may be too much to say that the declension from George Washington to Franklin Pierce and James Buchanan is an accurate reflection of the declining power and respect of the national government. But there can be no doubt that years of Jacksonian ascendancy and constant reiteration of the Jacksonian slogans, for example, "The world is governed too much" and "That government is best which governs least," had sharply curtailed the role of the federal government in the affairs of most Americans. State governments — chartering banks and railroads, building prisons and poorhouses, regulating grog shops, establishing bankruptcy procedures — were a good deal more active. But even here, "commonwealth" notions, which advocated state intervention to foster economic and social advancement for all, had lately lost appeal, so that state lawmakers, far from capitalizing on the passivity of Congress, generally followed its hands-off course.

Weak government was a luxury Americans had been able to afford because the nation's expanding agricultural economy needed scant regulation and because secure frontiers rendered large military establishments unnecessary. Moreover, during the 1840s Whigs and Democrats had reached something of a consensus on once-divisive issues such as the tariff, internal improvements, and a national bank. Limited government had come to seem not merely sufficient but desirable, a fundamental safeguard of individual freedoms. Inevitably, proposals for strong federal action on a matter of deep and conflicting concern—slavery—would cause special trouble.

II

In some respects, the nation's economy seemed little changed from Revolutionary days and before. An overwhelming majority of Americans (85 percent in 1850, 80 percent in 1860) still lived and worked on farms or in rural villages of fewer than 2,500 souls. In North and South alike, the typical agricultural unit was the family farm. Most Southern farmers owned no slaves; of those who did, nearly half held fewer than five. Even the work of the farm was performed in much the same way it had for centuries: with horse, ox, or mule; with plow, hoe, and hand-scythe; with muscle and sweat. Some experiments in scientific agriculture were being tried (Edmund Ruffin's *An Essay on Calcareous Manures* ran through five editions between 1832 and 1853), and on some of the larger farms in the North improved farm machinery, including McCormick's reaper, was coming into vogue. Most farmers, however, still favored traditional, soil-mining techniques; not until the Civil War would agriculture become truly mechanized.

Although all parts of the country depended for livelihood primarily upon farming, there existed important regional variations in the kinds of agriculture practiced. From early colonial times, Southern agriculture had been distinguished by its concentration on the production of staple crops through the use of slave labor. Thousands of Southern farmers (most owning their own lands) engaged in subsistence farming, growing enough crops to feed themselves and their livestock with perhaps a little left over to barter for necessities at a country store. But the wealth of the South depended on the production and export of one or another staple crop. Tobacco, the primary staple of the seventeenth and eighteenth centuries, was still a major crop in Virginia and Kentucky and of secondary importance in North Carolina, Tennessee, Maryland, and Missouri. Hemp, used for bagging and rope, was grown throughout the upper South, chiefly in Kentucky and Missouri. Rice, which required large gangs of slaves to cultivate and harvest, was a major crop in tidewater Georgia and South Carolina and a minor one in a few other coastal regions. Sugar cane, which like rice required much capital and many slaves to plant, cultivate, harvest, and refine, flourished on the rich delta plains of Louisiana and to a lesser extent in southeastern Texas and coastal Georgia. Elsewhere, cotton was king.

Cotton's commercial profitability had been negligible before the

1790s. By then, however, revolutionary advances in the textile industry (first in Great Britain, later in the United States) had created a powerful and growing demand for raw cotton. At first, this lucrative new market belonged exclusively to planters in the coastal regions of South Carolina and Georgia, for only there did special conditions make possible the cultivation of long-fibered, luxury cottons whose black seeds might easily be cleaned by hand. Upland, short-staple cotton, a hardy species that might be grown throughout most of the South but whose sticky green seeds took forever to separate from the fiber, became commercially feasible only after Eli Whitney unveiled his cotton engine ("gin," for short) in 1793. Whitney's gin, which could do the work of fifty men, revolutionized Southern agriculture and soon spread cotton cultivation far beyond South Carolina and Georgia. By 1850 the cotton kingdom covered most of the Deep South, sweeping westward from the Carolinas through eastern Texas and north into Arkansas, Tennessee, and here and there, Virginia. In 1791 the nation's cotton output totaled a mere 4,000 bales. By the eve of the Civil War, Southern farmers were producing some 5 *million* bales a year and cotton export shipments abroad (mainly to England) accounted for fully two-thirds the value of all American exports. One British traveler described Mobile, Alabama, in 1858 in terms that might have applied equally to Charleston, Savannah, Memphis, and other Southern commercial centers. It was, she said, a place where "people live in cotton houses and ride in cotton carriages. They buy cotton, sell cotton, think cotton, eat cotton, drink cotton, and dream cotton. They marry cotton wives, and unto them are born cotton children. . . . It has made Mobile and all its citizens."

Although in 1860 three-fourths of all Southern families owned no slaves and most who farmed tilled fewer than 80 acres, the plantation — an agricultural unit boasting twenty or more bondsmen — was the heart and soul of the Old South's economic life. This was so because by far the greatest production of staple crops came from plantations — all the sugar and rice, most tobacco, and at least 75 percent of the cotton. The big planters possessed not only the largest holdings but the most fertile and best situated lands. By mid-century the richest 10 percent in the Cotton South claimed more than half the region's agricultural wealth. Even the average slaveholder, according to one recent estimate, "was more than five times as wealthy as the average Northerner, more than ten times as wealthy as the average nonslaveholding Southern farmer." Thanks to rising prices for cotton and an attendant doubling in the average value of slaveholdings during the 1850s, by the eve of the Civil War a Southerner "who owned two slaves and nothing else was as rich as the average man in the North." Obviously, slaveholding was a highly profitable investment in the antebellum South and plantation owners an enormously privileged class.

The profits to be made from investments in slaves and land largely explain the slow pace of industrialization in the Old South. Except for William Gregg's cotton mills in Charleston and some iron and textile factories in Richmond (notably the Tredegar Iron Works), the slave states' manufacturing capacity was anemic at best. Despite the pleas of Southern nationalists who deplored their section's essentially colonial orientation to the North and called for a boycott of Northern goods and the establishment of "every description of manufacturing & of the mechanic arts," the South remained overwhelmingly agricultural. In 1860 only 15 percent of the nation's manufacturing establishments were located below the Mason-Dixon line, many of them small mills producing simple products: lumber, turpentine, cornmeal, and flour. The South's per capita investment in industry reached only a third of the national average and the value of its manufactured goods stood lower still.

Matters were obviously different in the free states where by mid-century the trend toward industrialization was well under way. One by one in the years following the War of 1812 the obstacles to a factory system—a preference for British goods, shortages of labor and capital, technological backwardness—had come tumbling down. By 1848 not only textiles, but boots, firearms, sewing machines, men's clothing, ironware, and dozens of other articles spewed from Northern factories. Many such establishments copied the so-called American System of Manufacture developed first by New England textile barons, a system that wholly integrated the process of production, from raw material to finished product, under a single roof. Only 20.6 percent of the North's labor force was directly engaged in manufacturing in 1850; 41.3 percent still wrested their living from the soil. But, at least north of the Potomac and Ohio rivers, the industrial revolution was well under way. Indeed, some regions (southern New England and parts of the Hudson and Delaware river valleys) were by the Civil War as heavily industrialized as most of Great Britain. New England as a whole manufactured in 1850 goods valued at $100 per person—more than double the national average and nearly ten times that of the South.

One essential ingredient in the rise of industrialism was the creation of an efficient system of transportation. By the 1840s, canals, steamboats, and especially railroads made possible the movement of goods and persons at a cost and speed unthinkable a generation earlier. Even contemporaries found the pace of transportation development astonishing. "When I first came to this country," wrote the German immigrant Francis Lieber, "I went from the Delaware to the Chesapeake in a confounded and confounding stagecoach. A few years later I had to go again to Washington and found a canal cut through Delaware . . . , and a year or so later, I crossed the same state on a railroad . . . , now I wait impatiently for a passage over the state, for aerial navigation is the next in order, all other means being exhausted." By mid-century the Northeast possessed a transportation network that was both modern and complete. During the 1850s, as rail construction spread into Ohio, Michigan, Indiana, and Illinois, the Northeast and Northwest became firmly linked, more tightly linked, indeed, than were the Northwest and the South by the river and rail system that connected those regions. (By 1860 Midwestern farmers shipped to the East four times as much corn and half again as much pork as they did to the South; a decade earlier they had sent southward two-thirds the corn and four times the pork that went to Eastern markets.) This would prove to be a fact of considerable importance in the critical days ahead.

The Southern railroad network, while by no means inconsiderable, was less fully developed than that of the North. Even after dramatic expansion during the 1850s, trackage within the future Confederacy came to roughly 9,000 miles — less than half the free states' total. Moreover, Southern railroads suffered from inadequate repair facilities and shortages of essential equipment, even cars and engines. By the Civil War a single Northern company, the Baltimore and Ohio, owned half as many passenger cars as the entire Confederacy; the Pennsylvania and Erie lines had nearly as many engines. Compounding such handicaps was the perverse decision of Southern railroads to lay track of various gauges (from 3 to 6 feet), necessitating expensive and time-consuming transshipment at numerous points. The Weldon Road, connecting Richmond with eastern North Carolina, was 4 inches narrower than the line from Richmond to east Tennessee, while a third road, from Richmond to Columbia, South Carolina, changed gauges three times en route. Such a system, augmented by river traffic and wagon roads, served adequately the needs of an agricultural economy in time of peace. Before long the burdens of war would lay bare its weaknesses.

The first half of the nineteenth century witnessed not only revolutions in transportation and (more tentatively) industry, but also a swing toward the city. In 1820 only thirteen settlements in the United States claimed over 10,000 inhabitants; New York City alone topped 100,000. By 1860 ninety-three cities boasted populations in excess of 10,000 and nine (including New York which had recently reached a million) reported more than 100,000 residents. During these four decades the city-dwelling population of the United States spurted from 7 percent to

20 percent, thrice the rate of rural growth in these years and faster than at any other time in our history.

Not only did the numerical size of American cities increase, thanks to growing farm surpluses, industrial advances, and European immigration, but their *physical* size also expanded. Population pressure plus improved urban transportation began slowly but inexorably to transform the preindustrial "walking city" into a larger, more complex, and impersonal place. At the end of the eighteenth century the radius of American cities seldom measured more than a mile; fifty years later it often ran to 4 or 5 miles. Clearly defined central business districts, socially and ethnically segregated residential neighborhoods, large-scale commuting, were by mid-century common features in all but the smallest American cities. By 1848 roughly one in five of Boston's businessmen traveled to work on steam railroads, and more than a half of all trains entering and leaving the city served stations within 15 miles of downtown Boston. The suburb, too, had come to stay.

Such urban progress, it must be noted, was a distinctly Northern phenomenon. Whereas fully a third of all New Englanders and citizens of the Middle Atlantic states lived in cities and towns by 1860, fewer than 10 percent of Southerners did. New Orleans was the Old South's only *thriving* city, the only one to rank among the nation's most populous fifteen. Like New Orleans, moreover, most leading Southern cities lay not in the region's heartland but along its perimeter: Atlantic coast ports or Ohio and Mississippi river towns. Towns in the interior often impressed visitors with their seediness and somnolence. "The houses are all poor and shabby, and have no shade to hide their tatters," a Michigan schoolteacher reported in 1858 of Satartia, Mississippi, the second-largest settlement in a rich Black Belt county. "It had flourished once with the trade and traffic of four or five stores. Those were its 'palmy days.' Now it has only two stores — poor low buildings; a tavern, dentist, doctor and shoemaker." Finally, the relative newness of most Southern cities greatly diluted their influence. In the rapidly urbanizing Northwest, towns were often built in advance of settlement, as spearheads for rural development: "first the railroad, then the town, then the farms," one contemporary recalled. In the West, "the city stamp[ed] the country," molding laws, social custom, and public opinion. Conversely, Southern towns commonly materialized only after the surrounding countryside was well settled. There, the country stamped the city. Rural values, which shaped attitudes toward commerce and wealth, kinship and tradition, honor and manliness, pervaded even the cities of the antebellum South.

Undergirding the economic advances of the period and sustaining a population that grew by leaps and bounds—from 17 million in 1840 to over 23 million in 1850 and more than 31.5 million by the Civil War—was the abundance, the material plenty of the land. Foreign visitors and immigrants especially were struck by the cornucopia of America. "Nature here offers a sustenance so immense to human industry that the class of theoretical speculators is absolutely unknown," observed Alexis de Tocqueville. "Everybody works, and the mine is so rich that all those who work rapidly succeed in acquiring that which renders existence happy. . . . This people is one of the happiest in the world." Settlers in the Wabash Valley gave similar testimony when they sang:

Way down upon the Wabash
Such lands were never known.
If Adam had passed over it,
This soil he'd surely own.
He'd think it was the Garden
He played in when a boy,
And straight he'd call it Eden
In the State of Illinois.

III

To many contemporaries and to historians who later wrote about these years, it seemed that material wealth, together with the absence of feudal encumbrances and the freedom from external threat which allowed Americans to join in the pursuit of riches wholeheartedly, had created a society remarkable for its openness, unpretentiousness, and ease of ascent. Compared to European nations the social (and geographic) mobility of white Americans was indeed striking. "Surely in no other Western society of the period," writes one historian, "could a self-taught merchant's apprentice have founded the manufacturing dynasty of the Massachusetts Lawrences; or a semi-literate ferry-boatman named Vanderbilt have gained control of New York City's transportation system; or the son of a London dried-fish shopkeeper named Benjamin have become Senator from Louisiana; or a self-taught prairie lawyer have been elected President of the nation."

Yet it would be wrong to swallow whole hog this image of America as the "happy republic." In the first place, 3.2 million black-skinned Americans were held in bondage and some 430,000 "free" Negroes were treated as pariahs in all parts of the country. So too, American women, whatever their relative freedom in comparison with their sisters in other lands, were still kept very much in submission by law and social conditioning alike. Only within a severely restricted "woman's sphere" might antebellum women find self-worth and challenge conventional notions of masculine superiority. And in the slave states special political and social—as well as economic—power rested in the hands of a small group (not more than 50,000) of planter oligarchs whose interests often ran counter not only to those of their chattels but to those of women and poor white men.

Moreover, recent studies show that at least in some parts of the United States wealth was not only malapportioned but becoming more so. In the South, while the concentration of holdings among slaveholders held steady during the 1850s, the proportion of white families owning slaves shrank, from nearly a third to barely one-quarter. And since the value of slaves skyrocketed, the economic gap between slaveowners and nonslaveowners was widening dramatically and portentously on the eve of the Civil War. Nor were such inequities confined to the South: in the big cities of the Northeast growing disparities of wealth might also be found. In New York City, for instance, the richest 1 percent of the population controlled fully half of the city's noncorporate wealth in 1845—a 10 percent increase since 1825. Similarly, Boston's richest 1 percent held 33 percent of that city's wealth in 1833, 37 percent in 1848. In such cities, moreover, self-made men—the Lawrences and Vanderbilts—were exceptions, not the rule. Most of the rich in 1850 were the sons of rich men. Of the richest New Yorkers in that year, only 5 percent came from "middling" or poor families.

Yet if American society at mid-century was not exactly egalitarian, it was undeniably one in flux. And this flux—this raw newness, this sense of the world in motion—produced a kind of psychic and cultural schizophrenia. On the one hand, Americans trumpeted their belief in the essential goodness of God and man, spoke soaringly of the potentiality of reform, boasted of having filled up a continent, of having devised the best system of government the world had ever known. Economic and technological advancement strengthened such feelings of pride, optimism, and confidence. At the same time, however, nagging doubts, vague feelings of dread, gnawed at American sensibilities. Electoral corruption and the raids of political spoilsmen produced in many Americans a strong mistrust of politicians. Railroad crashes and derailments, steamboat explosions, and labor exploitation, all contributed to a belief that economic and technological advancement was at best a mixed blessing. Ralph Waldo Emerson's complaint that "things are in the saddle" struck a responsive chord in the minds of many who feared that excessive materialism undermined the national character. When in

1858 Cyrus Field and his associates at last succeeded in laying a cable across the North Atlantic, New York City celebrated the occasion under a huge banner proclaiming "Peace on Earth and Good Will to Men." That same night prominent residents of Staten Island, to improve the value of their property, burned down a quarantine hospital in their midst, leaving its diseased inmates without shelter. Reflecting upon the day's events, the crusty conservative George Templeton Strong noted in his diary: "I fear that this millennium over which we've been braying is made of gutta-percha and copper wire and is not the real thing after all."

Americans sought relief from these tensions — produced by the discernible gap between the real and the ideal, what was and what ought to be — in several ways. Some found reassurance in religion, which had long offered means to reconcile sin and salvation; others sought it in an idealization of "Home, Sweet Home," stressing home and family as a bulwark against competitive strife and unwanted social pressures. Still others found relief in the period's immensely popular melodramas where villainy was confronted but overcome. Many more turned for comfort to nostalgic recollections of a simpler, more righteous past. Not only sentimental favorites like the "Old Oaken Bucket," but even political entreaties tapped such instincts. The Democrats' "Alphabetical Song," written for the 1840 presidential campaign, contained such couplets as these:

> *N* stands for National glory and fame
> Which Washington won for America's name.
> *O* stands for Old Times, when equality reigned,
> Ere the whigs had the altar of freedom profaned.

IV

For Southerners, of course, the gap between the ideal and the actual was particularly wide. The need to view slaves as both persons and property, as cheerful children and potential insurrectionaries, made the "confidence-dread syndrome" especially pronounced. Try as they might, Southern whites found it hard to convince themselves, not to mention the nation, that human bondage and American democracy were compatible.

Yet try they did. By the 1830s proslavery apologists had developed an elaborate defense of servitude as not merely a "necessary evil" but a "positive good," a boon to both masters and slaves. Slavery, declared its champions, was an institution of reciprocal benefits. To masters (and, at least indirectly, all whites) it offered political and social as well as obvious economic advantages. To the allegedly inferior African it offered security, protection, and cultural uplift. Slavery, asserted Chancellor William Harper of Virginia, had done more "to elevate a degraded race . . . to civilize the barbarous . . . to enlighten the ignorant, and to spread the blessing of Christianity among the heathen, than all the missionaries that philanthropy and religion had ever sent forth." Cultural advancement had its limits, of course, and slavery's defenders forcefully insisted that backward blacks stood far outside democracy's pale. Typical was the Louisiana planter who, when asked whether all men were created "free and equal as the Declaration of Independence holds they are," bluntly replied: "Yes. But all men, niggers, and monkeys *aint*." Indeed, to many, slavery's best defense was that it worked. Without it blacks would not labor and without black labor the South would soon become impoverished.

In defending slavery against its enemies, Southern whites, slaveholders and nonslaveholders alike, stood shoulder to shoulder. For some, this community of interest seemed a matter of economic necessity. Even when the slave system hurt them—by driving down crop prices, depriving them of markets, obstructing diversification, degrading manual labor—small, nonstaple-producing farmers depended on plantations to buy their crops, just as small-scale cotton growers often turned to the big planters for help in ginning and marketing their crop. The fear of job competition from emancipated bondsmen likewise helped rivet urban workingmen to the slave system. More still defended black slavery as essential to white freedom. For, it was believed, not only did slavery free white men from dependence on other whites for their meat and bread, but a slave "mudsill" kept even the poorest hillbilly off the bottom of the social heap. "Color alone is here the badge of distinction," wrote Virginia's Thomas Dew, "and all who are white are equal in spite of the variety of occupation." Above all, slavery seemed to offer the most effective means of controlling an allegedly shiftless, degraded, potentially dangerous race. This consideration led even some who doubted its justice reluctantly to support slavery. As one upcountry farmer told Frederick Law Olmsted in 1854,

> I wouldn't like to hev [the Negroes] free, if they was gwine to hang around . . . because they is so monstrous lazy. . . . Now suppose they was free, you see they'd all think themselves just as good as we . . . [Besides], how'd you like to hev a nigger steppin' up to your darter? Of course you wouldn't; and that's the reason I wouldn't like to hev 'em free; but I tell you, I don't

think it's right to hev 'em slaves so; that's the fac—taant right to keep 'em as they is.

Indeed it was just such men, nonslaveholding yeomen, who constituted most of the slave patrols that policed the Southern countryside.

The burdens of bondage, both physical and psychological, bore heavily on all slaves. Chattels personal, they might be bought and sold, rented out, gambled away, or claimed as an inheritance. Slave marriages lacked standing in law. (Masters sometimes performed mock weddings at which slave couples pledged to cleave together "until death or distance do you part.") Slave children legally belonged not to their parents but to their mother's master. Nineteenth-century slave codes provided minimal safeguards to slaves as persons—recognizing, as one Tennessee jurist remarked, that "a slave is not in the condition of a horse." Yet whenever conflict arose between a master's property rights and his slave's human rights, the courts invariably decided in favor of the former. And if slave codes became milder, as time wore on, with respect to the material treatment of slaves (a point at issue among historians), they unquestionably became more harsh with respect to manumission, education, and the status of free Negroes.

Everywhere oppressive, slavery nonetheless varied greatly from place to place, from time to time, from master to master. Household servants, for example, often possessed privileges denied most field hands; slaves on large plantations run by overseers were apt to be handled differently from those on small farms who worked elbow to elbow with their master; slaves in frontier regions might be driven harder than those in more settled parts; neighbors might provide for their chattels in disparate ways; even the same man might on different days show kindness and cruelty in varying measure. The most striking difference in the lives of slaves, however, was that between those who toiled on farms and plantations and those who resided in Southern towns and cities. By 1860 some half-million of the South's 4 million slaves might be found in urban settings. Most worked as domestics, while others filled a variety of other nonagricultural occupations: barber, baker, mill hand, bricklayer, riverboatman, among others. Often urban slaves were permitted to hire out their own time, even to find their own lodgings. "After learning to calk," recalled Frederick Douglass, "I sought my own employment, made my own contracts, and collected my own earnings; giving Master Hugh no trouble in any part of the transactions to which I was a party." "A city slave," Douglass claimed, "is almost a free citizen. [He] enjoys privileges altogether unknown to the whip-driven slave on the plantation."

Douglass exaggerated the freedom enjoyed by urban slaves, even before jittery whites began in the 1850s to tighten racial controls. But his observation about the relative disadvantage of plantation slaves was most certainly correct. Some slaves, it appears, found the physical chores of slavery light. One black woman reminisced, "Oh, no, we was nebber hurried. Marster nebber once said, 'Get up an' go to work,' an' no oberseer ebber said it, neither. Ef some on 'em did not git up when de odders went out to work, marster nebber said a word. Oh, no, we was nebber hurried." At times, at least, there seemed to be a kernel of truth in the maxim that it took two slaves to help one to do nothing.

Most slaves, however, worked—and worked hard—from sunup until after sundown, when housekeeping chores in the quarters (cooking, sewing, collecting firewood, tending gardens) were at last finished. Though there were exceptions, the work week usually ran from Monday morning to Saturday noon, with holidays at Christmas, Easter, and after the crop was laid by. On the large plantations, those counting thirty or more slaves (where nearly half of all bondsmen resided), masters usually divided their work force into two groups, field hands and household servants, with varying degrees of specialization and hierarchy within each.

To wrest loyal and efficient service from what was, after all, a captive labor force, slaveowners employed an informal system of rewards and punishments. Living conditions varied according to the means, disposition, and enlightenment of the master, but most slaves found their *material* circumstances at least marginally adequate. A diet heavy in cornmeal and salt pork produced vitamin deficiencies and a particularly high incidence of such enervating diseases as rickets, pellagra, and scurvy. The primitive state of nineteenth-century medicine meant woefully inadequate health care for blacks and whites alike. Shabby clothing adequate in summer often failed to fend off the cold in winter. The single-family cabins in which slaves were housed offered varying degrees of comfort: some were snug dwellings of clapboards, logs, or bricks; others "small, dilapidated and dingy" shacks. Still, although Spartan at best, the conditions of life were sufficient to keep slaves at their hoes and plows, and to make possible not merely a replenishment but a steady *increase* in their numbers. The fewer than 400,000 Africans imported into British North America before the close of the foreign slave trade in 1808 had become ten times that number by 1860. Nowhere else in the New World did slaves reproduce themselves.

Slaves whose conduct seemed particularly meritorious—for example, those who picked more than their quota of cotton, who added to the master's "property" by giving birth, or who informed on would-be insurrectionaries—often received special rewards. Such rewards (designed as object lessons for *all* slaves) took many forms: garden plots, money payments, passes to visit neighboring plantations, holidays, jugs of whiskey, or a few "hands" of tobacco—even a rare promise of freedom. On the other hand, slaves who sloughed off, stole, lied, cheated, challenged white supremacy, or tried to run away risked a panoply of physical and psychological punishments: shame, deprivation of privileges, short rations, sale and separation from one's family, and, above all, the lash. Few slaveholders were inherently sadistic and most found whippings distasteful. It was one of slavery's tragedies, however, that even those masters who preferred not to use the lash often felt compelled to do so lest they lose all control over their unwilling bondsmen. Thus a prominent South Carolina planter, tormented by his inability to govern through kindness, confided to a visitor that "if he lives 10 or 15 yrs. longer" his slaves would "gain ascendancy over him . . . [he] is sensible they are gaining on him: confesses [he] whips in a passion & half the time unjustly." Flogging, and the threat of flogging, remained always the primary instrument of slave discipline.

In surviving the ordeal of slavery, Southern blacks drew strength from a number of institutions and cultural traditions. Within the slave community, no institution was more crucial than the family. Though legally without standing, though it faced disruption whenever the master moved, died, or fell into debt, the slave family, one scholar has written, "was in actuality one of the most important survival mechanisms for the slave. In his family he found companionship, love, sexual gratification, sympathetic understanding of his sufferings; he learned how to avoid punishment, to cooperate with other blacks, and to maintain his self-esteem." For slave children, the family and its extended kinship network provided not only survival lessons (how to hold one's tongue before whites, how to display proper deference, how to create psychological "space") but role models of mature behavior—living reminders that slaves might become something more than submissive children. That black parents felt deeply the importance of family ties is borne out most clearly by the experience of Reconstruction: by the touching eagerness of partners to legalize their marriages once they were free, and by the remarkable stability of black marriages in the last third of the nineteenth century.

One of the most vital functions of the slave family was to assist in the transmission of a distinctive Afro-American culture, a culture constructed of African and American elements, but a culture nonetheless, one as rich as it was unique. That culture, moreover, both contributed to and gave evidence of the slaves' ability not merely to survive but to prevail under bondage. Unquestionably, slavery made difficult the reproduction of African cultural traditions in America. Few vestiges might be found in the Old South of the Africans' complex institutional and linguistic heritage, or of their distinctive forms of painting and sculpture. Music, however, and verbal art, proved more resilient. African-based folk tales, spirituals, and dances survived, affording slaves diversion, release, and a voice of their own. Despite masters' attempts to use religion as a means of social control ("He that knoweth his master's will and doeth it not, shall be beaten with many stripes"), slaves largely succeeded in blending African beliefs with biblical teachings to create a brand of Christianity all their own. That singularly joyful, life-affirming faith, and the emotional ceremonies that embodied it, bolstered slaves by joining them in communion with one another and with God, and by imparting the Lord's promise of deliverance hereafter. And in the person of slave preachers bondsmen found still another source of authority to which they might look for guidance, anchors for black pride and identity.

V

The crusade against American slavery was nearly as old as the institution itself. Although throughout the colonial period most Americans easily accepted slavery, some voices—notably the Puritan jurist Samuel Sewall and Pennsylvania Quakers John Woolman and Anthony Benezet, protested. The spirit of equality unleashed by the Revolution quickened and broadened such feeling sufficiently to blot out slavery in the North. Indeed, for a time it appeared that even in the South slavery had been gravely weakened. A good many Southern revolutionaries spoke abstractly of the evils of bondage, and private manumissions soared—especially in the upper South—during the 1780s and early 1790s. Yet, although Southerners continued for many years to justify their "peculiar institution" as a "necessary evil," it soon became apparent that little if any antislavery *action* would come from the South. When, for example, St. George Tucker proposed in 1796 a plan of emancipation so gradual that it would have taken nearly a century to complete, the Virginia House of Delegates tabled it swiftly, without discussion. The growth of domestic and European markets for cotton, and the effects of Eli Whitney's gin, of course did nothing to weaken the Old South's attachment to slavery.

It was left to Northerners, therefore, to develop a campaign against slavery. Yet even above the Mason-Dixon line abolitionism grew slowly, amid great hostility. Some feared that in challenging the right to hold human property, slavery's critics threatened the security of property generally. Others, "gentlemen of property and standing" often prominent in antiabolition mobs, objected as much to the abolitionists' means as to their ends. By harnessing modern techniques of organization and communication to appeal directly to ordinary citizens, over the heads of established local elites, abolitionists seemed to jeopardize long-standing patterns of deference and social control. The apparently close ties between American and British reformers merely strengthened the notion that the antislavery movement represented a conspiracy to undermine traditional sources of authority and to subvert the American way of life. Or, better, the abolitionists appeared to many Americans, right down to the Civil War, to menace American way*s* of life. Abolitionists were accused, that is, and with some justification, of seeking to replace diverse, traditionalist ways of life with one morally and socially homogeneous way of life.

While fearful conservatives stewed over reformist threats to the dominance of established elites, others found perilous—even un-American—the way abolitionists challenged "public sentiment" in an age that exalted majority rule. The "public mind," not holier-than-thou rabble-rousers, ought to determine the morality of national institutions. A belief in the sanctity of the U.S. Constitution which, nearly all agreed, forbade outside interference in the domestic institutions of any state, persuaded still others that, lacking the means to do good, abolitionists could only do harm. Finally, a deep-seated, nationwide prejudice against blacks heightened hostility to reformers who preached racial equality as well as emancipation. It was a select committee of New Hampshire's legislature, not Virginia's, which in 1839 formally declared: "Shall the land of Washington and Jefferson be surrendered to a race of slaves, without capacity, brutal, cowardly, groveling in their dispositions, upon whom nature has fixed the seal of perpetual inferiority? It is not to be believed."

Before 1830 abolitionists had favored a moderate, piecemeal, gradual approach to the liquidation of slavery. Much energy went into efforts to provide religious instruction for slaves and to encourage the voluntary return of free Negroes to Africa. In 1816 the American Colonization Society (ACS) was organized to promote this latter scheme and at first many abolitionists wished it well. Planters, it was reasoned, might more readily manumit their chattels if provision were made to remove them to Liberia, the ACS colony on the west coast of Africa. During the 1820s, however, reformers rapidly lost faith in colonization as an antislavery tactic. Evidence that free Negroes themselves decidedly opposed this scheme opened many eyes, as did the society's woeful lack of success in its main mission. Fewer than 1,500 American blacks settled in Africa under ACS auspices between 1820 and 1831. As William Lloyd Garrison's influential pamphlet *Thoughts on African Colonization* effectively demonstrated, far from facilitating emancipation, the ACS in fact hindered it by portraying free Negroes as debased, inferior, undesirable.

The manifest weakness of the American Colonization Society in resolving the slavery question was, then, one cause for the rise of a more radical abolitionism in the 1830s. There were other roots as well. Proslavery aggressiveness in the 1820s—praise for bondage as a "positive good," new obstacles to private manumissions, more stringent slave codes, admission of Missouri as a slave state—persuaded many philanthropists of the need for stronger countermeasures. Others took heart and a plan of action from British abolitionists whose abandonment of gradualism in favor of demands for "immediate emancipation" bore fruit in the West India Emancipation Act of 1833. Still others, touched by the spirit of an evangelical Protestantism which preached both free will and the need to *uproot* sin everywhere, called for immediate, uncompensated emancipation as essential to the redemption of a wayward nation.

At all events, the antislavery movement entered a second stage of development with the creation in 1833 of the American Anti-Slavery Society. Following the lead of the fiery Garrison (editor of the Boston *Liberator*) and such religiously oriented abolitionists as Theodore Weld, James G. Birney, and Lewis Tappan, abolitionists now sought, through moral appeals, to destroy slavery root and branch. To this end they published a flood of antislavery newspapers, magazines, pamphlets, and songbooks; distributed kerchiefs, medals—even chocolate wrappers—with antislavery messages; established a vast network of auxiliary societies; dispatched antislavery lecturers to every corner of the North; deluged Congress with petitions; and, for a time, sought even to win converts within the South.

Although in its earliest statements of principle the American Anti-Slavery Society endorsed political action as *one* means of attacking slavery, the antislavery crusade remained throughout the 1830s primarily a campaign of moral persuasion. By 1840, however, the movement entered a third stage as non-Garrisonian abolitionists organized the Liberty party—the first of a series of antislavery third parties designed to assault slavery with political weapons, within the framework of the Constitution.

In part, the shift of the antislavery impulse from moral persuasion to political action resulted from internal conflicts between the increasingly doctrinaire Garrisonians (who added to abolitionism such issues as women's rights, pacifism, and Sabbath reform) and church-oriented New York and Ohio abolitionists who protested Garrison's drift toward universal reform and believed that "a righteous and renovating" politics would give force to moral appeals. In part, the switch came because by 1840 the national Anti-Slavery Society, its tasks of proselytization and organization now largely complete, had come on hard times financially and seemed no longer effective as an instrument of abolition. But mainly the shift toward political action came in response to a series of events in the late 1830s and 1840s which thrust the slavery question into the very heart of national politics and greatly enlarged the numbers of those who favored the institution's curtailment, if not its utter destruction.

One such event was a controversy over the right of abolitionists to petition Congress on behalf of the slave. The issue arose in 1836 when the House of Representatives first passed a "gag rule" forbidding discussion or consideration of any antislavery petition. The abolitionists' response to this ban (not repealed until 1844) was to mount a massive petition campaign to dramatize slavery's threat to the freedom of all Americans. By forwarding a flood of antislavery petitions, they hoped "to take possession of Congress and turn it into a vast Anti Slavery Debating Society, with the whole country as an audience." In good measure, their hopes were realized. With antislavery Whigs such as former President John Quincy Adams, Seth Gates, and Joshua Giddings leading the antigag battle in the House, abolitionists gained a national forum for their ideas and won converts to their cause by identifying the "Slave Power" with the subversion of civil liberties. The gag rule controversy also persuaded many abolitionists of the need for more effective political weapons with which to defend traditional freedoms.

Still more decisive in provoking national debate on the merits of slavery and in forging a politics of abolition was the fight over the annexation of Texas. Both Andrew Jackson and Martin Van Buren had refrained from touching this hot potato, fearful of raising the slavery question. President John Tyler, however, seeking Southern support in the 1844 election, took it up. As his predecessors had feared, Tyler's bold decision aroused bitter exchanges over the status of slavery— without winning for himself his party's nomination, much less a return to the White House. Southerners insisted on a slave Texas "as indispensable to their security," while many Northerners (especially Whigs) reviled annexation as an outrageous plot to revitalize a monstrous institution. On February 28, 1845, the day Congress approved the admission of Texas to the Union, old John Quincy Adams wrote in his diary:

"The heaviest calamity that ever befell myself and my country was this day consummated."

More fateful by far, American annexation of Texas led directly and inevitably to war with Mexico, which still claimed that province as its own. And the Treaty of Guadalupe Hidalgo (1848) which ended that war, by ceding to the United States more than half a million square miles of Mexican soil made slavery beyond all doubt *the* issue in American politics. Would slavery be permitted to spread to these new lands, or would the region remain free soil, as Mexican law had decreed? "The United States will conquer Mexico," Ralph Waldo Emerson had predicted, "but it will be as the man swallows arsenic, which brings him down in turn. Mexico will poison us." It proved an accurate prophecy.

The Legacy of the Mexican War

2

Not all shared Emerson's foresight. Some, in fact, like a good many latter-day historians, refused to admit that slavery's status in the arid and barren Southwest was a legitimate issue. Daniel Webster dismissed the question as a "mere abstraction," while another contemporary insisted that "the whole controversy over the Territories related to an imaginary negro in an impossible place." Similarly, William Tecumseh Sherman told a Southern acquaintance in 1860: "If any calamity should befall our country in this question, the future historian would have the pleasant task of chronicling the downfall of the Great Republic because one class of [expurgated] would not permit theoretically another class of [expurgated] to go where neither party had the most remote intention to go, for I take it no sensible man, except an army officer who could not help himself, ever went to Utah, New Mexico or Arizona or even proposes to do so." Those who held such views could point to the 1860 census which listed only twenty slaveholders and forty-six slaves in all the federal territories.

Most Americans, however, were quick to perceive that the fate of slavery in western territories was a matter of crucial importance. To begin with, many Northerners genuinely feared (and Southerners hoped) that slavery would take root in the Southwest unless barriers were placed in its way. As James Russell Lowell's "Hosea Biglow" warned other Yankees:

> They may talk o' Freedom's airy
> Tell they're pupple in the face, —
> It's a grand gret cemetrary
> Fer the barthrights of our race;
> They jest want this Californy
> So's to lugh new slave-states in
> To abuse ye, an' to scorn ye,
> An' to plunder ye like sin.

Following the discovery of gold in California, reports appeared in Northern newspapers that companies of Southerners, "armed to the teeth," were being formed "for the express purpose of carrying slaves into California." Such reports were exaggerated but by no means wholly fanciful. Senator Jefferson Davis of Mississippi spoke of slave labor as essential to the development of commercial agriculture in southern California, while other Southerners boasted of slavery's perfect suitability to southwestern mining operations.

The question of slavery's extension also created concern because of the widespread belief that the institution must expand or die. "Keep it hedged up within the old field and it burns itself out," declared one New Hampshire congressman. "It is too improvident and exhausting a system for that and must seek a new, vigorous virgin soil to sustain it." Not only would the hedging in of slavery devalue Southern lands, but it would make increasingly burdensome and menacing an ever-larger, densely concentrated slave population. And, of course, slavery restriction would curtail the South's political power and hence its ability to fend off future assaults on the peculiar institution. There were serious flaws in the "expand or die" metaphor: slavery was both less wasteful and more resilient than contemporaries thought. But because most Northerners and Southerners believed it true, the argument lent urgency to the quarrel over slavery expansion.

A good many Northerners who cared little for the plight of slaves in Tennessee or Alabama nonetheless hoped to prevent slavery from spreading so as to protect their own selfish interests. Some were open racists wishing simply to keep "the territory free of negroes." Others, believing slave labor and free labor fundamentally incompatible, sought to defend the latter by denying any right to the former in the lands wrested from Mexico. Still others, more anti-South than antislavery, saw nonextension as a way of putting an arrogant Slave Power in its place. "They have trampled on the rights and just claims of the North sufficiently long and have fairly shit upon all our Northern statesmen and are now trying to rub it in," complained one salty New Englander in 1848, "and I think now is the time . . . for the North to take a stand and maintain it till they have brought the South to their proper level."

Honor as well as self-interest fueled this dispute. Northerners and Southerners alike perceived that the legal standing given to slavery in the territories would serve as a measure of the institution's moral acceptability in the nation. Free Soil advocates protested that any federal law making possible the introduction of slavery into California or New Mexico would require the active complicity of Northern representatives in the slave system. It was one matter to accept the constitutional safeguards thrown around the South's peculiar institution and to acquiesce in its existence where already rooted; it was a far different matter to be asked to bear a hand in its extension and revitalization. Prideful Southerners, on the other hand, bristled at talk of slavery restriction both because it stigmatized their society's most distinctive feature and because it threatened to deprive them, in John C. Calhoun's words, "of that perfect equality which belongs to them as members of the Union." To Southern whites, inequality signified slavery and they who knew it so well wanted no chains for themselves. "Death," vowed one of Calhoun's young disciples, "is preferable to acknowledged inferiority."

II

So momentous was the question of slavery expansion that proposals for its resolution sprouted almost as soon as the conflict with Mexico began. Scarcely eight weeks after Congress had declared war, in fact, on August 8, 1846, David Wilmot, a young Democratic representative from western Pennsylvania then serving his first term in Congress, attached to an appropriations bill a provision that slavery be excluded from any territory acquired from Mexico. Wilmot's Proviso, which deliberately copied the language of the Northwest Ordinance of 1787, carried in the House of Representatives, 83 to 64, along strict sectional lines. It died stillborn when the Senate failed to act before Congress adjourned. In subsequent sessions the proviso was brought forward time and again. Abraham Lincoln, a Whig representative in the Thirtieth Congress (1847–49), later claimed to have voted for the proviso "or the principle of it . . . at least forty times." Often, after angry debate, it passed in the House only to founder in the Senate where Southern influence prevailed. The principle it embodied, however—congressional prohibition of slavery in the territories—would become the ideological core of Free Soil and Republican parties.

Congressman Wilmot's motives in proposing a barrier against slavery expansion were mixed and only marginally philanthropic. Much of his concern was narrowly political. In part, at least, the proviso was designed to counter charges that the Slave Power had taken control of the Democratic party and that the Mexican War was being waged to enlarge slavery's dominions. Many Northern Democrats had themselves grown resentful of Southern dictation of party policy and looked upon the Wilmot Proviso as a way of standing up for their rights. As for the rights of black bondsmen, Wilmot showed scant concern.

I have no squeamish sensitiveness upon the subject of slavery, no morbid sympathy for the slave [Wilmot assured the House of Representatives in February 1847]. I plead the cause and rights of white freemen. I would preserve to free white labor a fair country, a rich inheritance, where the sons of toil, of my own race and own color, can live without the disgrace which association with negro slavery brings upon free labor.

Yet whatever the role of political and racial animus in framing the Wilmot Proviso, white Southerners were right to see it as a powerful challenge to the slave system everywhere—in states as well as territories. Wilmot himself admitted the emancipationist consequences of the proviso in a speech at Albany, New York, in October 1847. "Slavery has within itself the seeds of its own dissolution," he argued. "Keep it within limits, let it remain where it now is, and in time it will wear itself out." While Northern legislatures passed resolutions applauding the proviso, then, slave state representatives immediately denounced it as dangerous and insulting and issued proposals of their own for resolving the territorial question.

The most militant proslavery position—the direct antithesis of Wilmot's Proviso—is often called the "Calhoun doctrine," after the grim, haggard South Carolina statesman who developed it most fully. The federal territories, Calhoun contended in a speech to the U.S. Senate on February 19, 1847, were the common property of all the states, treasure purchased with the blood of young men from all parts of the nation. As such, citizens from every state had a right to migrate to any territory taking their property (slaves included) with them. Congress, as "joint agent" of the several states, had no constitutional authority to place restrictions on slavery in the common territories; and territorial governments, being merely the creatures of Congress, could not do what the parent body was forbidden to do. Thus, since ultimate sovereignty resided in the states, only when the people of a territory formed a state constitution might they rightfully pass upon slavery, one way or another. In short, every territory must be a slave territory. It was but a short step from this position to the one that in 1860 would splinter the Democratic party: namely, a demand for a federal code protecting slavery in the territories. "You will see," Calhoun informed one follower, "that I have made up the issue between North and South. If we flinch we are gone, but if we stand fast on it, we shall triumph either by compelling the North to yield to our terms, or declaring our independence of them."

Militant Southerners quickly rallied around Calhoun's "common property" doctrine, just as most Northerners—Democrats, at first, as well as Whigs—endorsed the Wilmot Proviso. To the orotund Thomas Hart Benton, these divergent theories seemed like the blades on a pair of shears: neither could cut by itself, but together they could sever the "map of the Union." Fearing such a result, moderates in both parties scrambled to put forward formulas for compromise.

One obvious solution to the controversy was to divide the territories between slavery, or at least the possibility of slavery, and freedom. Just such a compromise had defused an earlier crisis, when in 1820 Congress agreed to admit Missouri as a slave state (balancing it by the admission of Maine) but to ban slavery from the rest of the Louisiana Purchase above 36° 30′ N while permitting its establishment south of that line. No sooner had David Wilmot issued his call for free soil, in fact, than William Wick, a fellow Democrat from Indiana, offered a substitute amendment calling for extension of the Missouri Compromise line to any lands acquired from Mexico. Wick's amendment failed, 54 to 89, but many—including President James K. Polk, James Buchanan, John M. Clayton, and, for a time, Stephen A. Douglas—continued to find it appealing. Even many Calhounites, although denying the right of Congress to prohibit slavery anywhere, briefly backed the Missouri Compromise concept as an expedient solution to the territorial crisis. Calhoun himself fleetingly displayed a willingness to extend the 36° 30′ line to conquered territories, though he preferred that the initiative come from the North. Shelved during the 1850s, the Missouri Compromise principle would be resurrected during the winter of 1860–61 by politicians desperate to save a rapidly dividing Union.

A second proposal to end sectional conflict over the territories called upon Congress to let those most directly involved, the settlers themselves, decide whether to banish or admit slavery. First broached by Vice-President George M. Dallas, but given its fullest expression by Michigan's Lewis Cass, the Democratic candidate for president in 1848, popular sovereignty possessed undeniable appeal. Seemingly even-handed, it offered Northerners and Southerners an equal chance to set territorial policy on slavery. Moreover, by placing the decision in the hands of local pioneers, the doctrine both reaffirmed deeply held notions of popular rule and banished from Congress a sectionally explosive issue. Best of all, ambiguity concerning the moment at which territorial settlers might determine slavery's fate made possible widely divergent interpretations of its probable consequences. Northern advocates of popular sovereignty (nearly all of them Democrats) assured their constituents that a decision on slavery might be made promptly, just as soon as the first territorial assembly met. Since slaveholders would be reluctant to inhabit any territory until laws had been passed protecting their human property, an early judgment would almost certainly outlaw slavery. Southern politicians, on the other hand, sold popular sovereignty to slaveholders by insisting that a decision could be made only at the tag end of the territorial phase, when settlers drafted a state constitution and sought admission to the Union. In the interim (usually a period of several years), slavery would be recognized and protected as would any other form of property. Thus stated, popular sovereignty seemed indistinguishable from Calhoun's doctrine, just as the version peddled by Cass and company promised results no different from the Wilmot Proviso's. Only by keeping popular sovereignty's dissimilar meanings from colliding could Democratic leaders hope to maintain intraparty peace.

The simplest of all solutions to the quarrel over slavery expansion was the "No Territory" position. Traditionally opposed to territorial conquest, Whig leaders as diverse as Alexander H. Stephens (a Georgia congressman later to serve as vice-president of the Confederacy) and Thomas Corwin (a mildly antislavery senator from Ohio) hoped that by spurning new lands sectional conflict might be averted. As House Speaker Robert C. Winthrop of Massachusetts said early in 1848: "If the North can be prevented from uniting in such extension for fear the new territory would be slave & the South for fear it should be Free, we can put an end to all these projects of aggrandizement." The Treaty of Guadalupe Hidalgo, of course, rendered this plan inoperative, leaving Northern and Southern Whigs little room for cooperation on the nation's most pressing issue.

III

The events of 1848 showed just how dangerous the territorial dispute had become and how thorny would be its resolution. Not only did Congress continue its hostile and inconclusive debate over slavery's fate in the Southwest, but even a bill to organize faraway Oregon as a free territory produced bitter sectional exchanges. When in 1846 President Polk called for the organization of Oregon (whose northern border had at last been fixed at the forty-ninth parallel) nearly all expected the region to be free. Even so staunch a defender of Southern rights as Robert Barnwell Rhett of South Carolina admitted: "It is not probable that a single planter would ever desire to set his foot within its limits." But when Northern congressmen demanded that Oregon be organized without slavery, Southern representatives angrily protested. The exclusion of slave property from *any* territory, they insisted, would be an insulting and unconstitutional assault upon the institutions of the South. In August 1848 the free soil forces in Congress won the fight for Oregon, but only after insults, threats, and accusations of bad faith had magnified intersectional antagonism. Polk grudgingly signed the Oregon Bill, pointedly explaining that he did so only because Oregon lay north of the Missouri Compromise line.

Inevitably, the conflict over slavery expansion spilled over into the 1848 presidential campaign, even though both Whigs and Democrats sought to defuse the issue in order to preserve party unity and win the election. At their convention at Baltimore in May, the Democrats nominated the colorless Lewis Cass of Michigan for president and drafted a platform which, though condemning abolitionist troublemakers, made no mention of slavery in the territories. Cass's known endorsement of popular sovereignty of course bound the party informally to that formula. But by beating down attempts to clarify its meaning, Democrats were able to hawk popular sovereignty as a proslavery doctrine in the South and a surefire antislavery measure in the North. The Whigs went the Democrats one better. For president they nominated Zachary Taylor, a Mexican War hero, Louisiana slaveholder, and political neophyte; and to accommodate sectional disagreements on the territorial question they decided against a platform of any sort. Northern Whigs thus sought to capitalize upon Taylor's military fame and his presumed unwillingness to veto the Wilmot Proviso. At the same time, Southern Whigs touted the Hero of Buena Vista as one of their own, a more reliable champion of Southern rights than a Northerner like Cass.

Most Southerners, hoping that doctrinal looseness would yield political rewards, staunchly supported their party's ticket. In the North, however, a revolt of antislavery factions in both major parties led to the formation of the Free Soil party, a purely sectional party pledged to the Wilmot Proviso. As early as 1846, self-styled "Conscience" Whigs who believed slavery "a great moral, political, and social evil," had begun to attack not only the Slave Power but conservative, business-oriented "Cotton" Whigs who allegedly thought "more of sheep and cotton than of Man." The nomination of the slaveholder Taylor left such men "stunned stupefied outraged abased mortified and enraged to the last degree *beyond endurance.*" As it happened, a good many "Barnburner" Democrats (so labeled because critics likened their antislavery zeal to that of the Dutch farmer who torched his barn to get rid of its rats) were equally displeased with the nomination of Cass. In New York, where the Barnburner movement was strongest, a belief that Cass and his conservative "Hunker" allies had sabotaged Martin Van Buren's 1844 bid for the Democratic presidential nomination intensified such unhappiness. Meeting at Utica on June 22, 1848, the Barnburners proclaimed their political independence, whooped approval of a platform that denounced slavery as "a relic of barbarism which must necessarily be swept away in the progress of Christian civilization," and nominated Van Buren for president. Two months later, at Buffalo, New York, Barnburner Democrats joined hands with Conscience Whigs and Liberty party abolitionists from every Northern state to form a more broadly based Free Soil party. Van Buren, once "the catch-pole of slaveholders" but now a professed champion of slavery restriction (perhaps even of abolition in the District of Columbia), was again picked for president. As his running mate the Free Soilers chose the stiff-necked Charles Francis Adams, a Massachusetts Conscience Whig.

In some ways the Free Soil platform represented a watering down of the antislavery creed of the earlier Liberty party. Admitting the unconstitutionality of federal interference "with Slavery within the limits of any state," Free Soilers called simply for a congressional ban on slavery in the territories, an end to the admission of new slave states, and the withdrawal of all support for slavery where Congress possessed the right to act. The platform contained no criticism of racial discrimination, the Fugitive Slave Law of 1793, or the constitutional clause granting Southern states added representation in Congress for their slave populations. Yet in its demand for the denationalization of slavery and its forthright condemnation of the peculiar institution's basic immorality, the Free Soil creed provided a bridge between the principles of the Liberty party just disbanded and the Republican party yet to come. Owen Lovejoy, brother of the martyred abolitionist editor Elijah Lovejoy, pointed to this continuity of doctrine when he assured other Liberty men that "the principles of Liberty are in this [Free Soil] movement, undergird and surround it — the immediate object aimed at is one which we cordially approve, and the ultimate object is identical — the extinction of slavery."

Despite the Free Soil revolt and mutterings of dissatisfaction from Southern radicals like Calhoun and Alabama's William L. Yancey, the forces of nationalism — spurred as well as threatened by the late Mexican War — easily prevailed over those of divisive sectionalism in the election of 1848. Both Cass and Taylor drew substantial support in all parts of the country, with Taylor nailing down victory with electoral majorities both north and south of the Mason-Dixon line. Although a dozen Free Soil candidates won seats in the next Congress, that party's presidential ticket captured barely 10 percent of the popular vote and not a single electoral vote. National party attachments still held firm against the tugs of sectional interest, if only because both Whigs and Democrats had successfully papered over internal disagreements on the slavery question.

IV

By the time President Taylor took occupancy of the White House, the crisis over slavery had intensified. Not only had the discovery of gold in California (confirmed by Polk in his final message to Congress) lent urgency to the territorial issue, but a number of other slavery-related problems demanded attention. One arose from a conflict over the delineation of the Texas boundary with New Mexico: proslavery spokesmen championed the most extreme claims of the newest slave state, while free soilers supported the counterclaims of New Mexico, which seemed likely to become a free state. Another apple of discord was the South's resentment of Northern "personal liberty laws" which impeded the return of fugitive slaves. Although limited in their practical effect, such laws stung Southern pride, and by the late 1840s many were calling for a tough new federal statute to uphold the constitutional right of masters to a swift recovery of runaways. Still more friction arose over the status of slavery in the District of Columbia. For years, sensitive Southerners as well as Northerners and foreign visitors had found offensive the spectacle of slave auctions within the very shadow of the nation's capitol. Since slaveholders could auction off their human wares in nearby Baltimore, Annapolis, and Alexandria, why, many wondered, did Southern extremists hold out for the right to do so in Washington itself? Some, among them John G. Palfrey, Joshua Giddings, and Abraham Lincoln in the House of Representatives and John P. Hale in the Senate, now proposed that the ownership as well as the trade of slaves be abolished within the Federal District.

The widening rift between North and South prompted John C. Calhoun to convene a caucus of slave state congressmen in December 1848 to promote a united front against Northern aggression. That gathering's "Address," chiefly the work of Calhoun's pen, rehearsed a by-now-familiar litany of Northern wrongs and Southern rights. Southerners, this manifesto insisted, must "not be prohibited from migrating with our property, into the Territories of the United States, because we are slaveholders." Without parity in the territories an imbalance between slave and free states would grow inexorably until the later possessed the strength to impose universal emancipation—with all its horrors—upon a vanquished South. Although Calhoun had agreed to a slightly watered-down version in a bid for broad support, only forty-seven others (barely a third of the Southern contingent) set their names to his document. Moderate Democrats like Thomas Hart Benton and Sam Houston, who objected to the bellicose tone of the Southern Address, and nearly all Southern Whigs, who counted on Zachary Taylor to safeguard their region's interests and feared that Calhoun had in mind the destruction of their party, refused to sign. Still, the Southern Address exposed pervasive feelings of alienation and anxiety, and an ominous disillusionment with national parties as guardians of Southern rights.

The crisis deepened, and became still more alarming, during the spring and summer of 1849, at least when one listened to the radical voices in the South. In one Southern state after another, legislatures reaffirmed earlier resolutions against the Wilmot Proviso and took steps to cooperate with other slave states should that measure be enacted. President Taylor's shocking assurances to a Pennsylvania audience in August that "the people of the North need have no apprehension of the further extension of slavery," added to the South's distress and left Southern Whigs feeling stunned and betrayed. Talk of disunion was rife. Calhoun openly mused that "the alienation between the two sections has . . . already gone too far to save the union." He may have had in mind newspaper editorials like the one that appeared in the Sumter, South Carolina, *Banner,* contending that "the only remedy which will free . . . [the South] from Northern oppression, from the Wilmot Proviso and all its evil results, is the SECESSION OF THE SLAVEHOLDING STATES IN A BODY FROM THE UNION AND THEIR FORMATION INTO A SEPARATE REPUBLIC."

Equally ominous, in October 1849, Mississippi issued a call to all slave states, asking that they send representatives to a Southern convention at Nashville, Tennessee, early the following June "to devise and adopt some mode of resistance to [Northern] . . . aggressions." To many observers it seemed likely that this Nashville Convention might well point the way to disunion. Yet most Southerners and nearly all Northerners wished to avoid so calamitous an event, and pinned their hopes on the new Thirty-First Congress for a solution to sectional disputes.

The intensity of sectional feeling on the slavery issue showed itself first in the House of Representatives where for weeks a corporal's guard of Free Soilers and a half-dozen Southern "fire-eaters" prevented the election of a Speaker. At one point, when it appeared that one candidate had conspired to win Free Soil support by secretly promising to pack key committees with friends of the Wilmot Proviso, Robert Toombs of Georgia boiled over. Though until recently a Taylor Whig who had argued against Calhoun's schemes for Southern unity,

Toombs now warned the House that "if, by your legislation, you seek to drive us from the territories of California and New Mexico, purchased by the common blood and treasure of the whole people, and to abolish slavery in this District, thereby attempting to fix a national degradation upon half the states of this Confederacy, *I am for disunion.*" Finally, on December 22, after sixty-three ballots, the House selected Howell Cobb, a moderate Georgia Democrat, as Speaker and prepared to grapple with the issues dividing the nation.

The first plan of settlement came not from Congress but from President Taylor. An ardent nationalist who sought an end to narrow partisanship and sectional rancor, Taylor hoped to defuse the explosive territorial issue by admitting California and New Mexico directly to the Union as states. Some Southern Whigs had once been receptive to such a strategy, even though most expected both of these states to be free. By the time Taylor publicly embraced this plan, however, his close association with New York's Senator William H. Seward, his open opposition to slavery expansion, and Whig setbacks in Southern state elections had left the president with few supporters in the South. Nor, indeed, did Taylor's plan generate much enthusiasm among Northerners. Inevitably, then, others came forward with alternative plans for reconciliation: Senators Henry S. Foote, Stephen A. Douglas, Thomas Hart Benton, and the Great Compromiser himself—Henry Clay.

On January 29, 1850, the venerable Kentuckian (then seventy-three years old) rose to offer a compromise plan much broader in scope than any of the others. California, he proposed, should be admitted as a free state and Utah and New Mexico organized as territories without mention of slavery. Furthermore, Congress should induce Texas to surrender its extreme western boundary claims by offering to assume the $10 million Texas debt. Clay also suggested that slave trading (though not slavery itself) be suppressed in the District of Columbia, but that Southerners be given assurances that Congress contemplated no prohibition of the interstate slave trade. Finally, Clay proposed the enactment of a more stringent fugitive slave law.

This recipe for intersectional harmony was generally well received. Even a few Wilmot Proviso supporters, alarmed at the "distant thunder of disunion," thought well of it. But there was also loud and widespread opposition. Most Southern Democrats found the proposed settlement "utterly worthless and odious," a base surrender of Southern rights. Wilmot Proviso men, on the other hand, denounced Clay's proposals as flagrantly unjust: "sentiment for the north," fumed Senator Salmon P. Chase of Ohio, "substance for the south—just like the Missouri Compromise." Not only extremists found fault with the Kentuckian's compromise. President Taylor stuck firmly to the plan he had sketched in his annual message, and moderate Whigs like John Bell and Robert C. Winthrop, as well as Seward, refused to desert him for Clay.

Debate on Clay's compromise package, which began on February 5, revealed that party loyalty was rapidly crumbling under the weight of the slavery question. In the Senate, Wilmot Proviso Democrats like Benton and Hannibal Hamlin of Maine joined Northern Whigs (Daniel Webster and James Cooper excepted) in supporting Taylor's proposal for a piecemeal settlement, while Democrats Douglas, Cass, Foote, and William R. King worked backstage for Clay's plan. Opposing any form of compromise were the lone Free Soilers Salmon Chase and John P. Hale, and extreme advocates of Southern rights, among them John C. Calhoun and Jefferson Davis.

In April, after weeks of impassioned preliminary debate, the Senate referred Clay's compromise plan, along with alternate proposals, to a special committee of thirteen. On May 8, Henry Clay, as chairman of that committee, reported three bills that embodied his earlier resolutions. The first of these linked free statehood for California, territorial organization of Utah and New Mexico without restriction on slavery, and resolution of the Texas boundary problem. The second was a fugitive slave bill (patterned after one drafted by Virginia's James M. Mason), and the third suppressed the slave trade in the District of Columbia.

Clay seemingly hoped that by joining California statehood to the organization of Utah and New Mexico without the Wilmot Proviso he could sweeten the pill enough for Taylorites to swallow it. If so, he was soon disappointed. The president and his followers gave this "Omnibus Bill" a frosty reception, as did radicals both North and South. "This bill turns the whole of the territories into a slave pasture," cried Hale of New Hampshire, while Georgia's Robert Toombs warned that the passage of a measure so patently unfair would cause Southerners to swear "eternal hostility to your foul domination."

Still, the forces supporting the Omnibus Bill were strong—Clay, Webster, Douglas, Cass, and Foote—and for weeks no one could predict its fate. In July, however, the unexpected death of President Taylor (a victim, it was said, of too much Independence Day sun, followed by copious draughts of iced milk and cherries) suddenly strengthened the compromisers' hand. At once, the new president, Millard Fillmore, signaled an about-face in administration policy. His appointment of Daniel Webster as secretary of state in a wholly reconstituted cabinet was but the first of many signs that Clay's compromise now had a friend in the White House. Yet, even so, it proved impossible to enact the

Omnibus Bill in one chunk. Congress seemed stalemated, despite backstage pressure to win over irresolute opponents of the bill.

In the end, it was less such arm-twisting than a change in tactics that pulled the compromise through. On the last day of July the foes of compromise won an apparent victory when they succeeded in stripping the Omnibus Bill of all its provisions save for the organization of Utah. "Jefferson Davis' face grinned with smiles," reported the *New York Express*. Benton "bristled with delight" at having bested his old enemy Clay. Chase shook hands with Pierre Soulé of Louisiana. Seward danced "about like a little top." But this "carnival of joy" was short-lived. On August 1 the Senate passed the Utah Bill. Then, after the weary Clay had left to recuperate at Newport, Rhode Island, Stephen A. Douglas took charge and one by one steered the compromise bills safely through Congress. First came the admission of California as a free state, then an act organizing New Mexico without restriction on slavery (the boundary dispute with Texas having first been settled, the Texans getting $10 million for surrendering their most extreme claims), then the Fugitive State Act, and finally a statute abolishing the slave trade in the District of Columbia. By September 20, 1850, President Fillmore had signed them all into law and Congress adjourned, hoping that the nation's "five gaping wounds" (as Clay had called them) had at last been healed.

Those who looked closely at the process and results of the compromise, however, saw plainly that it had at best forestalled, not ended, sectional confrontation—that in important respects it was not a true compromise at all. Some issues had without question been clearly resolved: the Texas–New Mexico boundary dispute, the admission of California, and the buying and selling of slaves in the District of Columbia. But resolution of the dispute over fugitive slaves was more apparent than real, as would soon become plain. And the future of slavery itself in Washington was anything but certain. Potentially more serious, the organization of Utah and New Mexico without restriction on slavery left ambiguous the question of whether a territorial legislature might rule on slavery's status, or whether, as Southerners insisted, congressional "nonintervention" meant that slavery could not be excluded prior to statehood. With cause, Salmon P. Chase observed: "The question of slavery in the territories has been avoided. It has not been settled." Acceptance of the popular sovereignty formula would soon permit Stephen A. Douglas to claim that the Compromise of 1850 justified repeal of the Missouri Compromise restriction on slavery in the northern reaches of the Louisiana Purchase.

Indeed, analysis of the roll calls on the several compromise bills raises doubt as to whether there really was a compromise in 1850. Clearly there was not, as the historian David Potter observes, if by compromise one means an agreement in which each party to a dispute agrees to certain measures sought by the other. For balloting on the various compromise bills was strikingly sectional, each being enacted on the votes of a majority of one section (plus a small bloc of middle-of-the-roaders) despite the opposition of the other section. One might better call the settlement of 1850 a truce or an armistice, Potter suggests, than a genuine compromise.

V

Yet the substance, if not the process, of Clay's peace package seemed to be a compromise to most contemporaries. At first optimism over its healing power was widespread. Even critics sourly admitted that "the sickly air of compromise filled the land." Americans everywhere heaved sighs of relief that civil war had been averted.

In the South, the most immediate effect of the compromise was to shatter the secessionist movement that had been so threatening in 1849. In fact, Henry Clay's proposals, by offering Southern Whigs an attractive alternative to President Taylor's "unacceptable" plan, largely deflated the disunionists even before the compromise became law. The result was a marked shift in the South's attitude toward the Nashville Convention. Hopeful now that their interests could be protected within the Union, Southerners cooled noticeably toward talk of secession and any gathering which seemed to point in that direction. When it came time to select delegates to the Nashville meeting, only South Carolina and Mississippi showed any appreciable interest. "Of the eight millions of people in the Southern States," reported the *New Orleans Daily Crescent* in May 1850, "not ten thousand . . . [took part in] the appointments of the delegates . . . who will attend the Nashville Convention."

While still in the works, then, the compromise had doomed the Nashville Convention to failure. On June 3, 1850, delegates from only nine of fifteen slave states showed up at the Tennessee capital. Despite a goodly number of fiery-tongued extremists on hand, the tone of the gathering was surprisingly moderate. South Carolina's Robert Barnwell Rhett condemned Clay's proposal and scolded the South for being too forbearing and submissive. But most delegates, believing that "the disruption of the confederacy or . . . the abandonment of the territories to prevent such a result" would be a tragic mistake, expressed a willingness to "acquiesce" in the extension of the Missouri Compromise line to the Pacific—a solution long favored by such conservative Southerners as John Bell and James K. Polk. Realizing that they could not effectively denounce Northern aggressions until they knew the fate of Clay's plan, the Nashville Convention adjourned for six weeks. A second session, meeting after Congress had adopted the compromise measures, was even more pathetic than the first. Its representation was even more spotty and irregular than before, and the resolutions it passed—asserting state rights, upholding the right of secession, and criticizing the Compromise—passed largely unnoticed in the South.

The slave states had rejected disunion, at least for the time being. Yet by no means had they wholeheartedly or unreservedly embraced the Compromise of 1850. The colorful, free-spirited Sam Houston of Texas had been the only member of Congress from the Deep South to vote for *all* parts of the Compromise. Southerners still grumbled over the admission of California, settlement of the Texas-New Mexico border dispute, and suppression of slave sales in Washington. The consensus of Southern opinion was best represented by the Georgia Platform of December 1850, the work of a special state convention, which announced a conditional acceptance of the late Compromise. Though willing to accept the Compromise "as a permanent adjustment of this sectional controversy," Georgia proclaimed its determination "to resist, even (as a last resort) to a disruption of every tie which binds her to the Union"; any act of Congress abolishing slavery in the territories, the District of Columbia, or federal forts and navy yards within the South; any attempt to restrict the interstate slave trade; any ban on new slave states; or any interference with the Fugitive Slave Law.

Most other slave states followed suit, proclaiming a qualified adherence to the Compromise. Especially vehement was the insistence that Northerners attest their good faith by upholding the new Fugitive Slave Act. "Let this question of Slavery alone," cautioned one North Carolina newspaper, "take it out and keep it out of Congress; and respect and enforce the Fugitive Slave Law as it stands. If not, *we leave you!* Before God and man . . . if you fail in this simple act of justice, *the bonds will be dissolved!*" Secession, it was clear, had been set aside but not forgotten.

Northerners, too, quickly rallied around the Compromise. Even many former opponents now crossed their fingers and hoped that the Compromise had ended the sectional crisis once and for all. The friends of compromise were sure that it had. "There is, I believe, peace now prevailing throughout our borders," Henry Clay proclaimed in September 1850. "I believe it is permanent." And President Fillmore, in both his first and second annual messages to Congress, expressed his belief that the Compromise of 1850 was "a final settlement of the dangerous and exciting subjects which they embraced."

Such men proved poor prophets. For the truth was that however many might give support to the Compromise—with or without reservations—so long as there remained militant groups in North and South, the one committed to a crusade against the sin of slavery and the other to a defense of human bondage as a "positive good," any compromise involving slavery was bound to be fragile and short-lived. The decidedly sectional vote on the various components of the Compromise bespoke its essential weakness. Indeed, the Compromise began to crumble, and sectional tempers to flare anew, long before the explosion over the Kansas-Nebraska Bill in 1854. Debates at the next session of Congress (1850–51), in fact, showed that the slavery issue was still very much alive. Ironically, Southern friends of the Compromise were the first to open old wounds: Henry S. Foote set forth an entirely superfluous resolution declaring the Compromise a "definitive settlement of the questions growing out of domestic slavery," and Henry Clay requested a reexamination of means to suppress the African slave trade. "What have we heard of all this session?" grumbled Massachusetts senator Robert Rantoul. "'Quiet agitation'; and quieting agitation is the noisiest business we have." Matters had come to such a pass, groused Representative Charles Chapman of Connecticut, that were a congressman to die, a resolution of condolence could not pass without a rider reaffirming the Fugitive Slave Law.

Northerners, of course, also did their bit to keep the slavery question simmering in the aftermath of the Compromise. Harriet Beecher Stowe's wonderfully effective *Uncle Tom's Cabin* (published serially in the Washington *National Era* beginning in June 1851 and in book form early the following year) not only spread a sugar-coated antislavery message before literally millions of readers, at home and abroad, but by provoking an outraged Southern response touched off a far-reaching series of literary and journalistic exchanges on the meaning of human bondage. The visit to the United States of Louis Kossuth, exiled hero of Hungary's abortive bid for independence, added still more fuel to the sectional controversy. Although he tried to steer clear of the slavery question (thus alienating Garrisonian abolitionists), those who honored the "noble Magyar's" struggle for self-determination abroad inevitably passed implied censure on slavery at home. And "by turning the minds of all parties to the subject of universal liberty," Kossuth himself helped to keep antislavery agitation alive. "Every speech he makes is the best kind of Abolition lecture," Senator Benjamin Wade of Ohio exulted. "This is felt keenly by our Southern brethren."

The main source of sectional friction during these years, however, was the harsh Fugitive Slave Law. Viewed by Southerners as an essential part of the Compromise of 1850, the new statute—which denied alleged runaways the protection of habeas corpus, jury trial, and the right to give evidence—struck many Northerners as an "infamous" violation of basic civil liberties. While even moderates in the Deep South threatened secession if the Fugitive Slave Law were not faithfully executed, most Northerners deplored the law and supported it grudgingly if at all. Even such conservatives as Edward Everett, recently president of Harvard and a notorious abolitionist-baiter, pronounced the law unenforceable and expressed an unwillingness to obey it. Not even the Wilmot Proviso, rejoiced Charles Sumner, had offered such agitational advantages as the despotic extradition law. "This law," thundered the Reverend Charles Beecher,

> . . . is an unexampled climax of sin. It is the monster iniquity of the present age, and it will stand forever on the page of history, as the vilest monument of infamy of the nineteenth century. Russia knows nothing like it. . . . And nations afar off pause awhile from their worship of blocks of wood and stone, to ask what will those Christians do next.

Apart from serving as a fresh reminder of slavery's basic immorality, what most affronted Northerners was the way the Fugitive Slave Law authorized federal marshals to form local posses and to compel "all good citizens . . . to aid and assist" in the nasty business of slave catching. It was one thing to accept the existence of slavery in Southern states; it was an altogether different matter to be forced, under threat of heavy fine or jail sentence, to become an accomplice in the reenslavement of runaways—many of whom had for years lived blameless lives in Northern communities. Indeed, some argued that the Fugitive Slave Law served to nationalize slavery. "If the Free States are not Free Soil for every slave that escapes to them," warned the *Boston Commonwealth,* "then they are virtually slave territory."

As time passed, the initial uproar over the Fugitive Slave Law subsided. Union-minded Northerners preached the need to abide by all terms of the Compromise of 1850, and except in New England the return of runaways encountered scant opposition. Yet acts of resistance, though infrequent, were dramatic enough to keep sectional antagonism festering. Moderate groups still held the upper hand, as the formal endorsement of the Compromise by both major parties in 1852 made plain. Franklin Pierce of New Hampshire easily won that year's presidential election, thanks to the return of most Barnburners to the Democratic fold and Southern fears that the Whig candidate, Winfield Scott, would follow the lead of such Northern advisors as William H. Seward. Sectional tension, however, remained high, notwithstanding blustery reaffirmations of the Compromise's "finality." And the virtual collapse of organized Whiggery (Scott carried only four states, none in the Deep South) left the republic bound by but a single national party. It also created a political vacuum from which there would soon emerge a new, antislavery, Republican party.

"A Hell of a Storm"

Slavery, though the most fateful, was far from the only controversial issue of the 1850s. Questions such as temperance and immigration also aroused political passions during these years. The demise of the Whig party, in fact, owed much to its failure to define clear and distinctive stands on just such issues. Indeed, until 1856 it appeared that the principal challenge to Democratic ascendancy would come not from antislavery Republicans but from the antiforeign, anti-Catholic Native American party.

Nativism, especially anti-Catholic feeling, had been a powerful social force in America for centuries. What gave it intensity and transformed it into a lusty political movement was the massive immigration of Irish and German Catholics to the United States during the 1840s and 1850s. Between 1845 and 1854 nearly 3 million immigrants, "pushed" from their European homes by famine, political upheaval, economic dislocation, and religious dissatisfaction and "pulled" to America by glowing (often unrealistic) reports of freedom and opportunity for all, poured into the United States.

Such aliens, and particularly the Irish who settled primarily in the great cities of the Northeast—Boston, New York, Philadelphia, Baltimore—seemed to many Americans to pose a real threat to the established order and traditional values. Mainly Catholic in a land overwhelmingly Protestant, their demands for public support of parochial schools and the opening of teaching posts to Catholics struck many Protestants as a potential menace to the sacred concept of separation of church and state. The decided preference of Irish and German Catholics for the Democratic party, and their tendency to vote as urban bosses dictated, alarmed still others. Some blamed cheap immigrant labor for driving down the wages of American workers, while social reformers pointed to immigration as "the principal source of crime and pauperism in this county" and complained loudly of Irish hostility to the temperance and antislavery movements.

The logical political vehicle for such nativist feeling was the Whig party. Of the major parties it was the most solidly Protestant and, in its Northern branch, the most solidly antislavery. It also included the bulk of temperance advocates. The problem was that by the 1850s, when a sharp increase in the political participation of aliens made a political counterattack by nativists seem imperative, the Whig party was hopelessly ineffectual, divided within itself—a beached whale. Inevitably, then, those native-born Americans, especially laboring and middle-class Protestants in the Northeast who saw Catholic immigrants as a threat to such fundamental values as public order, political democracy, public education, and social mobility, sought some political third force to attack and neutralize that threat.

The party thus formed was an offshoot of the Order of the Star Spangled Banner, a secret nativist society formed in New York in 1849. In the 1850s its members became known as the "Know-Nothings" and their party as the Native American party. Its platform called for checks on the immigration of paupers and criminals, strict voter registration laws, and a twenty-one year probationary period for naturalized citizenship. Profiting from a growing sense that both Whigs and Democrats had become dangerously corrupt and unresponsive to the needs of the voters, the new party briefly enjoyed spectacular success. In 1854 Massachusetts Know-Nothings swept the field, electing 11 congressmen, a governor, all state officers, all state senators, and all but 2 of 378 state representatives. Even in the South, where concern over immigration and papal influence was marginal, Know-Nothings exploited Whiggery's collapse to win occasional victories.

Such triumphs were fleeting. As Horace Greeley had predicted, political nativism proved "as devoid of the elements of persistence as an anti-cholera or anti-potato rot party." Some voters turned away when the nativist party failed to make good on campaign promises to lengthen the naturalization period and deny aliens the vote. Others bridled at the order's secrecy, its ritualistic mumbo jumbo, its elaborate hierarchy, all of which exposed adherents to the charge of being undemocratic. Still others (especially those who had viewed the Know-Nothing party as a vehicle of political reform) found repellent the bully-boy tactics of nativists who in Baltimore, Cincinnati, Louisville, St. Louis, and elsewhere destroyed ballots and terrorized immigrants in order to win elections. What most crippled the Know-Nothings, however, was sectional conflict over the Kansas-Nebraska Act and competition from the new Republican party which formed in response to that measure.

II

By the early 1850s pressure from land-hungry settlers for the organization of the vast Nebraska territory, a region stretching north from the thirty-seventh parallel to the Canadian border between the Missouri River and the Rocky Mountains, had been intense. During the summer of 1853 the commissioner of Indian affairs (aptly named George Manypenny) removed one obstacle to white settlement by negotiating purchase treaties with the powerful tribes who had previously controlled these lands. That fall two groups of pioneers, one from Missouri and the other from near Council Bluffs, Iowa, settled in the Kansas River district at Fort Leavenworth. There they established territorial governments which, though extralegal, showed the impatience of Westerners for the opening of fresh lands in Nebraska.

Yet obstacles still remained. Most serious was the opposition of Southerners to any territorial bill that denied them equal rights— including the right to hold slave property, despite the Missouri Compromise ban on slavery in this very region. The recent admission of California as a free state strengthened the South's determination to prevent Nebraska's organization as free soil. In March 1853 all Southern senators, save those from Missouri, united to defeat by a whisker a bill (already approved by the House) which would have organized the part of the Nebraska territory that is today Kansas without slavery. By the time the Thirty-Third Congress convened in December 1853, Missouri too had swung into line, opposing organization of Nebraska if slaveholders were excluded. Indeed Senator David R. Atchison, who, admitting the finality of the Missouri Compromise, had in March voted to organize Nebraska as a free territory, now vowed to see Nebraska "sink in hell" before he would vote to make it free soil. The hot-tempered Missourian, anticipating a stiff fight for reelection against the formidable Thomas Hart Benton, found himself bolstered in his newfound resolve by editorials like that in the St. Louis *Republican* which warned: "If Nebraska be made a free Territory then will Missouri be surrounded on three sides by free territory, where there will always be men and means to assist in the escape of our slaves. . . . With the emissaries of abolitionists around us, and the facilities of escape so enlarged, this species of property would become insecure, if not valueless, in Missouri."

Still another impediment to the establishment of a government for Nebraska was sectional rivalry over the construction of a railroad to the Pacific coast. Congress had expressed an unwillingness to support more than one transcontinental road, and Southerners, who favored a line from New Orleans to the Pacific by way of El Paso and the Gila Valley, rightly saw an unorganized Nebraska as a hindrance to construction along a central route. Since many Eastern politicians opposed any federally subsidized Pacific railroad, Northwestern champions of a transcontinental line recognized their dependence upon the backing of Southerners and the need, therefore, to soothe apprehensions about the rights of slaveholders in Nebraska.

None saw this more clearly than did Stephen A. Douglas of Illinois, chairman of the Senate Committee on the Territories. A devoted nationalist and Jacksonian Democrat, Douglas looked upon the organization of Nebraska and the construction of a Pacific railway as interconnected parts of a magnificent program not just of western but of *national* development. He asked in 1853,

> How are we to develop, cherish and protect our immense interests and possessions on the Pacific, with a vast wilderness fifteen hundred miles in breadth, filled with hostile savages, and cutting off all direct communication? The Indian barrier must be removed. The tide of emigration and civilization must be permitted to roll onward until it rushes through the passes of the mountains, and spreads over the plains, and mingles with the waters of the Pacific. Continuous lines of settlement with civil, political and religious institutions all under the protection of law, are imperiously demanded by the highest national considerations. These are essential, but they are not sufficient. No man can keep up with the spirit of this age who travels on anything slower than the locomotive, and fails to receive intelligence by lightning. We must therefore have Rail Roads and Telegraphs from the Atlantic to the Pacific, through our own territory.

From the moment he entered Congress, in the mid-1840s, Douglas had worked to give life to his dream. His advocacy of a Pacific railroad over a central route was well known, as was his support for free western homesteads, a transcontinental telegraph line, and an overland mail service. Repeatedly he had introduced bills to establish a territorial government for Nebraska. The narrow defeat of the latest such measure, in March 1853, left Douglas bitter but hopeful, and when the Thirty-Third Congress convened nine months later he was prepared to make a new stab at organizing Nebraska, this time in such a way as to win Southern backing.

Douglas found his solution in the Compromise of 1850. Arguing that passage of the Utah and New Mexico acts now made popular sovereignty the accepted national policy toward slavery in the territories,

Douglas presented to Congress on January 4, 1854, a bill for the organization of Nebraska which, without directly repealing the Missouri Compromise line, left settlers free to decide the slavery question for themselves. Apparently Douglas hoped that by simply sidestepping the Missouri Compromise he could curry favor with Southerners without giving needless offense to Northerners. If so, he was soon brought to earth by slave state representatives who reminded him that unless it was *explicitly* repealed the 1820 restriction would remain in effect until Nebraska voted to set it aside. Not only powerful Democrats such as Senators James M. Mason, and R. M. T. Hunter of Virginia, Andrew P. Butler of South Carolina, and Missouri's Atchison, but Southern Whigs, desperate to prove themselves reliable defenders of Southern rights, insisted that the Missouri Compromise ban on slavery north of 36° 30′ be expressly repealed.

Bowing to such pressure, Douglas on January 23 submitted to the Senate a revised measure that categorically overturned the Missouri Compromise. Popular sovereignty, unencumbered, would settle the fate of slavery in a vast domain once set aside for freedom. (The practical meaning of popular sovereignty—might a decision against slavery be made before a territory became a state?—was deliberately left ambiguous.) The revised bill also divided Nebraska into two territories: Kansas to the west of Missouri, and Nebraska abutting Iowa and Minnesota, thus encouraging speculation that one would become slave, the other free.

As Douglas had predicted, repeal of the Missouri Compromise (which he himself had once proclaimed "a sacred thing, which no ruthless hand would ever be reckless enough to disturb") kicked up a "hell of a storm" throughout the North. In Congress, a handful of free soilers issued an "Appeal . . . to the People of the United States." Skillfully drafted, mainly by Senator Salmon P. Chase of Ohio who proudly called it "the *most valuable* of my works," that address indicted the Kansas-Nebraska Bill "as a gross violation of a sacred pledge; as a criminal betrayal of precious rights; as part and parcel of an atrocious plot to exclude from a vast unoccupied region immigrants from the Old World and free laborers from our own States, and convert it into a dreary region of despotism, inhabited by masters and slaves." First published in the Washington *National Era* and the *New York Times* a day after Douglas had introduced his revised ordinance, the "Appeal" was soon reprinted in newspapers across the North. In city after city petition campaigns were mounted and mass rallies staged to protest the "Nebraska infamy" and Northern "doughfaces" who endorsed it. To men like Abraham Lincoln (then riding circuit in central Illinois) it was especially alarming that Douglas, a *Northerner* with no direct stake in slavery, had sponsored a measure that potentially enlarged slavery's pastures. The Slave Power, which had previously been "warring on the defensive side," seemed suddenly aggressive, bent on the overthrow of all legal barriers to bondage.

Not only, then, did such conservative Whigs as Hamilton Fish and Thomas Ewing now stand shoulder to shoulder with Whiggish liberals and seasoned Free Soilers in condemning Douglas's "treasonable scheme," but many Democrats joined in. In Cincinnati, 1,000 "unquestioned and adamantine" Democrats signed a call for a Nebraska protest meeting; in Chicago, both the chairman and principal speaker at the city's first anti-Nebraska rally were prominent Democrats. "The Nebraska peace measure is working as might be expected," wrote one of Franklin Pierce's New Hampshire friends. "Everybody almost is ready for a rebellion." Douglas himself would ruefully admit, "I could travel from Boston to Chicago by the light of my own effigy."

All the same, Douglas escorted his bill unscathed through the halls of Congress. In the Senate, the measure passed easily, 37 to 14, on the votes of 14 free state Democrats and Southerners of both parties. John Bell of Tennessee and Sam Houston of Texas were the only Southern senators voting "nay." In the House, however, the battle was much hotter and closer. Insults and threats came thick and fast, and more than once drawn pistols sent shivers through the chamber. Here defections among Northern Democrats were more serious than in the Senate and at one point 66 of 92 free state Democrats voted against the bill, temporarily defeating it. In the end, however, by means of political arm-twisting lost in the mists of history, enough Northern Democrats were added to a once-again solid Southern contingent to secure passage by 113 to 100. As expected, President Pierce, heavily dependent upon Southern support for the success of his domestic and foreign programs, signed the Kansas-Nebraska Bill on May 30, 1854.

The forces of sectionalism were dramatically apparent in the Kansas-Nebraska decision. An examination of the combined tally in the House and Senate shows that nearly 90 percent of all Southerners in Congress voted for Douglas's measure, while 64 percent of the Northern representatives cast ballots against it. Sectional pressures simply overwhelmed the moribund Whig troop: on the decisive roll call every one of fifty-two Northern Whig senators and representatives voted "nay," while three out of every four Southern Whigs voted for passage. Yet within the Democracy, partisan loyalty still counted for much; without it repeal of the Missouri Compromise barrier would have been impossible. In the end 56 percent of all Northern Democratic congressmen braved charges of truckling to slaveholders and voted as their party leaders told them to—in favor of the Kansas-Nebraska Bill. Just how long such party regularity could be sustained in the face of sectional currents that had now demolished organized Whiggery remained to be seen.

In light of all the protest and schism the Kansas-Nebraska Act touched off, much of which its author had anticipated, it is worth pondering Douglas's motives in presenting it and promoting it so vigorously. In his own eyes, and those of his champions, Douglas had merely responded to western pressure to open fresh lands for settlement, thereby making possible the integration and development of the American republic all the way to the Pacific. He had not sought the overthrow of the Missouri Compromise, but some concession to slavery had been necessary to secure Southern cooperation in the organization of Nebraska. It had been a price worth paying, for settlement of the central plains would, he predicted, "impart peace to the country & stability to the Union." Criticism was to be expected; but, Douglas assured one Georgia Democrat, "The storm will soon spend its fury, and the people of the north will sustain the measure when they come to understand it."

Without wholly discounting the senator's own explanation for his actions, one may admit that narrower, less noble impulses also played a part. Political considerations clearly counted for much. For Douglas, the Kansas-Nebraska measure offered a chance to curry Southern support for his presidential ambitions, gratify Westerners eager for new lands and a Pacific railroad, and strengthen the Democratic party by burning off unreliable elements and reaffirming its commitment to popular rule. Moreover, by paving the way for construction of a railway to the Pacific by a central or northern route, the Kansas-Nebraska Act promised benefits not only to his region but, thanks to real estate holdings in Chicago and Superior City, Wisconsin, to Douglas's pocket as well.

Finally, one should bear in mind what was perhaps the greatest of all Stephen Douglas's shortcomings: his failure to understand that slavery was a moral as well as a practical issue. Having at best a lukewarm aversion to the institution (he was, in fact, absentee manager of nearly 150 slaves in Mississippi, a legacy from his first wife), Douglas found it hard to grasp other men's attachment to the Missouri Compromise and their fury at its repeal. Characteristic of his attitude toward the peculiar institution was his statement to a Tennessee audience in 1858:

Whenever a territory has a climate, soil, and productions
making it the *interest* of the inhabitants to encourage slave property, they will pass a slave code and give it encouragement.
Whenever the climate, soil, and productions preclude the
possibility of slavery being profitable, they will not permit it.
You come right back to the principle of dollars and cents.

Believing that geographic conditions and popular sovereignty would
keep Nebraska free, and convinced that slavery was a question of
secondary importance anyway, Douglas proudly accepted responsibility
for a measure thousands bitterly assailed. "I passed the Kansas-
Nebraska Act myself," he boasted. "I had the power of a dictator
throughout the whole controversy in both houses."

Whatever the motives behind it, the consequences of the Kansas-
Nebraska Act were momentous beyond anticipation. Douglas himself
lost standing in the North without appreciably strengthening his
political support in the South. His attempt to sell popular sovereignty as
an antislavery doctrine had backfired, for as one historian notes,
"When Douglas, with a broad wink at the southerners in Congress, invited them to vote for popular sovereignty as a device for overthrowing
the guarantees of freedom north of 36° 30′, he permanently discredited
his own doctrine in the eyes of any potential antislavery supporters."
Moreover, Northern Democrats paid dearly for their party's role in
overturning the Missouri restriction. In the congressional elections of
1854 and 1855, free state Democrats suffered crushing reverses, losing
all but twenty-five of the ninety-one seats they had held on the eve of the
Kansas-Nebraska explosion. Southern Democrats, having managed to
hold their own (sixty-seven seats in 1854, sixty-three in 1856), now outnumbered their Northern colleagues in the House of Representatives by
more than two to one. Although the balance in the Senate remained
closer than in the House, and although the Pennsylvania Democrat
James Buchanan captured the presidency in 1856, the nation's sole intersectional party had acquired a distinctly Southern cast. Most significant, by galvanizing Northern advocates of free soil and destroying
what remained of a national Whig party, the Kansas-Nebraska crisis
prepared the way for an antislavery alliance mightier than any that had
gone before.

III

None were quicker to condemn the Nebraska "infamy," nor to
glimpse the political opportunity it afforded, than the Free Soilers. Hav-

ing kept their spirits high, party lines firm, and principles intact, despite repeated electoral setbacks and attempts by the major parties to muffle the slavery question, Free Soilers rejoiced at the growing popularity of their principles. "Our position is now rather enviable," cheered Joshua Giddings as the Nebraska storm began to brew. "We lead the hosts of freedom." While some like Giddings hoped that anti-Nebraska defectors from the Whig and Democratic parties might rally under the Free Soil banner to battle the newly aggressive Slave Power, most third-party veterans agreed that the crisis at hand required the formation of a powerful new antislavery coalition. "This war with slavery is too radical, too difficult, too long, too big for success without a power constructed especially for it," one Maine Free Soiler asserted. "Cromwell needed a better army and so do we." All, however, were determined to bind the new party to the broad antislavery principles contained in the Free Soil platforms of 1848 and 1852.

The Kansas-Nebraska upheaval also raised the hopes of Northern Whigs. Some optimists predicted that the "honest, reflecting" masses, recalling the unanimous opposition of Northern Whig congressmen to Douglas's bill, would turn in this "hour of trouble to the Whig party." "Never were our political skies more bright and cheering," boasted one Whig editor in Ohio. Like the Free Soilers, however, most free state Whigs early saw the utility of a completely new political party. The "betrayal" of Southern Whigs, who had chosen section over party in voting to obliterate the Missouri restriction, left Whigs in the North no choice but to forge some new partisan alliance "or be forever the vassals of imperious task masters." Besides, the issues that had once defined Whiggery — banks, tariffs, roads and canals — had of late lost force, making political reorganization relatively painless. "Well," one Illinois Whig concluded in April 1854, "Whig, Democrat & free soil are now all 'obsolete ideas,' and all bygones are gone forever — and what shall we do next? What but unite on *principle* instead of *party.*"

Even some Democrats were sufficiently outraged at the repeal of the Missouri Compromise line to join willingly with antislavery Whigs and Free Soilers in creating a new opposition party. Deep-seated loyalties, a solicitude for traditional Jacksonian programs, and fear for the Union should politics become sectionalized kept most Democrats in line. But disenchantment with Southern dictation of policy and a heightened sense of impotence as the party fell under the sway of "Whiggish" thinkers like William L. Marcy and James Buchanan combined with genuine antislavery convictions to persuade a fair number of Democrats that the time had come to form new political allegiances. Some jumped ship sooner than others, but by 1856 perhaps 15 percent of the Republican party's strength came from former Democrats, among them such leaders as Gideon Welles, Preston King, Francis P. Blair, and David Wilmot.

The first steps toward a fusion of these disparate anti-Nebraska elements came while Congress was still debating Stephen Douglas's bill. On February 22, 1854, Free Democrats in Michigan met at Jackson and fashioned a state ticket headed by Kinsley S. Bingham, a "Free Soil Cass man" in 1848, and two former Whigs. Six days later, antislavery Whigs, Democrats, and Free Soilers in Wisconsin gathered in Ripon's Congregational church and vowed, should the Kansas-Nebraska Bill pass, to form a new "Republican" party dedicated to slavery restriction. That May, some thirty members of the U.S. House of Representatives likewise adopted the name "Republican" and agreed on the necessity of a new political organization to check Southern aggressions. By mid-summer statewide anti-Nebraska fusion conventions had been convened in Vermont and throughout the Middle West. Elsewhere in the North, anti-Nebraska forces cooperated closely, often nominating overlapping slates, but without, as yet, formal union.

Not all of these new coalitions christened themselves Republican, and the intensity of antislavery conviction varied from state to state. As a rule, where political abolitionism had been a force of long standing, as in Vermont, Michigan, and Wisconsin, the new party seized the name Republican and endorsed resolutions similar to the Free Soil platforms of 1848 and 1852: excoriating slavery as "a great moral, social, and political evil," demanding its abolition in the nation's capital and its exclusion from federal territories, urging repeal of the Fugitive Slave Act, and seeking an end to the admission of any more slave states. Where, on the other hand, radical elements were weak, Whiggery still hardy, or political nativism strong, alliance occurred under other names (Whig, People's, Union) and on platforms limited to a restoration of the Missouri Compromise. There were times, indeed, when it appeared that "a perfect chaos of party movements" had replaced the once-stable Whig-Democratic party system. In Maine, for example, Republicans not only battled pro-Nebraska Democrats (who sought to make the state's liquor law the main issue), but challenged anti-Nebraska Democrats allied with anti-Republican Whigs, and nativist Know-Nothings. The process of realignment would be neither smooth nor easy.

Before Republicans could establish themselves as the chief rivals of the "proslavery" Democratic party, they had to overcome the pretensions of the Know-Nothings, who by 1854 boasted a powerful, well-drilled organization reaching into all parts of the nation. What made the Native American party a threat to fledgling Republicans was that despite its attempts to still sectional controversy, many *Northern* Know-Nothings combined antipathy for Catholics and foreigners with moderate antislavery sentiments. All three antagonisms merged, in fact, since nativist hostility centered mainly on the Irish, most of them Catholic and bitter foes of abolition. Each of these aversions, moreover, responded to apparent threats to what native-born Northern Protestants perceived as the American way.

An early sign that Republicans, not Know-Nothings, would prevail came in February 1856 with the election of Nathaniel P. Banks as speaker of the U.S. House of Representatives. A former Know-Nothing of Democratic origins, the Bobbin Boy of Massachusetts had lately switched his allegiance to the Republican party, and with the speakership up for grabs in a three-cornered contest between Republicans, Democrats, and Native Americans, House Republicans shrewdly promoted Banks's candidacy in hopes of splintering the nativists and drawing all antislavery representatives into the Republican camp. After a bitter struggle stretching over nine weeks and 132 inconclusive ballots, a weary House elected Banks Speaker by 3 votes over William Aiken of South Carolina. Republicans were predictably ecstatic, for in the speakership they now claimed a national prize of great practical and symbolic value. Equally inspiriting, perhaps a third of Banks's support had come from nativists now willing to "act alone with the pure Republicans" — strong evidence that Republican, rather than Know-Nothing, fortunes were on the rise. "The Republican Party is now inaugurated," exulted New York's Thurlow Weed. "We can now 'work with a will.'" Just as predictably, Southerners reacted with alarm. "The election of Banks has given great hopes to our enemies," Georgia's Robert Toombs observed, "and their policy is dangerous in the extreme to us." "It seems to me," fretted Albert Gallatin Brown of Mississippi, "that the Union of our fathers is hopelessly lost."

The Republicans took another step forward in the process of party building three weeks after Banks's victory. On February 22, representatives of all free states and five slave states met at Pittsburgh to perfect national party machinery and to arrange for a nominating convention at some later date. Despite the presence of such radicals as Owen Lovejoy, Joshua Giddings, and George W. Julian, the temper of this Pittsburgh gathering was notably restrained. Most Republicans, hoping to solidify their gains among antislavery Know-Nothings and to secure support from slaveless Southerners, agreed with Horace Greeley that for the time being the new party's platform should confine itself simply to "making every territory free." Except for attacking the Pierce administration and demanding the early admission of Kansas as a free state, the Pittsburgh platform did just that. Nothing was said about slavery in the District of Columbia, the Fugitive Slave Law, or the admission of new slave states to the Union. A proposed plank condemning nativist bigotry never really had a chance, especially after anti-slavery Know-Nothings wired from that party's national convention in Philadelphia: "The [Native] American party no longer unite. Raise the Republican banner. No further extension of slavery. The Americans are with you." Radicals could only hope that the Republican national nominating convention, called for mid-June at Philadelphia, would take a stronger stand.

As it happened, events of that spring substantially radicalized Republican attitudes toward slavery and the Slave Power, and gave a powerful boost to the party's fortunes. In May the nation learned that proslavery ruffians had pillaged the free state stronghold at Lawrence, Kansas, and that, a day later, Congressman Preston Brooks of South Carolina had caned Charles Sumner nearly to death as the Massachusetts abolitionist sat at his desk in the U.S. Senate. Many Southerners excused, even approved, both actions—Lawrence, they said, was infested with lawless abolitionists and Sumner deserved "chastisement" for his vicious, ad hominem attacks upon the South. Northerners were outraged. To champions of free soil the events of May underscored the violence endemic to slavery and heightened a determination to stand up to Southern "bullies." William Cullen Bryant struck a common note when in the *New York Evening Post* he observed:

> Violence reigns in the streets of Washington . . . violence has now found its way into the Senate Chamber. Violence lies in wait on all the navigable rivers and all the railways of Missouri, to obstruct those who pass from the free states into Kansas. Violence overhangs the frontiers of that territory like a storm-cloud charged with hail and lightning. Violence has carried election after election in that territory. . . . In short, violence is the order of the day; the North is to be pushed to the wall by it, and this plot will succeed if the people of the free states are as apathetic as the slaveholders are insolent.

The caning of Senator Sumner was especially significant, for it not only buttressed Republican charges of Southern arrogance and threats to free speech but lent credence to reports of proslavery "massacre, rapine and murder" in Kansas. As one sympathizer assured Sumner, "The north needed in order to *see* the slave aggression, one of its best men Butchered in Congress, or something else as wicked which could be brought home to them. Had it not been for your poor head, the Kansas outrage would not have been felt at the North." "Bleeding Kansas" and "Bleeding Sumner" now became Republican rallying cries, and those who had chafed at the timidity of the Pittsburgh platform looked confidently for better things from the forthcoming convention in Philadelphia.

In good measure, the delegates who assembled in Philadelphia's Musical Fund Hall on June 17 fulfilled such expectations. Led by such antislavery activists as David Wilmot, Thaddeus Stevens, Joshua Giddings, John P. Hale, Charles Francis Adams, and Owen Lovejoy, the convention swiftly and enthusiastically approved a platform far more radical than that framed earlier in Pittsburgh. Short, forceful, and direct, the new credo reiterated old Liberty and Free Soil demands that the federal government destroy slavery wherever constitutionally empowered to do so, called upon Congress to "prohibit in the territories those twin relics of barbarism—polygamy and slavery," and urged the prompt admission of Kansas as a free state. In addition to such antislavery planks, the platform endorsed federal assistance in river and harbor improvement and in the construction of a railroad to the Pacific, "by the most central practicable route." Finally, in a gentle rebuke to Know-Nothingism, the Republicans invited the support of all who shared these principles and decried legislative attempts to impair the security of any group.

Republican radicals were delighted with this platform, slightly less so with the nominations which followed. Preconvention skirmishing had already narrowed the list of likely candidates; now the delegates at Philadelphia centered their attention on two names: John C. Frémont and John McLean. (William H. Seward, a favorite of many radicals, was persuaded by his New York advisors to keep his candidacy "pickled away" until 1860.) Of the two, Frémont fit the Republican bill most neatly. A colorful man of forty-three whose youthful vigor seemed appropriate for a leader of the young Republican party, Frémont had acquired considerable fame as a western explorer, California free soiler, and son-in-law of the redoubtable Thomas Hart Benton. Aside from a short stint as senator from California, he lacked political experience, but in a way this was an advantage. Closely identified with no party or policy, save for a moderate attachment to free soil-free labor doctrines, Frémont found favor with Republicans of all stripes. Even radicals, persuaded that the Pathfinder would run a good race and stand up to the South, thought him an appealing candidate. McLean, a graying Supreme Court justice from Ohio, drew support from old-line Whigs who contended that his popularity among Know-Nothings might help carry such key states as Pennsylvania. Most delegates, however, thought McLean simply too old, cautious, and colorless, and too timid in his antislavery beliefs, to lead a vibrant new party. A straw ballot showed 359 votes for Frémont, 190 for McLean. With "three times three perfect Davy Crockett war-whoops" the convention then made Frémont's nomination unanimous and, as a sop to conservatives, picked William L. Dayton of New Jersey as his running mate.

Republicans in 1856 faced opposition from two quarters. In February the Know-Nothings, after most "North American" delegates had seceded in protest against the party's refusal to repudiate the Kansas-Nebraska Act, nominated Millard Fillmore for president. In a way, it was a curious choice. Fillmore, whose daughter had been tutored by nuns, was by no means anti-Catholic, and though privately initiated into the mysteries of Know-Nothingism he had never attended a meeting of the order. His conservative Unionism, however, made Fillmore attractive to "South Americans" and the die-hard Whigs who in September added their endorsement to his candidacy. The Democrats, passing over the incumbent Pierce and Stephen A. Douglas, settled on Pennsylvania's drab (though safe and seasoned) James Buchanan. A known friend of the South, Buchanan was blessed in having been out of the country as minister to Great Britain during the Kansas-Nebraska dispute. Though unhappy with the doctrine of popular sovereignty and its violent heritage in Kansas, he willingly embraced the party platform which praised that still-ambiguous doctrine as "embodying the only sound and safe solution of the 'slavery question.' "

While the Republicans centered their lively campaign upon the "crime against Kansas" and the need to check an ever-more aggressive "slaveocracy," their opponents portrayed Republicans as the party of disunion. "The Union is in danger and the people everywhere begin to know it," Buchanan warned early in the canvass. "The Black Republicans must be, as they can be with justice, boldly assailed as disunionists, and this charge must be re-iterated again and again." His partisans were only too happy to comply. Leading Democratic newspapers, including the *Washington Union, Richmond Enquirer,* and *Charleston Mercury,* forecast an immediate breakup of the Union should Frémont triumph. In South Carolina, Senator Sumner's assailant Preston Brooks — himself a campaign issue, in Republican eyes — announced that if Frémont were elected the slave states would be duty-bound not just to dissolve the Union but to "lay the strong arm of Southern freemen upon the treasury and archives of the government." James Mason, Howell Cobb, John Slidell, Henry Wise, and many others echoed such views.

Frémont personally came in for hard knocks, charged with being illegitimate (true), a closet Catholic (false), and a man whose sole claim to fame was "that he was born in South Carolina, crossed the Rocky Mountains, subsisted on frogs, lizards, snakes and grasshoppers, and captured a woolly horse." But though the whispered imputation of Catholicism may have cost Frémont the support of some nativists, the belief that his election would drive proud Southerners from the Union hurt him most. Even such hidebound Whigs as Rufus Choate and the sons of Daniel Webster and Henry Clay threw their support to "Old Obliquity," James Buchanan, believing that he and not Fillmore was the man most likely to defeat Frémont and thereby forestall secession and civil war. In the end, Benton himself abandoned his son-in-law and stumped vigorously for Buchanan (whom he loathed), convinced that the election of a purely sectional president would precipitate bloody disunion.

With Buchanan virtually invincible in the Cotton South and Frémont the odds-on favorite in New England, New York, and the upper Midwest, the campaign centered in the southern tier of free states stretching west from New Jersey and Pennsylvania through Indiana and Illinois. Pennsylvania, outstripped only by New York in the number of its electoral votes, received special attention. The Democrats blanketed the state with imported spellbinders like Reverdy Johnson, William E. Preston, and Howell Cobb, preaching the menace of "black Republicanism" and the need for "fair play in Kansas." Though strapped for funds, Republicans responded to the challenge with prodigious, if sometimes disorganized, efforts of their own. "I suppose there are about two hundred orators, great and small, now stumping Pennsylvania for Frémont," one Republican editor reported as the campaign drew to a close.

In the end, the Democrats won the battle for Pennsylvania and with it the presidential election. Besides Pennsylvania, Buchanan carried New Jersey, Indiana, Illinois, California, and every slave state but Maryland, which went for Fillmore. Frémont, whose name was not even on the ballot in ten Southern states, captured eleven free states— all, except for Ohio, lying north of those claimed by Buchanan. Above the forty-first parallel the Democratic candidate carried scarcely a county, even in the states he won. Not since 1812 had the fault lines of a presidential election been so starkly sectional.

Republicans were disappointed but far from disheartened at the outcome of the 1856 campaign. Although Buchanan had claimed 174 electoral votes to Frémont's 114 and Fillmore's 8, Republican leaders drew cheer from the popular tally which showed that Frémont and Fillmore together outpolled Buchanan by some 400,000 ballots. Even in the free states Frémont had lost, the Democratic party's strength showed signs of decay. If, as now seemed likely, Fillmore's Northern partisans should cast their lot with the Republicans, the chances of victory in 1860 looked rosy. The capture of Pennsylvania and the switch of a few thousand votes in Indiana or Illinois would do the trick. Benjamin Wade of Ohio expressed the upbeat mood of most Republicans when, soon after the election, he informed an associate, "I am rejoiced to see that our party, though beaten, is not conquered. . . . Before six months have expired our enemies will find, that one more such victory will result in the utter annihilation of their party."

While most Democrats exulted in their victory, a good many, especially in the Deep South, fretted that Republican optimism was well founded. The astonishing Northern support for Frémont, observed one of Jefferson Davis's Mississippi friends, "shows that the *immediate* future . . . is big with peril. Besides this, the few northern States that went for Buchanan were carried by considerable giving way on principle, and the signification of our victory is greatly weakened. . . . As it is, the democracy have the offices four years more, and that is all." Southern moderates hoped to use those four years to fortify their section's interests within the Union. Specifically, they hoped to use their influence with the Buchanan administration to secure full rights to slave property in the territories and an end to "this continual and irritating agitation of the slavery question." Southern radicals, however, persuaded that the "very organization" of the Republican party "evinced a hostility to the Southern States," began to urge creation of "a separate confederacy, as the only means of warding off the continued and increasing assaults of the Northern people." The events of Buchanan's presidency—in Washington, northern Virginia, and the grassy plains of Kansas—would soon give such ultras the upper hand.

"And the War Came"

Those who elected James Buchanan president of the United States had hoped that by "harmony and concession" he might unify the Democratic party and put an end to sectional bitterness. Buchanan himself, in his inaugural address, decried the long and sterile agitation over slavery. By leaving the peculiar institution alone in the states, he observed, and by letting popular sovereignty determine its status in the territories, intersectional goodwill might be restored. Yet, as it turned out, Buchanan presided over and contributed to the fragmentation of his party, the last important institutional link binding North and South. And, of course, the issue that disrupted the Democrats was the very slavery issue he had so desperately hoped to resolve.

I

For a decade Democratic party unity had depended upon the blurred meaning of popular sovereignty. So long as the ability of territorial settlers to outlaw slavery prior to the formation of a state constitution remained ambiguous, intraparty peace was possible. Early in President Buchanan's administration, however, certain events greatly narrowed the meaning of popular sovereignty and led ultimately to the splintering of the Democratic party.

The first such event was the Supreme Court's decision, delivered on March 6, 1857, in the case of *Dred Scott* v. *Sandford*. Dred Scott had been born a slave, in Virginia, sometime near the beginning of the nineteenth century. In 1830 he moved with his master, Peter Blow, to St. Louis where, upon Blow's death, he was sold to Dr. John Emerson, an army surgeon. Between 1834 and 1838 he accompanied Emerson to Fort Armstrong, near Rock Island, Illinois, and Fort Snelling in Wisconsin Territory. Situated on the west bank of the Mississippi River, near what is now St. Paul, Minnesota, Fort Snelling fell within the portion of the Louisiana Purchase closed to slavery by the Missouri Compromise. For the better part of five years, then, Dred Scott had resided on free soil. After his return to St. Louis and Emerson's death in 1843, Scott, his wife, and two daughters passed into the hands first of Mrs. Emerson and, later, of her brother John F. A. Sanford.

In 1846, perhaps prompted by members of the Blow family, who had remained friendly with their former slave, Dred Scott brought suit for his freedom. The case went first to the circuit court of St. Louis County where in 1850 the jury agreed with Scott's contention that his residence in a free state and a free territory had made him a free man. Two years later, however, an appeal to the Missouri Supreme Court reversed this finding. Following Chief Justice of the United States Roger B. Taney's opinion in *Strader* v. *Graham* (1851), the Missouri justices ruled that whatever the effect of his residence on free soil, Dred Scott's status was determined by Missouri law once he returned to that state. And that law, two of the three justices decided, left Scott a slave.

Dred Scott having by now come under the control of Sanford, a citizen of New York, his lawyers were able to file a new suit on Scott's behalf in the federal circuit court at St. Louis. When in May 1854 that court also rejected Scott's claim to freedom, his attorneys appealed the decision to the U.S. Supreme Court. After much delay, *Dred Scott* v. *Sandford* (a clerk misspelled the defendant's name) came before the nation's highest court in mid-February 1856.

That *Dred Scott* v. *Sandford* was a case of no ordinary interest was apparent in the stature of the counsel engaged by both sides. Attorneys for Scott were Montgomery Blair, eldest son of Andrew Jackson's trusted advisor Francis P. Blair, and George Ticknor Curtis, one of the country's most outstanding lawyers and brother of Supreme Court Justice Benjamin R. Curtis. Arguing for the other side—nominally John Sanford but actually the slaveholding South—were Reverdy Johnson of Maryland, a former attorney general and perhaps the most distinguished member of the American bar, and Henry S. Geyer, senator from Missouri. Increasing turmoil in Kansas (which included the "sack" of Lawrence and John Brown's retaliatory massacre of five proslavery settlers at Pottawatomie Creek) added to the significance of the case and heightened hopes that a judicial resolution of the territorial question might soon be forthcoming. President Buchanan further stimulated interest in the case when, in his inaugural address, he observed that the court's impending decision would provide a final settlement to the dispute over slavery in the territories and urged "all good citizens . . . cheerfully [to] submit, whatever this [decision] may be."

Buchanan, it now appears, already knew at the time of his inaugural (thanks to communications from Justices John Catron and Robert

C. Grier) that the *Dred Scott* decision would deal broadly with the question of slavery in the territories. He also knew that the court's opinion would declare the Missouri Compromise restriction, and any other congressional or territorial prohibition of slavery, unconstitutional. When he asked that all good citizens happily acquiesce in the decision at hand, therefore, he was asking nothing less than that Republicans should renounce the principle on which their party had been founded and that Douglas Democrats should surrender their beloved doctrine of popular sovereignty, at least as most understood it.

The Supreme Court's decision, handed down two days after Buchanan took office, did not come altogether as a bolt out of the blue. A year and a half earlier Attorney General Caleb Cushing had prepared for President Pierce a well-publicized brief which maintained that the Missouri Compromise was invalid since it denied states north of 36° 30′ freedom to decide the question of slavery for themselves. For weeks, moreover, Washington had buzzed with rumors that a majority of the high court's justices stood poised to repudiate the power of Congress to outlaw slavery in any territory. Nonetheless, the *Dred Scott* decision came as a shock to most Americans and produced an electrifying effect throughout the North.

In passing judgment on Scott's claim to freedom, the Court had first to consider the question of jurisdiction. Could Scott, or any Negro of slave ancestry, claim citizenship in the United States and hence the right to bring suit in federal courts? To this question no clear-cut answer emerged from the separate opinions written by the nine justices. James Wayne of Georgia and Peter V. Daniel of Virginia joined Chief Justice Taney, who penned the "opinion of the Court," in ruling against Negro citizenship. Historically and constitutionally, Taney contended, Negroes "had no rights which the white man was bound to respect." Ohio's John McLean and Benjamin Curtis of Massachusetts, however, held that blacks were eligible for citizenship, while the other justices took no position on the issue. All, however, proceeded to consider the merits of the case. And all, except Samuel Nelson of New York, addressed the crucial question of congressional authority over slavery in the territories—especially the constitutionality of the Missouri Compromise. This willingness to move beyond mere technical judgment and to consider the case in its broadest bearings derived, among other reasons, from public pressure on the Court somehow to "settle" an already vexing, and potentially disastrous, issue. Most Northerners, of course, hoped that the Court's "settlement" would uphold congressional barriers to slavery expansion. Southerners, on the other hand, prayed for a decision that would vindicate their honor by repudiating laws antagonistic to the peculiar institution.

Given the Court's composition, it is hardly surprising that the South's prayers were answered. All seven of the Court's Democratic justices upheld the lower court's ruling that Dred Scott's sojourn in Illinois had not set him free since Missouri laws governed his status once he had returned to St. Louis. Moreover, all five Southern justices, together with Buchanan's surrogate, Grier of Pennsylvania, held that Scott's residence at Fort Snelling did not affect his status as a slave because the Missouri Compromise ban on slavery in that region was unconstitutional. The power of Congress over the territories, Chief Justice Taney maintained, was limited to their preparation for admission as states, and any infringement of a slaveholder's right to full enjoyment of his private property violated the due process clause of the Fifth Amendment. Congressional authority over slave property, said Taney, extended only to "guarding and protecting the owner in his rights." By implication, territorial legislatures, being the creatures of Congress, were also constitutionally forbidden to interdict slavery, although Taney alone made the point explicit. Only McLean, the Court's sole Republican, and Benjamin Curtis, a Whig, dissented from these opinions. Both held that Scott's stay in Illinois had forever loosed his bonds and that the Missouri Compromise restriction was valid.

President Buchanan, Justices Taney and Wayne, and a great many others had dreamily hoped that good citizens everywhere would accept the *Dred Scott* decision as a lasting settlement of the rancorous dispute over slavery in the territories. They should have known better. Indeed, the circumstances as well as the outcome of the decision did more to provoke than to allay sectional antagonism. That a decidedly pro-Southern decision had been rendered by a Court controlled by Southerners was bound to cause trouble. Though initially disposed to sidestep the question of congressional power over the territories, Justice Grier agreed in the end to concur with Taney lest it "appear that the line of latitude should mark the line of division in the court." Yet except for Grier, the lines *did* coincide—a fact which encouraged complaints that the Court had abandoned judicial impartiality to tamper with a purely political question. The solidly Democratic credentials of the Court's proslavery majority simply reinforced such protests. And the Court's action in taking up the merits of the case after ruling that as a Negro Dred Scott had no standing before it prompted charges of extrajudicial behavior. Such accusations were, in fact, mistaken. Taney, at least, thought it necessary to declare the Missouri Compromise restriction unconstitutional in order to fortify his jurisdictional argument, namely that Dred Scott lacked standing *both* because he was a Negro *and* because he was still a slave. Nonetheless, the notion that the *Dred Scott* decision represented the worst sort of political usurpation quickly gained currency in Republican and free soil Democratic circles.

Coming as it did in the wake of the Kansas-Nebraska Act, the *Dred Scott* decision struck many Northerners as not only dangerous in itself but alarming evidence of a slowly unfolding conspiracy to force slavery into every corner of the land.

> Seventy years ago [the Harrisburg, Pennsylvania, *Telegraph* editorialized in 1859] the Democrats drew a line around the States, and said to the Slave Trader, "thus far you may go, but no farther." This was the Jeffersonian Proviso. Thirty years ago they rubbed out part of the line, and said to him, "You may go into the lands South, but not into the lands North." This was the Missouri Compromise. Five years ago they rubbed out the rest of the line, and said to him, "We leave it to the Settlers to decide whether you shall come in or not." This was the Nebraska Bill. Now they turn humbly to him, hat in hand, and say, "Go where you please; the land is all yours, the National flag shall protect you, and the National troops shoot down whoever resists you." This is the Dred Scott decision.

The threat of a Slave Power conspiracy against freedom everywhere, long a staple of antislavery rhetoric, now became the stock-in-trade of Republican editors and politicians. A whispered exchange between Chief Justice Taney and President Buchanan at the 1857 inaugural seemed a sinister reminder of the recent "collusion" of Douglas and Pierce on the Kansas-Nebraska Bill. "Stephen and Franklin and Roger and James," claimed Abraham Lincoln, had plotted to protect slavery in the territories. And, he warned, unless Northerners awoke to the dangers at hand, the conspirators' next step might well be another Supreme Court decision denying the right of any *state* to prohibit slavery. Even some antislavery Democrats discerned in the *Dred Scott* decision "a conspiracy between a portion of the Supreme Court Judges, Buchanan and the South . . . to retard the progress of freedom, and confirm the claims of the slave power to universal supremacy."

Such apprehensions, while overblown, derived from a clear-eyed perception that of late Democratic policymakers had cooperated in the expansion rather than restriction of slavery's dominion. This alarming trend, as Lincoln took pains to point out, gained strength both from the "care-not" attitude implicit in popular sovereignty and from Taney's ruling that "as beings of an inferior order" black Americans possessed no rights that federal courts need respect. If the trend were to be reversed and slavery placed where the Founding Fathers had left it — on the path to extinction — the unholy alliance of planters and Northern "doughfaces" would have to be destroyed. Such was the lesson Republicans drew from the *Dred Scott* decision. "The remedy," editorialized the *Chicago Tribune,* "is union and action; the ballot box. Let free States be a unit in Congress on the side of freedom. Let the next President be Republican, and 1860 will mark an era kindred with that of 1776."

Republicans were not alone in their unhappiness over the *Dred Scott* ruling. Southerners, to be sure, made no secret of their satisfaction at having received such impressive validation of their position. Taney's opinion, crowed the *Augusta Constitutionalist,* "covers every question regarding slavery and settles it in favor of the South." And the initial response of Northern Democrats was to circle wagons and defend the high court's decision against Republican attack. Most found it easy to endorse Taney's judgment against black citizenship and *congressional* regulation of slavery in the territories, and the chance to vilify their opponents as lawless foes of judicial authority was too delicious to pass up.

Yet far from resolving the simmering dispute over popular sovereignty, the *Dred Scott* decision had underscored party differences over the doctrine's meaning. To hold the support of their free soil constituencies, Northern Democrats now scrambled anxiously to show that despite Taney's contrary pronouncement, popular sovereignty might still work in antislavery ways. Some simply dismissed Taney's assertion that territorial legislatures lacked authority to interfere with slave property as *obiter dictum* — merely one judge's opinion on a point peripheral to the case in hand. Stephen A. Douglas took a different tack, arguing that the right to take slaves into a territory would remain "a barren and a worthless right" unless buttressed by local police regulations. This principle of "residual popular sovereignty," as it has been called, briefly found favor even among some slave state congressmen. Most white Southerners, however, were quick to denounce it. Before long they would be demanding a federal slave code for the territories to give *Dred Scott* v. *Sandford* its intended effect. The ominous rift in the Democratic party thus remained wide and, thanks to the crisis in Kansas, soon grew wider still. (Dred Scott, the "small, pleasant-looking negro" at the center of this political storm, gained his freedom from a new master soon after the Supreme Court denied it, working until his death sixteen months later as a hotel porter in St. Louis.)

II

While Roger Taney's *Dred Scott* opinion theoretically undercut the Northern version of popular sovereignty—that territorial legislators might prohibit slavery if they chose—the proslavery constitutional convention in Lecompton, Kansas, threatened to make a mockery of it in practice. Indeed, from the moment Kansas opened for settlement, ballot-stuffing Missourians, at one time led by Senator Atchison himself, had done their best to insure that the popular will spoke with a Southern accent. So fraudulent had been the first territorial election, in fact (the ballots cast outnumbered eligible voters by more than two to one), and so outrageously proslavery the actions of the legislature thus elected, that in protest free state settlers established a rival government of their own.

For two years these hostile groups clashed, sometimes violently, over such matters as disputed land claims as well as the status of slavery. The ugliest incident came in the spring of 1856, hard on the heels of the proslavery attack on Lawrence. On the night of May 24, John Brown, a messianic, footloose abolitionist from Ohio led four of his sons, a son-in-law, and two other men to a proslavery settlement at Dutch Henry's Crossing on Pottawatomie Creek. Under cover of darkness they dragged from their beds and murdered in cold blood five proslavery pioneers. All were horribly mutilated. For a time it appeared that full-scale war would erupt on the Kansas plains. Atchison spoke of killing "every God-damned abolitionist in the district"; Jim Lane, leader of a large, well-armed free state army, promised the same fate to all proslavery settlers; and for a time "Bleeding Kansas" was more than just a slogan. By fall the sagacity and evenhandedness of a new governor, John W. Geary, brought a temporary restoration of order to the territory. Tension still ran high, however, and the slavery question was still far from resolved, when shortly before Franklin Pierce left office the proslavery legislature at Lecompton called for the election of delegates to a constitutional convention in preparation for Kansas's admission to statehood.

Certain that it would be rigged against them, free state settlers decided to boycott the election rather than commit themselves to its results. The outcome, then, was predictable: out of 9,000 registered voters only 2,000—mostly proslavery settlers—cast ballots. The constitutional convention scheduled to meet at Lecompton in September 1857 would be a distinctly proslavery affair.

Soon after the Lecompton deliberations began, free state forces demonstrated the moderate *antislavery* disposition of most Kansans by winning control of the regular territorial legislature. For this triumph they could thank the newly arrived Democratic governor, Robert J. Walker. A Mississippian of Pennsylvania origins, Walker boldly tossed out hundreds of fraudulent proslavery ballots, thereby sealing the free staters' victory. (One set of returns Walker rejected came from Oxford, a cluster of some half-dozen cabins, where 1,628 votes were counted for proslavery candidates. Upon examination it was discovered that nearly all the names on the official return had been copied, in order, from the *Cincinnati Directory.*)

As if to give point to their anger at Walker's "unwarranted" intervention, the Lecompton delegates nonetheless proceeded to draft a proslavery constitution. Describing the right to slave property as "inviolable," standing "before and higher than any constitutional sanction," the Lecompton constitution not only protected the title of slaveholders to the roughly 200 slaves already in Kansas but forbade amendment for seven years. Worse still, so far as free staters were concerned, instead of submitting the whole constitution to the voters for approval or disapproval, the Lecompton Convention decided to permit a referendum solely on "the constitution with slavery" or "the constitution without slavery." The only difference was that the latter choice would ban the further importation of slaves into Kansas. Either way, bondsmen presently held in the territory (and their offspring) would remain enslaved. Either way, Kansas would become a slave state. Without question, drastic liberties had been taken with the doctrine of popular sovereignty.

Governor Walker, who had gone to Kansas with firm assurances that President Buchanan and the cabinet shared his conviction "that the actual *bona fide* residents of the Territory, by a fair and regular vote, unaffected by fraud or violence, must be permitted, in adopting their State Constitution, to decide for themselves what shall be their social institutions," now protested against the Lecompton farce and urged Buchanan to repudiate it. "I doubt if three hundred men wish to fasten slavery on Kansas," he argued; "no party stands for slavery; the people will fight before they let this cheating document, which means slavery both ways, go through." Northern Democrats like George Bancroft and John Forney made similar pleas. But Buchanan, in a decision disastrous for his party, his presidency, and the Union itself, rejected such advice. Recognizing that 112 of his 174 electoral votes in 1856 had come from slave states, aware that Southern Democrats now greatly outnumbered Northern Democrats in both houses of Congress, and taking counsel primarily from such old Southern friends as Howell Cobb, Jacob Thompson, and John Slidell, Buchanan decided to abandon principle—

and Walker—and to throw his weight behind the Lecompton constitution.

He did so despite overwhelming evidence that the vast majority of Kansans wanted no part of slavery. Free staters had boycotted the partial referendum prescribed by the Lecompton Convention, with the result that 6,266 had favored the constitution with slavery, 567 without. A congressional investigating committee later determined that nearly 3,000 of these ballots were fraudulent. Two weeks later, on January 4, 1858, a second referendum took place. Authorized by the territorial legislature, it offered Kansans a chance to pass judgment on the *whole* constitution. This time, with most of the proslavery faction standing aside, 138 voted for the constitution with slavery, 24 for the constitution without slavery, and 10,266 against the constitution altogether. The battle for Kansas was "already fought," New York's Republican senator William H. Seward boasted in February, "it is over."

Many Southerners agreed. Few expected Kansas to be a slave state for long. The antislavery disposition of most settlers was unmistakable; natural conditions seemed inhospitable to slavery; and the number of slaves in the territory had fallen drastically in the last year, from nearly 300 to barely 100. But the South's honor was at stake, and the likelihood that Kansas would in any event soon become a Northern prize, only increased Southern anger at those who opposed the Lecompton constitution. Some, it is true, mainly Whigs, protested the "barefaced fraud and cheating" of the Lecompton forces and cautioned against investing Southern pride in so lost a cause. Even Edmund Ruffin of Virginia, already pressing for Southern independence, admitted that most Kansans disapproved of slavery. If the Lecompton constitution were forced upon them, he said, the South would secure "an apparent gain and victory . . . , but in a bad cause, and the slavery feature . . . [would] be certainly struck out of the constitution within a year after Kansas . . . [became] a state."

A great many more, however, insisted on making Lecompton a test of the South's ability to find equality within the Union. The South, explained Senator John Slidell of Louisiana, was "struggling for the maintenance of a principle, barren, it is true, of present practical fruits, but indispensable for our future protection." If Kansas were denied admission because slavery "nominally and temporarily exists there," he asked, "what may we expect when application shall be made by a state of which it will be a real and enduring institution?" Not since Texas had a slave state joined the Union, and the decision on Lecompton would show whether Northern majorities would ever again give the South its due. For the first time since 1850 mutterings of disunion rippled through the South. "If Kansas is rejected," Governor Joseph E. Brown of Georgia told Alexander H. Stephens, "I think self respect will compel the Southern members of Congress . . . to vacate their seats and return to their constituents to assist them in drawing around themselves new safeguards for the protection of their rights in the future. When the Union ceases to protect our equal rights, it ceases to have any charms for me." To Senator James H. Hammond of South Carolina a constituent wrote: "Save the Union, if you can. But rather than have Kansas refused admission under the Lecompton Constitution, let it perish in blood and fire."

Republicans, of course, saw things differently. The "Lecompton swindle," they complained, was but the latest in a long series of perversions of popular sovereignty—the latest step, indeed, in the "slaveocracy's" campaign to give the peculiar institution new life and scope, and to curtail the freedoms of Northern whites. First Kansas-Nebraska, then Dred Scott, and now Lecompton—all had been framed to that end. Republicans found particularly alarming the clause in the Lecompton constitution which placed the right of slave property "higher than any constitutional sanction." Such a doctrine, alongside Taney's *Dred Scott* ruling, seemed evidence of a "great Conspiracy to carry Slavery by Federal authority into all the States." Republicans could have but one response to the Lecompton constitution, Abraham Lincoln told a party gathering in May 1858. "It should be throttled and killed as hastily and as heartily as a rabid dog."

Southerners had expected this reaction from the "black Republicans." What they had not bargained for, however, was the opposition of popular sovereignty's most forceful advocate, Stephen A. Douglas, and a substantial number of other Northern Democrats. Denouncing the partial referendum on the Lecompton constitution as a "system of trickery and jugglery," Douglas warned: "If this constitution is to be forced down our throats, in violation of the fundamental principle of free government, under a mode of submission that is a mockery and insult, I will resist it to the last." Heedless of political costs, Douglas defiantly joined with Republicans to attack Lecompton and its backers. "By G——d sir, I made Mr. James Buchanan," he blustered, "and by G——d sir, I will unmake him."

The sight of the Little Giant openly at odds with President Buchanan and the dominant element of his own party delighted Republicans. "Never have I seen a slave insurrection before," chortled Senator Wade of Ohio. Some prominent Republicans, including Horace Greeley of the *New York Tribune* and Senators James Dixon and Henry Wilson, so welcomed Douglas's break with the administration that they supported his bid for reelection to the Senate against Abraham Lincoln. Such a reward, they reasoned, might encourage others to defy the Slave Power. A good many Northern Democrats also applauded Douglas's anti-Lecompton stand. Especially in Illinois support for the senator's position was, as he had foreseen, widespread. "I don't see how you could have taken any other course, and sustained yourself at home," one partisan observed. "Had you gone the other way, the Dem[ocratic] party in the State would have been routed horse foot and dragoon." Even many Democrats in the border states, mindful of Douglas's "former eminent services to the South," took his assault on Lecompton in stride. The lower South, however, reverberated with denunciations of Douglas's "treachery," a betrayal made all the more heinous by his pretense of friendship for the South. "This defection of Douglas," confessed one South Carolinian, "has done more than all else to shake my confidence in northern men on the slavery issue, for I have always regarded him as one of our safest and most reliable friends." Not only, therefore, did Douglas's defection all but destroy chances for Democratic harmony in the critical months ahead, but it gravely weakened Southern confidence in partisan politics as a defense against Northern, antislavery majorities. Radicals who insisted that "a Slaveholding Confederacy should be . . . the *ultimate* aim of every Southern patriot" now found more receptive audiences than ever before.

With help from the Little Giant, Republicans in Congress successfully scuttled the Lecompton constitution. Administration pressure kept all but two Democratic senators from joining Douglas's revolt, and the Lecompton Bill carried in the upper chamber, 33 to 25. In the House, however, Republicans and some twenty Douglas Democrats forced a deadlock by passing a substitute measure requiring that the Lecompton constitution be resubmitted to Kansas voters in a closely policed referendum. This deadlock was broken when administration forces engineered a face-saving compromise, the English Bill, which cloaked resubmission (anathema to Southerners) in the guise of a land grant plebiscite. Framed by Representative William H. English, an Indiana Democrat, this measure offered Kansans a customary grant of public lands and prompt admission to the Union if they accepted the Lecompton constitution. If they rejected it, the residents of Kansas would have to wait indefinitely for statehood and federal lands. Republicans and Douglasites protested this "bribe" to make Kansas a slave state, but though the English Bill became law they need not have worried. In August, Kansans in a fair election rejected Lecompton resoundingly. For the first time in years, that troubled land knew peace.

The political wounds of the Kansas struggle, however, would

plague the nation for years to come. Sectional hatred flamed as never before. In the North, resentment over Southern efforts to extend slavery by force, fraud, and cajolery grew wider and deeper. In the South, the Kansas dispute drew moderates and radicals closer together, heightened feelings of isolation and betrayal, and strengthened acceptance of secession as a legitimate—if not yet timely—remedy for Southern wrongs. And everywhere signs of a growing tendency to violence foretold dangerous days ahead. Men now came armed to Congress as they had to Kansas, and respectful discourse often went by the boards. In February 1858, Congressman Lawrence Keitt of South Carolina attempted to throttle Galusha Grow while the Pennsylvania Republican was drumming up anti-Lecompton votes on the Democratic side of the House. A small-scale melee followed in which Mississippi's William Barksdale lost his wig, while Henry Clay's son James, standing atop his desk, drunkenly shouted for order. Soon thereafter, when Senator James Green of Missouri threatened Pennsylvania's Simon Cameron with bodily harm following an exchange of insults in the Senate, Cameron signed a mutual defense pact with fellow Republicans Benjamin Wade and Zachariah Chandler which bound the three to "carry . . . into the coffin" any quarrel forced upon them by Southern "bullies." Never was the pact implemented, but that it had been thought necessary and proper was in itself alarming.

For the national Democratic party the Lecompton crisis was truly disastrous. President Buchanan's gamble that the popularity of Democratic economic policies (restraints on banks and paper currency) would prevent the party's Northern wing from joining Douglas's revolt failed miserably. In the 1858 congressional races Douglas Democrats and Buchanan Democrats battled one another as bitterly as they did the Republicans, at ruinous cost to the Northern Democratic party. When Buchanan took office, the House of Representatives included fifty-three free state and seventy-five slave state Democrats. Two years later, after the fallout from Lecompton, there were still sixty-nine Southern Democrats in the House, but only thirty-one Northern Democrats, twelve of them anti-Lecomptonites. The Panic of 1857, which hit the North especially hard, was partly to blame for this loss. And Democrats fared better in Northern statewide elections than in congressional contests; this fed Douglas's presidential hopes for 1860. Nationally, however, the Democratic party was a party divided, and in Congress Stephen Douglas and his friends found themselves hopelessly outnumbered, dependent upon Republican support to beat back the South's most exorbitant demands.

Exploiting Democratic divisions, Republicans emerged from the

Lecompton fight stronger than ever. A gain of some seventeen seats in the 1858 elections meant that their party would control the House of Representatives in the Thirty-Sixth Congress. Also pleasing was the continuing trickle of anti-Nebraska Democrats, among them a former Iowa party chairman and a recent governor of Kansas, into the Republican camp. At the same time, however, resolution of the Kansas crisis robbed Republicans of their most dramatic issue, clouded differences between themselves and the Douglas Democrats, and raised new questions about the need for so narrowly sectional a party.

III

Facing a promising but uncertain future, Republicans divided over the approach most likely to bring their party victory in 1860. Some conservatives, weary of "the everlasting cry about negroes, Bleeding Kansas, etc.," recommended that the slavery issue be soft-pedaled, even set aside, and that greater attention be devoted to questions of political economy, especially the tariff. Others suggested fusion with Douglas Democrats or Whig/Know-Nothings, even if it required a watering down of the party's antislavery creed. Mainstream Republicans, however, rejected such advice and instead responded warmly to William Seward, Abraham Lincoln, and others who preached strict adherence to antislavery principles and spoke of an "irrepressible conflict" between slavery and freedom. Only by reaffirming slavery's basic immorality and repudiating the "care-not" attitude implicit in popular sovereignty, Lincoln repeatedly asserted during his unsuccessful 1858 campaign for the Senate, could the Republican party maintain a distinct identity and thwart attempts to legalize human bondage throughout the United States.

To dramatize the inherent evil of slavery, and to remind voters that the territorial issue was but part of a broader, more fundamental conflict, Republican legislatures in several Northern states passed new personal liberty laws designed to shield alleged runaways from the hated Fugitive Slave Act of 1850. Similarly, New York Republicans proposed in 1859 a bill to free automatically all slaves brought into the state by Southern tourists. By underscoring the Republican party's antislavery commitment, such measures helped to distinguish Republicans from their Northern rivals—including Douglas Democrats who had joined the fight against the Lecompton constitution not because it sanctioned slavery but because it flouted popular sovereignty.

Southerners, already outraged at the "loss" of Kansas, the "Irrepressible Conflict" and "House Divided" speeches of Seward and Lincoln, and the apostasy of Stephen Douglas, reacted angrily to this "mock[ing] at constitutional obligations." In obstructing enforcement of the Fugitive Slave Act, as in thwarting the admission of a slave state, Republicans had trampled on requirements that Southerners had set down in the Georgia Platform of 1850 and afterward as essential for their continued participation in the Union. "Black Republicans," it seemed, had declared war upon the institutions of the South. Some moderates as well as radicals now supported measures of military preparedness to ready the South for any contingency. Pronouncing disunion "a great though not the greatest calamity," Jefferson Davis urged the Mississippi legislature in November 1858 to establish a state armory for the repair, improvement, and manufacture of arms, "including cannon and their carriages; the casting of shot and shells, and the preparation of fixed ammunition."

The South's bunkerlike perspective became still more pronounced following John Brown's reckless foray into northern Virginia in mid-October 1859. With the moral and financial assistance of a small group of prominent Eastern abolitionists known as the "Secret Six" (Gerrit Smith, Theodore Parker, Samuel Gridley Howe, George L. Stearns, Thomas Wentworth Higginson, and Franklin B. Sanborn), Brown planned to seize the federal arsenal at Harpers Ferry in order to secure weapons for the band of insurrectionary slaves he expected would flock to his side. As a military undertaking, the Harpers Ferry raid proved a dismal and tragic failure. Thanks partly to his own mistakes of generalship, John Brown's private war against slavery was over within thirty-six hours of its beginning. The whole operation, Abraham Lincoln later observed, "was so absurd that the slaves, with all their ignorance, saw plainly enough it could not succeed"; not a single slave voluntarily joined Brown's band, and those he pressed into service abandoned him at first opportunity. Before being trapped in the arsenal's engine house, the ragtag invaders had killed four persons (including the mayor of Harpers Ferry and a Negro baggage master) and wounded nine. Of his eighteen-man "army," ten (including two of Brown's sons) had been killed, and five, the badly wounded John Brown among them, were taken prisoner. (Interestingly, the Marine detachment from Washington which crushed Brown's ill-advised campaign, was commanded by Lieutenant Colonel Robert E. Lee and Lieutenant J. E. B. Stuart.) Captured on October 18, Brown was indicted *and* tried for treason against the state of Virginia a week later, convicted on November 2, and hanged on December 2. As he calmly ascended the gallows, the prisoner handed one of his jailors a note: "I John Brown am now quite *certain* that the crimes of this *guilty land* will never be purged *away* but with Blood."

Without question, the Harpers Ferry invasion made vastly more difficult a peaceful resolution of sectional differences. In the North, Republicans scrambled to parry Democratic charges that, in Stephen A. Douglas's words, Brown's raid was the "natural, logical, inevitable result of the doctrines and teachings of the Republican party." The party press condemned the attempted insurrection as "fatally wrong," "utterly repugnant," the product of misguided fanaticism. New Hampshire's Senator John P. Hale spoke for most Republicans in Congress when he assured Southerners that his political associates "have never made, and never will make, an appeal to slaves. . . . Their appeal, so far as I know, is to the enlightened conscience and the patriotism, not of the slaves, but of their masters."

Some Northerners, however, deplored not Brown's violent expedition but his execution and the "blood-stained" institution he had sought to destroy. On the day after Brown's capture, Henry David Thoreau spoke of Harpers Ferry as "the best news America ever had," and, anticipating Brown's execution, compared it to the crucifixion of Christ. Likewise, Ralph Waldo Emerson, in a lecture titled "Courage," described Brown as "the saint . . . [whose] martyrdom . . . will make the gallows as glorious as the cross." Expressions so radical as these were rare, but many Republicans who denounced Brown's means came openly to praise his motives and to blame slavery and the Slave Power for the blood spilled at Harpers Ferry. The violence in Virginia, such men argued, was of a piece with the bloodshed in Kansas, filibustering in Central America, suppression of free speech in the South, and the code duello — all offshoots of the violence inherent in slavery itself. John Brown's crimes were no worse than those of "border ruffians" and slave catchers, and he, at least, had striven to free, not to enslave or oppress.

Jittery Southerners, apprehensive and insecure about their peculiar institution, always fearful of slave uprisings, and perhaps subconsciously troubled with feelings of guilt, exploded in fear and rage over John Brown's raid. None took comfort from Republican repudiation of Brown's methods and few found reassurance in the anti-Brown "Union" rallies staged by Northern conservatives. Harpers Ferry, nearly all agreed, was "the natural fruit" of "black Republican" doctrine; it was "fact coming to the aid of logic," as Robert Barnwell Rhett put it. And the old-line Whigs and Democrats who made up the "Humbug Union Meetings" in Northern cities were not only politically weak (as Republican victories in 1859 state elections revealed) but unreliable.

"Will the conservative sentiment in the free States be able to roll back the tide of wild fanaticism which finds its *root in the conscience of a people*?" one South Carolina radical asked. "Never," he concluded. "For the conservatism itself is rotten to the core. Not one perhaps of all those men who would thus sweep back the ocean of abolitionism with a broom, but are conscientiously convinced that slavery in principle is wrong and that the institution is evil." It stung proud Southerners to fury that so many Northerners put the blame for Harpers Ferry not where it belonged—on the mad, self-righteous John Brown and his "black-hearted abolitionist" allies—but on the South's peculiar institution. "We cannot stand such insults and outrages as those of Harpers Ferry without suffering worse than the death of citizens," Virginia's governor Henry Wise told the state legislature in December, "without suffering dishonor, the death of a state."

Feeling isolated, besieged, dishonored, and physically imperiled as never before, white Southerners strove frantically to erect new defenses against enemies both from without and within. Local vigilance committees sought to uncover other John Browns, to uproot subversion wherever it might be found. Men were flogged, tarred and feathered, and forced to flee for their lives because of the merest suspicion about their loyalty to the South and its institutions. Slave patrols were strengthened and free Negroes subjected to stricter controls. State arsenals stocked additional supplies of arms and munitions, while militia companies drilled with renewed zeal. Here and there boycotts were proclaimed against Northern merchandise. More than 200 medical students withdrew from the University of Pennsylvania to protest Harpers Ferry and to uphold the worth of Southern institutions. "Let Virginia call home her children!" proclaimed Governor Henry A. Wise at a welcoming rally in Richmond. To insure correctness of belief as well as behavior, still stricter standards of thought control were imposed. Not only Hinton R. Helper's *The Impending Crisis* (1857) but books less openly critical of slavery were publicly burned. Certain newspapers were seized and suppressed. Alabama debated a resolution designed to shut out abolitionist ideas by licensing only those teachers who had resided in the state a decade or more. Some fearful souls now found the very process of free inquiry dangerous and seditious, and they opposed not merely *Northern* educators but education itself.

The chief effect of John Brown's foray was, of course, to strengthen the hand of the fiery advocates of secession, Rhett, Ruffin, Yancey, A. G. Brown, and others. Their talk of an abolitionist conspiracy against Southern lives and property now seemed much more credible than before and the belief that disunion was preferable to continued submission to Northern aggressions swelled perceptibly. In a dramatic stroke, the crusty Ruffin confiscated some of the cast-iron pikes with which Brown had intended to arm insurrectionary slaves, mailing one to each Southern governor, bearing the label "*Sample of the favors designed for us by our Northern brethren.*" Slaveholders and nonslaveholders alike could grasp this message. Throughout the South even one-time moderates threatened disunion should a Republican be chosen president in 1860.

Sectional antagonisms, inflamed by the raid on Harpers Ferry, continued to burn long after John Brown's body began "a-mouldering" in the grave. In Congress, Northern and Southern representatives traded insults and accusations over responsibility for the raid and waged a fierce battle for the speakership of the House. Rather than accept a Northerner from *either* party, Southern radicals resorted to filibuster, parliamentary delay, and open threats of disunion. Menace hung in the air for weeks on end, and many members came to their desks well armed. "The only persons who do not have a revolver or a knife are those with two revolvers," claimed James H. Hammond. Finally, after a deadlock lasting from December 5 to February 1, 1860, William Pennington, a conservative Republican from New Jersey, won the prize. But for the intransigence of a cluster of extreme "Southern rights" Democrats, John A. McClernand, a prominent Douglas Democrat from Illinois, might have been elected Speaker of the House. It was a harbinger of things to come.

Southern opposition to the pet Republican economic measures — free homesteads, a protective tariff, and construction of a Pacific railroad — added to sectional discord in the Thirty-Sixth Congress and demonstrated that the contest between free labor and slave labor comprehended fundamental disagreements over economic development and social order. Republicans ballyhooed their program as crucial to the development of a mixed, integrated, national economy, one beneficial to transportation and industry as well as agriculture. Southerners, on the other hand, charging that Republican policies would favor Northern at the expense of Southern interests, joined President Buchanan to defeat them.

As always, however, the territorial question provided the main bone of contention between North and South. In February 1860, Senator Jefferson Davis set the stage for the final — and fatal — struggle over this issue by demanding the enactment of a federal slave code for the territories. Davis's purpose was twofold: (1) to assert the right of slaveholders to protection from the kind of "unfriendly legislation" that Stephen A. Douglas had said might allow territorial settlers to banish slavery, notwithstanding the *Dred Scott* decision; and (2) to brand as miscreants those Northern Democrats who followed Douglas's lead. Although the Senate Democratic caucus (and, informally, President Buchanan) approved Davis's proposal, it had no earthly chance of enactment, and even some staunch defenders of Southern rights questioned the political wisdom of so divisive an act on the eve of the Democratic national convention. Davis, however, hoped to shape the agenda for that convention and advertise the Little Giant's unacceptability to the South. And some Southern radicals, it would appear, pressed for a federal slave code expressly to split the Democratic party and pave the way for disunion.

Against this ominous backdrop the most fateful presidential campaign in American history was played out. The Democrats convened first, at Charleston, South Carolina, between April 23 and May 3. Neither the time nor the place were conducive to party harmony. Charleston, though a charming city, was ill equipped to handle so large a gathering. Crowded, cramped, and expensive quarters; price-gouging shopkeepers; temperatures that hovered in the 90s; and the prospect of a long session (made still bleaker by the exhaustion of whiskey supplies); all frayed delegates' nerves. Worse, Charleston was a hotbed of secession, the home of Robert Barnwell Rhett; the city's streets and the convention hall itself thronged with radicals whose pro-Southern fervor exerted a subtle influence.

Although Southern Democrats had come to control the congressional wing of their party, Douglas Democrats enjoyed something better than parity nationally. When the convention opened, therefore, Douglas claimed the backing of a bare majority of delegates — enough to control the platform but (because of the party's long-standing two-thirds rule) not enough to secure his nomination without Southern support. That there would be trouble over both the platform and the nomination had been clear for some time. In January, Alabama Democrats had vowed to bolt the national convention unless the party endorsed a congressional slave code for the territories, and three days before the Charleston meeting got under way delegates from seven states in the Deep South agreed to walk out should the renegade Douglas be nominated. The Douglas camp was equally determined to resist such pressure. "We are not in a condition to carry another ounce of Southern weight," warned one of Douglas's confidants; caving in to the South's slave code ultimatum, free state Democrats believed, would be both a surrender of principle and an act of political suicide. Few, then, were much surprised when Douglas's backers, by a vote of 165 to 138, won the party's approval of a platform that pointedly omitted any mention of a federal slave code. Thereupon, some fifty delegates from eight Southern states, led by Alabama's William L. Yancey ("Prince of Fire-Eaters") stalked out of the convention.

Unable to nominate Douglas, who fell short of the necessary two-thirds even after the Southern radicals pulled out, the remaining delegates adjourned to reconvene at Baltimore on June 18. At the same time, Yancey and company decided to meet a week earlier at Richmond. Given a second chance, Douglas captured the nomination of the "National Democrats," with Herschel V. Johnson of Georgia as his running mate. After waiting to see what action the regulars would take, the Southern dissidents, strengthened by fresh defections from seven other slave states, selected a proslavery ticket headed by John C. Breckinridge of Kentucky and Joseph Lane of Oregon. Division had come to the Democratic party as it would soon to the nation.

Poised to profit from this Democratic schism were the Republicans who met at Chicago in May. The task before them was to select a presidential candidate and draft a platform appealing to antislavery voters yet capable of winning over conservative Whig-Native Americans whose support for Fillmore (especially in the border free states) had cost Frémont victory in 1856. The delegates accomplished this task less by trimming their principles than by capitalizing on a stiffening of anti-Southern attitudes throughout the North in the wake of Dred Scott, Lecompton, and "Bleeding Kansas"; talk of seizing Cuba and reopening the African slave trade; and demands for congressional protection of slavery in the territories. New planks calling for a protective tariff, free homesteads, and full observance of immigrant rights made the 1860 Republican platform a somewhat broader document than that of 1856. Yet slavery remained the party's primary concern, and the resolutions dealing with it went basically unchanged. Denouncing popular sovereignty as "deception and fraud," the platform explicitly denied the power of any legislative body to legalize slavery in a territory. Democrats might gibe that the Republican credo was "like the pedlers [sic] suspenders: 'short enough for any boy and long enough for any man.'" But even radical Republicans applauded the principles set forth at Chicago.

Likewise, the nomination of Abraham Lincoln over the front-running William H. Seward and half a dozen other candidates, derived as much from widespread respect for Lincoln's rock-solid antislavery beliefs as from consternation over the New Yorker's reputed radicalism. Although his bold attacks on nativism and the notoriety of his "higher law" and "irrepressible conflict" speeches cost Seward the support of most conservatives, many Republicans had grown mistrustful of his recent waffling on the slavery question. Especially unsettling were Seward's encouragement of Douglas, his growing receptivity to popular sovereignty, his vote to admit Oregon despite its Jim Crow constitution, and his recent Senate speech which had conciliatorily referred to the South as the "capital states" and to the North as the "labor states." Seward seemed to be "seeking an opportunity to distinguish himself as a compromiser," concluded one Maine Republican. "But he ought to consider that the day for compromises has long since gone by."

Lincoln, on the other hand, had emerged as a serious national candidate precisely because he so forcefully and eloquently resisted any lowering of his party's standard. In dozens of speeches during the fall and winter of 1859–60 throughout the Middle West, New York, and New England Lincoln thundered against slavery's basic immorality and advised Republicans to shun debilitating compromise. "Republicans believe that slavery is wrong," he told Ohio audiences in 1859, "and they insist, and will continue to insist upon a national policy which recognizes it, and deals with it, *as a wrong*. There *can* be no letting down about this." Lincoln had, of course, other attractions. Having kept his distaste for nativism private, he offended neither Know-Nothings (as had Seward) nor foreign-born voters. A Westerner of Whiggish roots he left no doubt of his support for Republican economic policies. He possessed the undivided allegiance of Republicans in Illinois, a critical state. But it was because he caught so well the prevailing antislavery temper of his party that many delegates were ready to turn to Lincoln once the bids of their favorite sons fell short. After trailing Seward on the first two ballots, Lincoln won nomination on the third. It augured well for Republican fortunes that Lincoln had received his strongest backing from the very states that had cost Frémont victory in 1856 — Indiana, Illinois, and Pennsylvania.

In May, conservative Whigs and former Know-Nothings, the residue of the now-defunct Native American party, had formed the Constitutional Union party. Pledged simply and vaguely to a defense of the Constitution, the Union, "and the enforcement of the laws," the new party's standard-bearers, John Bell of Tennessee and Edward Everett of Massachusetts, became the chief adversaries of Breckinridge Democrats in the South, just as Lincoln and his running mate Hannibal Hamlin became the principal opponents of Douglas Democrats in the North. So wide and deep had the sectional fault line become, that south of Virginia, Kentucky, and Missouri, Lincoln did not appear on the ballot. Nor did Breckinridge in Rhode Island, New York, and New Jersey.

Tariffs and homesteads, railroads and immigrants, political graft and corruption, all figured in the 1860 election. The most fundamental issue, however, remained the rights and wrongs of slavery and the largely unspoken fear of disunion should an antislavery president be chosen. Republicans and Southern Democrats both pooh-poohed such fears, but Douglas as well as Bell shared them fully. Indeed, when early gubernatorial elections in Pennsylvania and Indiana foretold a Republican victory in November, Douglas manfully declared: "Mr. Lincoln is the next President. We must try to save the Union. I will go South." He did just that. The closing weeks of the campaign found him in Tennessee, Georgia, and Alabama, bravely urging "every good citizen" to frustrate the schemes of secessionists. He was as anxious as anyone to see the Republican ticket defeated, Douglas told a Montgomery audience; but "if Lincoln is elected, he must be inaugurated."

The November returns, and the Deep South's reaction, confirmed Douglas's fears. Abraham Lincoln swept every free state but New Jersey, which he split with Douglas. Douglas, though second in the popular vote, captured only Missouri, in a squeaker over Bell. Breckinridge carried eleven slave states (though he won outright majorities in only four), and Bell prevailed in Virginia, Kentucky, and his native Tennessee. Although he could claim scarcely 40 percent of the popular vote, Lincoln had picked up 180 electoral votes—57 more than all his opponents combined. The purely sectional Republican party—a party not even recognized by ten Southern states—had now seized control of the executive branch of the federal government. A president publicly committed to the eventual destruction of slavery, an institution he had labeled "a moral, social and political evil" would soon occupy the White House. It was precisely because abolitionists like John Greenleaf Whittier cheered "the triumph of our principles—so long delayed" that white Southerners recoiled in alarm. The Unionism Stephen Douglas had taken such pains to buttress now faced a graver challenge than ever before. Even the pro-Douglas *Atlanta Confederacy* threatened: "Let the consequences be what they may—whether the Potomac is crimsoned in human gore, and Pennsylvania Avenue is paved ten fathoms in depth with mangled bodies, or whether the last vestige of liberty is swept from the face of the American continent, the South will never submit to such humiliation and degradation as the inauguration of Abraham Lincoln."

IV

The slaveholding South had good reason to take alarm at Lincoln's victory. Its perception of the Republican party as first and foremost an antislavery instrument was fundamentally correct. Even conservative Republicans, who stressed the danger of Slave Power aggression and showed scant concern for those in chains, damned slavery as a "blighting institution" and sought a congressional barrier against its spread. The events of the 1850s—Kansas-Nebraska, Dred Scott, Lecompton and "Bleeding Kansas," proslavery designs on Cuba, and talk of reopening the African slave trade—had progressively radicalized party moderates, producing a heightened sensitivity to the immorality of slavery and a determination, in Lincoln's words, to pursue its "ultimate extinction" throughout the land.

There were limits, of course, to the antislavery steps Republicans might take. Northern conservatism remained a force to be reckoned with, especially within the Democratic party and among property-conscious Republican businessmen. Virtually all Republicans admitted that the Constitution forbade outside interference with the domestic institutions of Southern states. Moreover, despite Lincoln's election the South was by no means impotent within the national government. It still controlled the Supreme Court, much of the federal bureaucracy, and, with the aid of Northern Democrats, could hold its own in Congress. Lincoln himself, though sincerely opposed to slavery, was no wild-eyed abolitionist. A Kentuckian by birth (his father had served on the Hardin County, Kentucky, slave patrol), he could count many Southerners, even slaveholders, among his friends and relatives. Alexander H. Stephens, a fellow Whig in the Thirtieth Congress, admitted that "in point of merit as a man I have no doubt Lincoln is just as good, safe and sound a man as Mr. Buchanan, and would administer the Government so far as he is individually concerned just as safely for the South and as honestly and faithfully *in every particular.*" Lincoln lent credence to this characterization by offering a cabinet post (soon declined) to John A. Gilmer, a North Carolina Unionist.

Still, Lincoln's triumph was a palpable menace to the South. Quite aside from the long-range damage to be expected once Congress and the Supreme Court also came under Republican control (namely, exclusion of slavery from all territories, abolition in the District of Columbia, an end to the interstate slave trade, repeal or drastic modification of the Fugitive Slave Law), the new president, acting solely on his executive authority, might make no end of mischief. By appointing Republicans to judgeships, collectorships, postmasterships, and other positions in the South he could foster an antislavery influence dangerous not only to the peculiar institution but, once it reached the slave quarters, to the very lives of Southern whites. Such patronage, moreover, might spawn Republican organizations in the South destructive to the unity on which the region's special culture depended.

In fact, Lincoln's election itself, independent of the policies he and his party might be expected to pursue, represented an assault on the honor and well-being of the South. By electing a candidate pledged to slavery's destruction, the Northern majority had grossly insulted the South and proclaimed its determination to make vassals—slaves—of Southern whites. To prideful Southerners, the voters' verdict amounted to "a declaration of war against our property and the supremacy of the white race," a slap in the face that demanded retribution. More practical considerations also fueled Southern indignation at Lincoln's victory. Many fretted that slave property, its value dependent upon an expectation of future returns, "must be greatly depreciated" under a "black Republican" administration. The *Charleston Mercury* estimated that "the submission of the South to the administration of the Federal Government under Messrs. Lincoln and Hamlin, must reduce the value of slaves in the South, one hundred dollars each," a loss to the region of more than $400 million. Worse yet, as slave prices skidded, planters in the upper South (where slavery was deemed a marginal investment) would feel pressure to sell off their chattels. Then, worried the *Mercury,* "the Frontier States [will] *enter on the policy of making themselves Free States.*" Meanwhile, word of the election of an antislavery president seemed in itself sufficient to promote bloody insurrections against the "master race." Finally, magnifying all such fears, was the fear of the unknown. Abraham Lincoln would be the *first* Republican president and history offered no reassurances concerning his probable behavior in office.

Southern radicals—men like William L. Yancey of Alabama, Robert Barnwell Rhett of South Carolina, T. R. R. Cobb of Georgia, and Edmund Ruffin of Virginia, men who for years had agitated for disunion as the best means of protecting and advancing Southern interests—now saw their opportunity and moved swiftly to capitalize on the flurry of indignation following Lincoln's election. For the past year and more, such "fire-eaters" had threatened secession in the event of a Republican triumph in 1860. Now they had to make good those threats or admit they were just so much hot air.

The disunionist argument appealed both to practical interests and regional pride. Not only did Republican ascendancy threaten the right to property in slaves, and with it racial control, moral and cultural superiority, and economic well-being, but it dishonored a people who had made honor a way of life. Thus the Mississippi secessionist Albert Gallatin Brown clamored for resistance to "submissionists" at any price. "If it should cost us the Union, our fortunes, our lives, let them go," he cried. Better ruin than meek submission "to a disgrace so deep and damning." The Republicans, claimed others, were bent upon using the power of "Lord King Numbers" to subvert republican government, to force "complete subjection and political bondage, degradation, and ruin" upon the South. Now having gained the upper hand, warned a South Carolina "Minute Man," the Republican "tyrants" meant "to reduce you and your wives and your daughters on a level with the very slaves you buy and sell." Liberty, safety, prosperity, and self-respect all demanded the dissolution of a once-nurturing but now oppressive Union.

In winning support for their position, Southern disunionists possessed certain advantages. Above all, they had the advantage of urging action instead of inaction, of taking the offensive instead of the defensive, labeling caution cowardice. The reckless counsel of the secessionists was simply more exciting than that of Unionists who advocated a policy of wait and see. It somehow seemed a good deal more patriotic. Fears that separation would precipitate civil war were easily brushed aside. "You may slap a Yankee in the face and he'll go off and sue you," some said, "but he won't fight." Secessionists also benefited from the growth of Southern nationalism in recent years. This sense of the South as a nation unto itself derived more from shared fears and resentments than from a common, unique cultural identity. Yet rightly or wrongly, many Southerners had come to believe that theirs was a distinctive way of life. Just as Northerners boasted of a social system that exalted free labor, unabashed materialism, and social mobility, so many Southerners had come to insist upon the superiority of a culture rooted in slavery, a culture which, it was said, placed honor, generosity, devotion to family and community, and the maintenance of social order above "progress" and material gain. Such events as the Panic of 1857, which hit the commercial Northeast much harder than the agricultural South, seemed evidence of the superiority of Southern institutions, while Fugitive Slave Law violations, John Brown's raid, and Republican victories buttressed the notion that only through secession might such institutions be preserved.

Southern Unionists—strongest in the upper South, among former Whigs, and in regions with relatively few slaves—countered with arguments of their own. Far from protecting slavery, they insisted, secession would place it in peril, for secession (despite the sweet talk of fire-eaters) was bound to lead to war, and war to emancipation. "I consider slavery much more secure in the Union than out of it," Alexander H. Stephens declared. Other forms of property would be similarly endangered, as would, indeed, the lives of all Southern whites. The French Revolution had spawned a massive slave insurrection in Santo Domingo, more than one Unionist noted; who could say that a Southern revolution would not produce the same result? As the Georgian Stephens sagely observed, "Revolutions are much easier started than controlled, and the men who begin them, even for the best purposes and objects, seldom end them." Before embarking on so uncertain a journey, Unionists cautioned, the South should await some overt act of Northern aggression. "Let revolution come when the Constitution is trampled upon," the Lexington *Kentucky Statesman* advised; "let not resistance be predicated upon the purpose of even a successful party, to trample upon it. . . . Wait, wait, wait, and if we fail to preserve the Union with a Constitution intact, then let us have a UNITED SOUTH."

One should be careful not to exaggerate the differences between the secessionists and their opponents within the South, for there were substantial areas of agreement between them. On the one hand, very few Southerners looked to disunion as an end in itself. Even ardent secessionists would have remained faithful to the Union had they been persuaded that Southern rights would be respected. On the other hand few Unionists were willing to sacrifice Southern rights to the Union. Most vigorously defended the slave system and shared the belief that secession was a constitutional, not merely revolutionary, right and that no state should be forced to remain in the Union.

So evenly balanced were the advocates of immediate, separate state secession and the Unionists or "cooperationists" (a term that included both those who believed that Southern independence could succeed only if all slave states acted in concert and those who favored delay as a way of buying time and forestalling disunion), that had not South Carolina moved so quickly, unilaterally, history might have taken a different turn. South Carolina, the most alienated and undemocratic of Southern states, did, however, move with astonishing swiftness. Its legislature, already in session to cast the state's electoral votes (South Carolina being the only state unwilling to leave this decision to the voters), provided on November 10, 1860, for an election of delegates to a constitutional convention to meet on December 17. On December 20 that convention unanimously adopted an ordinance of secession.

Within a month and a half six other states from the Deep South, emboldened by South Carolina's example, had followed suit: Mississippi, Florida, Alabama, Georgia, Louisiana, and Texas. In several of these states the vote was exceptionally close, notably in Georgia, Alabama, and Louisiana. Without the intimidation of secessionist mobs, the outcome might well have been different. In every case, however, "straight-out" secessionists made the most of their majorities, beat down (except for Texas) attempts to submit ordinances of secession to a popular referendum, and carried their states out of the Union. On

February 7, 1861, delegates from six of these states (representatives from Texas arrived later) met at Montgomery, Alabama, and adopted a provisional constitution which offered explicit protection to slave property and deleted the general welfare clause but otherwise closely resembled the Constitution of the United States. Even the ban on the African slave trade was preserved. Two days later they chose Jefferson Davis and Alexander H. Stephens as president and vice-president of the Confederate States of America. The gravity of the moment was captured best by Mary Chesnut, whose husband James, until recently a U.S. senator from South Carolina, was one of the Montgomery delegates. "This Southern Confederacy must be supported now by calm determination and cool brains," she wrote. "We have risked all, and we must play our best, for the stake is life or death."

The disunionists had played their hand well. Their dream of an independent Southern nation was now a reality. Yet those who looked closely at the results of the secession conventions found cause for concern as well as satisfaction. For example, support for disunion was clearly weakest among nonslaveholders and in counties with relatively few slaves. The basis for the later complaint that the Civil War was "a rich man's war and a poor man's fight" could already be discerned. More immediately alarming to those who gathered at Montgomery was the unwillingness, for the present, of the upper South to join in. Without the wealth, manpower, and resources of states like Virginia, Tennessee, and North Carolina, the survival of a Southern Confederacy seemed much in doubt. Yet, throughout the upper South, secession conventions either never met or concluded that Lincoln's victory was insufficient cause for separation. Such caution and restraint is perhaps best explained by the region's comparatively smaller stake in slavery. Proportionately, about half as many white families in the upper South held slaves (20.6 percent) as did those in the seven states of the original Confederacy (37.2 percent); similarly, the percentage of slaves in the Deep South (47.5 percent) was more than double that in the upper South (22.6 percent). The border slave states were deeply disturbed at the prospect of a "black Republican" in the White House. But their fears of race warfare and economic disaster being less acute than those of whites in the Black Belt, their economic ties to the North being closer and their faith in the political process greater, they swallowed the bitter pill of Lincoln's election and waited to see what time would bring. Still, although the upper South resisted disunion, a determination to oppose the coercion of any seceding state was widespread. Before long Jefferson Davis and his compatriots would exploit that determination to draw proud Virginia and three other states into the Confederacy.

Fearing such a development, which could only increase the likelihood of civil war, moderates in both North and South worked desperately to concoct some compromise to stave off further defections and entice already-departed states to return. In Congress, both the House and Senate established special committees to explore plans of conciliation. The most comprehensive such plan was that sponsored by the venerable Kentucky Unionist John J. Crittenden, two of whose sons later served as major generals in opposing armies during the Civil War. The key element in Crittenden's scheme was the old and oft-rejected proposal to extend the Missouri Compromise line to the Pacific, banning slavery in territories north of 36° 30' but establishing and maintaining it in all territory "now held, or hereafter acquired" south of that line. This hoary recommendation—made especially obnoxious to Northerners by its positive recognition (not merely toleration) of slavery below 36° 30' and its inducement to southerly expansion—also became the centerpiece of an intersectional peace conference which met at Virginia's initiative in Washington in February.

For many reasons, the compromisers' efforts came to naught. Legislative measures could scarcely erase the hopes and fears released by the Republican triumph of 1860, and even in the border states support for compromise proved halfhearted. The Deep South had long since set its course, and by 1861 its few representatives in Washington persistently rebuffed the very notion of healing concessions. Concessions, in any event, were not forthcoming. Republican congressmen, angered at slave state intransigence, fearful of alienating their party's antislavery core, and determined to thwart attempts by Southern "bullies" to reverse the verdict of the ballot box, steadfastly refused to surrender or impair the Chicago platform.

Those Republican congressmen who resisted capitulation to Southern demands found themselves bolstered by their constituents below and by President Lincoln above. Although he refrained from public statements during the months between his election and his inauguration, Lincoln privately made plain his hostility to any trimming on the basic matter of slavery in the territories. To Southern friends he sent assurances that his administration would not attack slavery in the states or in the District of Columbia, that it would leave alone the interstate slave trade, enforce the Fugitive Slave Law, and urge the free states to repeal their personal liberty laws. (Four Northern states complied.) Lincoln even endorsed a proposed Thirteenth Amendment which would have forever prohibited federal interference with slavery in the states. But on the territorial question, he refused to budge. Characteristic was his advice to Congressman Elihu Washburne of Illinois (December 13, 1860):

> Prevent, as far as possible, any of our friends from demoralizing themselves, and our cause, by entertaining propositions for compromise of any sort, on *'slavery extension.'* There is no possible compromise upon it, but which puts us under again, and leaves all our work to do over again. Whether it be a Mo. line, or . . . Pop. Sov. it is all the same. Let either be done, & immediately filibustering and extending slavery recommences. On that point hold firm, as with a chain of steel.

Lincoln also left no doubt of his belief in the perpetuity of the Union and his determination, as president, "to execute the laws and maintain the existing government." Repeatedly he denied any plan of aggression or coercion against the South. There was "no need of bloodshed and war," he told a Pennsylvania audience. "I am not in favor of such a course; and I may say in advance that there will be no bloodshed unless it is forced upon the government. The government will not use force, unless force is used against it." At the same time, Lincoln clearly indicated that he would take whatever steps were necessary to uphold national authority—to collect federal revenues and to protect or recapture government property throughout the United States.

When the Fort Sumter crisis arose, therefore, President Lincoln was ready to act moderately but firmly, aware of both military and political considerations. Despite cabinet opinion in favor of withdrawing Major Robert Anderson's small force from its untenable position in the heart of Charleston harbor, Lincoln decided on an attempt to reprovision (not reinforce) the fort. Such a gesture would fulfill his announced intention of holding forts and federal property in the South; and, should South Carolina oppose the relief expedition (as it did) the opprobrium of initiating civil war would rest with the South. The Confederacy, feeling the need to strike a blow that would join the upper South with the lower, tested Lincoln's resolve by firing the first shot, on April 12, 1861—the honor going to Virginia's "Father of Secession" Edmund Ruffin. That shot, as Jefferson Davis and others had hoped, provoked federal retaliation and propelled Virginia, Arkansas, North Carolina, and Tennessee into the Confederacy. It also began the bloodiest war in all of American history.

Call to Arms

Blissfully oblivious of the carnage to come, Americans North and South responded to the onset of hostilities with reckless enthusiasm. On April 15, 1861, two days after Fort Sumter fell, President Lincoln issued a proclamation calling forth 75,000 state militia to put down an insurrection "too powerful to be suppressed by the ordinary course of judicial proceedings." Although it precipitated the final round of secession, this step—and others Lincoln took soon after: blockading Confederate ports, suspending the writ of habeas corpus between Philadelphia and Washington, enlarging the regular army and navy—won hearty support throughout the free states. Volunteering proceeded so briskly that the president's modest quota was soon subscribed, and some governors enrolled surplus regiments lest "the ardor of the people" be repressed. Belief that the war would be short, that "those fellows down South are big bluffers . . . [who] would rather talk than fight," fed a spread-eagle patriotism that muted old antagonisms and drew even most Northern Democrats into the struggle to save the Union. "The assault upon Fort Sumter started us all to our feet, as one man," wrote the Philadelphia jurist Horace Binney; "all political division ceased among us from that very moment. There is among us but one thought, one object, one end, one symbol—the Stars and Stripes."

In rallying free state Democrats to war against the "Montgomery mutineers," none worked more heroically or more effectively than Senator Stephen A. Douglas. Although he had repeatedly assailed Lincoln and the Republicans during the tense months prior to Fort Sumter, once the first shots had been exchanged Douglas acted swiftly and wholeheartedly to bolster the administration's resistance to disunion. Calling on the President as soon as he learned of Sumter's surrender, Douglas not only approved Lincoln's call for 75,000 volunteers but suggested that the figure be raised to 200,000. "You do not know the dishonest purposes of those [Confederate] men as I do," he explained. And when, soon afterward, a friend asked the senator what should be done with the many Confederate sympathizers still in Washington, Douglas bitterly exclaimed: "If I were President, I'd convert them or hang them all within forty-eight hours." A week later Douglas set out for Illinois where, on April 25, he delivered a widely publicized speech to a joint session of the Illinois legislature at Springfield in which he boldly proclaimed that "the shortest way to peace is the most stupendous and unanimous preparation for war." A May Day address in Chicago brought a still sterner message. "There can be no neutrals in this war," Douglas insisted; "only patriots and traitors." Barely a month later the Little Giant lay dead, a victim of years of overwork and heavy drink. Had he lived, the cooperation between Northern Democrats and Republicans which marked the first months of the Civil War might have lingered a bit longer, and the divisive influence of such "Copperheads" as Clement Vallandigham and Fernando Wood counted for less.

Such was the hope and elation that swept the North after Fort Sumter's fall that even many avowed pacifists gave their blessing to Lincoln's war efforts. With few exceptions, "nonresistant" abolitionists like William Lloyd Garrison and John Greenleaf Whittier interpreted the Civil War as "the chastisement which Divine Providence is inflicting on the nation" for its complicity in slavery. Crediting their crusade of moral suasion for having precipitated this mighty confrontation, they now embraced "righteous violence" as the means by which slavery might at long last be destroyed. Though they would complain about the tardiness of Lincoln and the Republicans in embracing emancipation as a legitimate war aim, most abolitionists backed the military subjugation of the South. It was, after all, James Sloan Gibbons, an antislavery Quaker possessed of "a reasonable leaning toward wrath in cases of emergency," who penned the words for Stephen Foster's "We Are Coming, Father Abraham, Three Hundred Thousand More," an instantly popular song sung at recruiting rallies throughout the North.

Those in the North who pledged support to the war effort often did so in pursuit of special goals. Abolitionists sought an end to slavery and the establishment of racial democracy in America; Westerners wished to reclaim free navigation of the Mississippi River from St. Louis to New Orleans and to reestablish their once-lucrative trade with Southern markets; Yankee bankers and businessmen sought the restoration of political stability, a recovery of Southern debts, and the resumption of commercial relations with the South; Eastern conservatives hoped to restore respect for "order, government, and law"; and many young New England Brahmins looked to civil war to bring personal fulfillment as well as renewed toughness to a nation gone soft. All, however, agreed at the outset on more general objectives: to crush the rebellion, restore the

Union, and tutor the South in the more progressive ways of the North. Governor Alexander W. Randall expressed the determination of many when he told a special session of Wisconsin's legislature in May 1861: "This war began where Charleston *is*; it should end where Charleston *was*. These gathering armies are the instruments of His vengeance, to execute His judgment; they are His flails wherewith on God's great Southern threshing floor, He will pound rebellion for its sins!"

The South, too, greeted the onset of hostilities with noisy enthusiasm and faith that a "virtuous and gallant people in a good cause never have failed." Lincoln's call for troops to suppress the rebellion drove Virginia, North Carolina, Tennessee, and Arkansas into the Confederacy and rendered uncertain the loyalty of Kentucky, Missouri, and, briefly, even Maryland. Throughout Dixie, Unionists changed colors or went underground. Volunteers flocked to enlist in such numbers that by July 112,000 troops had been mustered into service and another 200,000 turned away for want of arms. One elderly Virginian, after sending five sons and a black servant off to camp, wrote to the governor: "I have but one single daughter and she desires me to say to your Exc. that if you will furnish her with *Suitable Arms* she will undertake deeds of daring that will astonish many of the sterner sex. And if these with their Gallant Officers & Comrades are not enough to satisfy *Northern Averice* [*sic*] *and fanaticism,* you can have the remaining strength of your most obt Servant, Thos. G. Spencer." Planters tendered the services of slaves, railways offered discounts on military traffic, churches took up collections and donated their bells for the casting of cannon, the young ladies of Lucy Cobb Institute in Athens, Georgia, contributed $120 to the Confederate coffers. In these and countless other ways Southerners displayed support for a war most expected would be both short and glorious. A few, Jefferson Davis and Robert E. Lee among them, foresaw a protracted struggle. Most, however, remained through 1861 confident of a quick Southern victory, certain that when it came to fighting one Confederate "could whip or hurt four Yankeys."

Like the Yankee enemy, those who threw their support to the Confederacy acted from a variety of motives. Most fundamentally, of course, they fought in defense of their homes and a way of life, rooted in slavery, deemed superior to the fanatical, cold-hearted, money-grubbing ways of the North. Honor, self-determination, social and racial stability, all stood in peril if the Confederacy collapsed. Some Southerners had more special agendas. Preservation of the plantation system, for example, was of paramount importance to the planter class and time would show that many would pursue this goal even when it clashed with the maintenance of Confederate independence. Some echoed Yankee Brahmins like Francis Parkman and Oliver Wendell Holmes in expressing hopes that the war would add something Spartan to the Southern character. A good many patrician conservatives, moreover, looked to the war to shut off currents of class conflict and reestablish the hegemony of the "better sort"—those "men of property & of education, who from the very fact of ownership of the soil and its production and from their education are alone qualified to be the ruling class."

II

For a time, the excitement following the first clash of arms was sufficient to keep recruiting officers busy, to fill army and navy rolls without resort to special incentives or coercion. At first, indeed, troops poured forth beyond the capacity of state and federal authorities to arm, feed, drill, or equip them. Some early recruits paraded for a time with broomhandle "muskets," and some Confederate soldiers had only shotguns to fire in the battle of Shiloh, a year after the war began. By 1862, however, both armies had gone far toward fulfilling their material needs, while enlistments showed signs of slackening.

Though military victories—notably those at Bull Run, Ball's Bluff, and Wilson's Creek—kept Confederate morale high throughout most of 1861, Southern armies were the first to feel the pinch, simply because they had a much smaller manpower pool to tap. With only 1,140,000 white males of military age, compared to three and a half times that many in the Union states, the Confederacy depended upon near total mobilization to hold its own in the field. Although its army's strength rarely rose above half the Federals' total, the Confederacy put at least 80 percent of its young white men under arms during the course of the Civil War (as against roughly 50 percent in the North). The availability of 3.5 million slaves for labor on the home front made possible such a *levee en masse,* but left the Confederates nonetheless vulnerable to cracks in morale.

By the end of 1861 many short-term enlistments had expired, twelve-month volunteers talked eagerly of going home, and Southern boys no longer rushed to enlist. Word of military drudgery and hardship, of suffering and death even in "victorious" battles, filtered home and led many to recalculate the price of glory. From Columbia, South Carolina, a recruiting officer wrote in November: "[My job] is a sinecure because there are no troops coming in . . . —the deep-mouthed curse, the fierce shout, the wild rush to arms and vengeance aint here."

Battlefield reverses, which gave evidence that the war would be long and punishing, so depressed enlistment enthusiasm that in April 1862 the Confederate government passed the first military conscription law in American history. By the terms of this statute every able-bodied white male between the ages of eighteen and thirty-five (soon raised to forty-five) was subject to military duty for three years or, if less, the war's duration. Although it broke sharply from the Minuteman tradition of past wars, and although a few like Georgia's Governor Joseph E. Brown protested that it trampled on states' rights, most Confederates readily accepted the draft as essential to their continued independence. Even the Conscription Act of February 1864 which, said scornful Yankees, robbed cradle and grave by making all between seventeen and fifty eligible for service, found favor in the South as a necessary, if desperate, war measure.

Protest developed, however, over a provision that allowed persons hiring substitutes to escape military service. Scarce supply and heavy demand soon drove the asking price of eligible substitutes far beyond the means of most citizens, prompting charges of elitism. The actions of unscrupulous brokers and dishonest substitutes (one man sold himself to twenty clients) compounded public dissatisfaction, and in December 1863 the Confederate Congress forthrightly closed the proxy loophole. Even more controversial were the special exemptions that Congress established in an attempt to maximize the Confederate war effort. Among those shielded from the draft were public servants, ministers, teachers, editors, nurses, factory and railroad workers, miners, and telegraph operators. The mad dash to such "bomb-proof positions" as these caused scandals aplenty, but none which equaled in divisive effect the Confederate decision in October 1862, to excuse from service one planter or overseer on each plantation of twenty slaves. Nothing did more to provoke the cry that this was "a rich man's war and a poor man's fight" than the infamous "twenty Negro law."

Even without the abuses that attended it, so alien a concept as military conscription was bound to carry a stigma, South and North. A Georgia editor probably came close to the mark when he declared that "most of our young men would just as soon be sent to the penitentiary for a term of years as to be conscripted." Yet the very taint that adhered to draftees made conscription a useful goad to volunteering. This fact was certainly much in mind when early in March 1863 the Union government passed a conscription law of its own. The Enrollment Act, as it was called, specified that every fit male citizen between twenty and forty-five was liable to three years of military service. Exemptions were much more limited than in the Confederacy, but those drafted could escape duty if they hired an acceptable substitute or, until 1864, paid a $300 commutation fee. In implementing the draft, the War Department set state quotas which, if not met by volunteering, were to be filled by conscription. As expected, the onus of conscription, plus generous federal, state, and local bounties to those who enlisted, allowed Northern states to fill most of their quotas with volunteers. Only some 6 percent of the Union's fighting men (46,000 draftees and 118,000 substitutes) entered service under the Federal conscription system. Even more than the enemy, which netted about one-fifth of its forces through conscription, the Union army was an army of volunteers.

The North's great edge in manpower was but one of the advantages which, before their stunning defeat at Bull Run, led many Yankees to predict certain, swift victory. The Union's ability to sustain its soldiers and sailors also far outstripped the Confederacy's. Its industrial capacity was vastly superior. In 1860 the North boasted six times as many factories and workshops as might be found in the South, with a productive capacity at least ten times greater. When the Civil War began, Northern states annually produced fifteen times as much iron, thirty-eight times as much coal, fourteen times as many textile goods, thirty times as many boots and shoes, and thirty-two times as many firearms as did the Confederate states. A single county in Connecticut produced in 1860 firearms valued at ten times those manufactured below the Mason-Dixon line. The free states also possessed a disproportionate share of skilled industrial workers, and though the Confederates wisely granted draft exemptions to expert craftsmen, at times the loss of a single technician would hamstring production. When, for example, Federal raiders killed John Jones, a skilled barrel straightener, the Richmond Armory's output fell by 369 rifles a month during the prolonged period it took to train his replacement. So, too, with four times the bank deposits and nearly twice the specie reserves, the North's financial condition was much healthier than the South's. Even when it came to agriculture the North enjoyed an edge. In 1860, half of the nation's corn, four-fifths of its wheat, and seven-eighths of its oats came from beyond the Confederacy's borders. Likewise, when war began the loyal states claimed many more horses, cows, and sheep (and fewer mules, cattle, and hogs) than did the South.

The North also benefited from a decidedly superior transportation system. Not only was its rail network more than twice as extensive as the South's (21,973 miles of track, compared to 9,283 in the Confederacy), but it enjoyed a marked advantage in locomotives, rollingstock, engine works, repair facilities, and skilled mechanics. The Union's unmatched ability to repair or replace damaged equipment soon became a source of wonder and despair to hard-pressed Southerners. One detachment of Confederate troops, it was said, later excused its failure to blow up a tunnel to check General Sherman's advance through Georgia by saying, "Oh, hell! Don't you know that old Sherman carries a *duplicate* tunnel along?" In addition to its rail superiority, nearly all the registered shipping lay in Northern hands when the war began.

Although clearly outmatched in manpower and materiel, the Confederacy possessed important advantages of its own, advantages which shaped the South's military strategy and kindled hopes of independence made good. Most fundamentally, the Confederates had no need to "win" this war—they had merely to prevent the North from winning. Southern independence, that is, depended not upon the conquest and occupation of Union territory, or even the annihilation of Yankee armies. Rather, it rested on the Confederates' ability to make their own subjugation so costly and difficult as to cause the North to lose heart and give in. A related advantage, of course, was that for Southerners the war's essential purpose—defense of the homeland—was more readily grasped, more emotionally arousing, than the North's somewhat abstract pursuit of reunion. In time many Southerners would place defense of the homestead above the homeland. Planters would withhold slaves from Confederate service and trade cotton with the enemy; worried privates and corporals would desert their posts to answer family calls for help. But for a time at least the South's defensive mission was easily understood and gave special unity to its war effort.

So long as the Confederates held to a defensive position, moreover, they could substantially neutralize the Union's superiority in manpower. Fighting a war of resistance, taking advantage of interior lines and familiar terrain, having no need to hold conquered territory, garrison cities, or defend long lines of supply, the gray armies could make do with many fewer men than an attacking force would require. As William Tecumseh Sherman noted in his *Memoirs,* an invading army grows smaller as its advances—needing to post detachments along the way to guard supply depots, railroad bridges, and the like—whereas a defending army grows larger as outlying soldiers fall back to prepared positions to the rear. Often it took the North as many men to protect its supply lines as it did to fight battles. Guerrilla bands (Mosby's Rangers, Quantrill's bushwhackers, and many others) abetted a defensive strategy by cutting rail lines, burning bridges, ambushing Federal patrols, and in other ways throwing the invaders off stride.

The defensive position of the Confederates was still further enhanced by the introduction of the rifle. In earlier conflicts, including the Mexican War, the basic infantry firearm had been the smoothbore musket, a weapon so laughably inaccurate that, as Ulysses S. Grant remarked, "at the distance of a few hundred yards a man might fire at you all day without your finding out." (In 1861 crack marksmen from an Illinois regiment gave experimental proof of Grant's observation by firing 160 smoothbore shots at a flour barrel 180 yards away; only 4 of the bullets hit the target!) During the late 1850s, however, the U.S. Army had begun converting to more accurate and deadly muzzle-loading rifles and by the second year of the Civil War most soldiers on both sides were armed with such weapons, usually American Springfields or British Enfields. Able to stop an attack at 400 yards and to kill at half a mile, the rifle revolutionized tactics by overpowering bayonet and cavalry charges, diminishing artillery's offensive role, and greatly increasing the advantage of the defense. Especially when entrenched, defenders bearing rifles could stand their ground against a much larger attacking force. "The rifle and the spade," one expert concludes, "had made defense at least three times as strong as offense."

Geography also worked in many ways to the South's advantage. The very size of the Confederacy—larger than any European nation, save Russia and Turkey—gave room for maneuver, delay, and strategic withdrawal and compounded the difficulty of conquest. "They may overrun our frontier states and plunder our coast but, as for conquering us, the thing is an impossibility," Virginia's George W. Randolph assured his daughter in October 1861. "There is no instance in history of a people as numerous as we are inhabiting a country so extensive as ours being subjected if true to themselves." In the West, it is true, major rivers, the Mississippi, the Cumberland, the Tennessee, offered the Yankees avenues of invasion; but in the much-fought-over Virginia theater the Rappahannock, Rapidan, York, Chickahominy, and James rivers ran athwart the main Union line of advance. The fertile valley of the Shenandoah, angling toward Washington but away from Richmond, favored the diversionary raids of Stonewall Jackson and Jubal Early and was used by Robert E. Lee in his Gettysburg campaign of 1863. West of the Shenandoah, the Allegheny Mountains safeguarded approaches to Virginia and other South Atlantic states.

Fighting in defense of their homeland, the Confederates also benefited from familiarity with the terrain, an advantage made greater by the absence, until well into the war, of reliable maps. Before the Civil War the only careful geographical surveys were those made in the Far West. Accurate military maps existed for no part of the United States until after the war began. In his Western campaign in 1862, General Henry W. Halleck depended on maps he got from a bookstore, and the Confederate commander P. G. T. Beauregard foiled Halleck's pursuit after the capture of Corinth, Mississippi, by removing all road signs. It was 1863 before the Army of the Potomac had reliable maps of northern Virginia. Indeed, General Sherman complained of "extremely defective" maps during his Carolina campaign, only weeks before hostilities ceased. The Confederates' maps were no better, of course, but at least Southerners knew their own countryside.

Taking cognizance of the strengths as well as the weaknesses of their position, Confederate leaders groped their way toward a suitable military strategy. Purely guerrilla warfare was out of the question, partly because it seemed a dishonorable way to give battle but mainly because it would have jeopardized control over slavery. A more conventional defensive strategy, however, had the double advantage of helping the South to compensate for its numerical inferiority and showing the world that, in Jefferson Davis's words, the Confederacy asked merely that "the people of the United States should cease to war upon us, and permit us to pursue our own path to happiness, while they in peace pursue theirs." Still, a strategy too passively defensive carried risks of its own. Making Southern soil the battleground would exact fearful economic costs and place a heavy strain on Confederate morale. If, moreover, the North were permitted to apply its vast preponderance of power everywhere, weak points on the Confederacy's perimeter might well collapse. Some prominent figures (Robert Toombs, Henry A. Wise, General Beauregard, among others) therefore urged an aggressive policy from the outset and complained when the South's victory at First Bull Run was not followed by a quick march on Washington.

What emerged, then, was a partial accommodation to both views, an "offensive-defense" designed to husband the South's resources and prevent the enemy from applying fatal pressure on *all* points by attacking him at *selected* points and at times of the Confederacy's choosing. Surprise and rapid concentration of forces, it was hoped, might annihilate Union armies or at least hold the invader at bay long enough to demoralize the North, win foreign recognition, and secure Confederate independence. Robert E. Lee, the boldest and most ardent devotee of this "offensive-defensive" strategy, ultimately concluded that only victories on Northern soil would break the Yankees' spirit — hence his invasions of Maryland and Pennsylvania in 1862 and 1863. The decisive victories never came, however, because rifled weapons proved so deadly to both sides that no single battle could be said to have produced crucial results. All too often the Confederacy's deliberate departures from defensive warfare served only to multiply casualties and squander scarce equipment. In exactly half of the twenty-two major battles of the Civil War, the Confederates attacked. When they did they suffered nearly twice as many casualties (117,000 to 61,000) as when they defended. Thus there was more than a little truth in the remark of one unreconstructed rebel who, after the Civil War, answered a Federal officer's taunt "Well we whipped you" by retorting: "No, we just wore ourselves out whipping you."

Northern strategy evolved slowly and haltingly, as much in response to expanding political goals as to changing military circumstances. At first, in keeping with Lincoln's determination that suppression of the rebellion "not degenerate into a violent and remorseless revolutionary struggle," Union strategy was tentative, restrained—even passive. Soon after Fort Sumter's fall, Winfield Scott, commanding general of the U.S. Army, offered a plan designed to pressure the seceded states back into the Union with minimal loss of blood. His "Anaconda Plan," as it was somewhat derisively called, proposed a naval blockade of Confederate ports to seal off trade with Europe and occupation of the Mississippi River line to cut off the western Confederacy. This done, Scott believed, little more in the way of military action would be required since time and economic distress would allow Southern Unionists to regain the upper hand and return their states to the Union. Scott's plan had much to commend it. The blockade and control of the Mississippi were to become major elements in the Union's blueprint for victory. The weakness of Scott's thinking lay in his gross underestimation of Confederate resolve and his total disregard for Northern impatience.

More in tune with the popular mood were those who cried "Forward to Richmond!"—an entreaty to which even Lincoln and Scott succumbed and which led to the sobering defeat at Bull Run. If nothing else, First Bull Run made Northerners painfully aware that this would be a long and costly conflict and that victory would depend upon full utilization of the Union's superior resources. Congress responded in July 1861 by authorizing the enlistment of 500,000 three-year volunteers and an additional 24,000 army regulars. With the concurrence of General George B. McClellan, who replaced Scott as supreme Union commander in November 1861, President Lincoln now embraced a strategy of simultaneous advances calculated to exploit the North's numerical superiority and to minimize the South's ability to concentrate its forces over interior lines. By threatening the enemy "with superior forces at *different* points, at the *same* time," he suggested, "we can safely attack one, or both, if he makes no change; and if he *weakens* one to *strengthen* the other, [we can] forebear to attack the strengthened one, but seize and hold the weakened one, gaining so much."

To this strategy of coordinated, simultaneous advances, which the

Union pursued fitfully at first but more effectively after Ulysses S. Grant became general in chief in March 1864, was added a growing commitment to a policy of total warfare. This decision to move beyond territorial conquest to "a strategy of annihilation" derived from a growing awareness of the need for sterner measures to overcome dogged, often brilliant, Southern resistance. Hopes that gingerly warfare for purely territorial objectives would facilitate reunion evaporated following a series of Union defeats and close calls in 1862. By 1863 the Northern government was firmly committed to a strategy of total war aimed not only against the enemy's armies but against its social and political system as well. Politically the new policy meant confiscation of rebel property, emancipation, and the recruitment of black soldiers. Militarily it meant remorseless assaults on gray armies, on their logistical base, and on the morale of the Southern people. What had begun as a war of limited ends had become indeed a violent and vengeful revolutionary struggle.

III

In making strategic calculations, both North and South paid careful attention to foreign as well as domestic affairs. The Confederates understood clearly that the success of their bid for independence depended in large measure upon securing recognition and assistance from the European powers, especially Great Britain and France. And the North, of course, deemed it just as essential that such aid not be forthcoming. In retrospect one can see that the cards were probably stacked against the South from the beginning, if only because diplomatically the Union had the same advantage the Confederacy enjoyed in military affairs: it had no need to win over Britain and France, only to keep them neutral. The warring American camps, however, believed European intervention to be a real possibility, especially in 1861 and 1862, and each waged a vigorous diplomatic campaign to win favor abroad.

Confederate hopes for European assistance were rooted in a blind faith in the power of King Cotton. "No, sir, you dare not make war on cotton," Senator James H. Hammond of South Carolina had declared in 1858. "No power on earth dares make war upon it. Cotton is king." Nearly all Southerners shared Hammond's conviction, and when the Civil War came they were sure that King Cotton would see them through. It was well known that something like 80 percent of all raw cotton used in the important textile industries of Great Britain and France was grown on the farms and plantations of the American South.

It would be easy, Southerners were certain, by exploiting European dependence on their snowy fiber, to win diplomatic recognition of Confederate independence and naval assistance in breaking the Federal blockade. "That little attenuated cotton thread, which a child can break," Georgia's Benjamin H. Hill boasted in July 1861, "nevertheless *can hang the world.*" The English themselves seemed aware of their subordination to King Cotton. Two weeks before the shooting began, in fact, *Punch* rhymed:

> Though with the North we sympathise,
>   It must not be forgotten
> That with the South we've stronger ties,
>   Which are composed of cotton,
> Whereof our imports mount unto
>   A sum of many figures
> And where would be our calico
>   Without the toil of niggers?

This obsessive confidence in the coercive powers of cotton was, as one historian notes, an illusion at first as comforting and later as shattering as "the belief of the French people prior to World War II in the impregnability of the Maginot line."

The first step in exerting the power of King Cotton was the imposition of an embargo on cotton exports. Better than the still-leaky Union blockade, such a measure would insure a cotton famine in Europe and produce irresistible pressure from textile magnates and workers for intervention on behalf of the Confederacy. This embargo was imposed and enforced for the most part extralegally (occasionally even illegally) by state and local officials or public safety committees. Yet the Confederate Congress encouraged it and the Southern people gave it overwhelming support during the early years of the Civil War. During 1861 and much of 1862 the cotton embargo was virtually airtight. Eventually, the ban on exports was slowly relaxed until it ceased altogether, mainly because the Confederates had come to realize the need to trade cotton for desperately needed supplies.

In the meantime, however, the Confederate Congress had approved two other measures designed to put pressure on Britain and France. The first of these was a law passed in March 1862 providing for the destruction of all cotton or tobacco in any danger of falling into enemy hands. In consequence, by 1865 some 2.5 million bales of cotton had gone up in smoke. Responding to popular demand, Congress also agreed to a joint resolution urging curtailment of cotton cultivation. Partly as a result of this appeal and state statutes which gave it teeth (though mainly because planters, uncertain of markets for cotton, voluntarily switched to food crops), cotton production fell precipitously: from 4.5 million bales in 1861 to 1.5 million in 1862 and 450,000 in 1863.

For a time it appeared that King Cotton diplomacy might succeed. By the fall of 1862 the effects of the Federal blockade and the South's curtailment program were being felt in both England and France. Over 330,000 British workers had lost their jobs, as mills in Lancashire and elsewhere curtailed operations or shut down altogether; two-thirds that many French mill hands were also unemployed during the winter of 1862–63. The English liberal Richard Cobden's warning to Charles Sumner, that "unless cotton comes in considerable quantity before the end of . . . [1862] the governments of Europe will be knocking at your door," reflected a widespread belief that Great Britain and France would brook no lasting interruption of American cotton supplies. To those abroad who contemplated intervention to secure continuing shipments of Confederate cotton were added the voices of English conservatives. Such men identified the Union with imperialism, materialism, and the rampant democracy they sought to still at home; Confederate states they perceived as "communities of Englishmen still living in the 18th century," the locus of a superior culture worthy of independence.

Southern hopes of European assistance burned brightest in the first year and a half of the war, and faded steadily thereafter. Queen Victoria's proclamation of neutrality (May 14, 1861), together with a similar pronouncement from the French government, stopped short of recognizing Confederate sovereignty but did extend belligerent status to the South. And with this status came such practical prerogatives as the right to solicit loans and purchase arms abroad, put commerce raiders to sea, and gain access to prize courts. Though it also upheld the Northern blockade, the queen's proclamation, which came before Charles Francis Adams, the first Republican minister to the Court of St. James, had reached his post, outraged Union leaders and encouraged the South to expect more overt assistance in the months to come.

The *Trent* affair also stirred hopes of British intervention on behalf of the Confederacy. For when in November 1861 Captain Charles Wilkes of the USS *San Jacinto* stopped the British mail steamer *Trent* in Bahamian waters, seized the Confederate diplomats James M. Mason and John Slidell then bound for London and Paris, and carried his captives to Fort Warren prison in Boston harbor, a "typhoon of fury" swept through England. "You may stand for this," Prime Minister Lord Palmerston stormed to his cabinet, "but damned if I will!" The foreign secretary, Lord John Russell, swiftly drafted an ultimatum demanding the prisoners' release and an apology for Wilkes's "piratical" actions. Even the staid London *Times* called for war against the high-handed Yankees, and France made plain its support of the British position. Unhappily for the South, the Lincoln administration adroitly defused this crisis by releasing the Confederate envoys on a technicality— Wilkes, explained Secretary of State Seward, had erred in seizing only Mason and Slidell instead of the entire ship. Soon forgotten, the incident nonetheless strained relations between Great Britain and the United States and bolstered Southern faith that Europe would before long actively intervene in the American Civil War.

The likelihood of European intervention rose during the summer and early fall of 1862, though less because of the *Trent* affair or the cotton famine than because of Confederate military victories—the Seven Days' campaign and Second Bull Run—which emboldened Southern sympathizers overseas. In Britain the staggering casualties resulting from such battles produced humanitarian protests and increased pressure for some sort of peacemaking initiative. Foreign Secretary Russell was an early convert to this view and on September 14 Prime Minister Palmerston, observing that the Union Army "got a very complete smashing" at Bull Run and that "even Washington or Baltimore may fall into the hands of the Confederates," privately suggested that Britain and France join in proposing to the North and South an "arrangement upon the basis of separation." Russell heartily concurred, adding that "in case of failure, we ought ourselves to recognize the Southern States as an independent state." Three weeks later William E. Gladstone, chancellor of the exchequer, publicly endorsed such proposals in a speech at Newcastle. "There is no doubt," he said, "that Jefferson Davis and other leaders of the South have made an army; they are making, it appears, a navy; and they have made what is more than either—they have made a nation."

In the event, however, neither Britain nor France proved willing to risk intervention. By 1863 King Cotton diplomacy lay in tatters. In Europe's decision to remain neutral, hardheaded calculations of national self-interest were most important. The failure of the interventionist movement in 1862 stemmed more from growing doubts of the Confederacy's ability to establish and maintain its independence— underscored at a propitious moment by General McClellan's repulse of Lee's army at Antietam Creek, September 17, 1862—than from abstract judgments of right and wrong in the American conflict. Palmerston testified to the paramountcy of such considerations when on the eve of Antietam he wrote: "If the Federals sustain a great defeat, they may be at once ready for mediation and the iron should be struck while it is hot.

If, on the other hand, they should have the best of it, we may wait awhile and see what may follow."

Southern hopes that the threat of a cotton famine would induce Britain to break the Union blockade and recognize the Confederacy were by no means groundless. Gladstone's pro-Confederate speech at Newcastle derived at least partly from his anguish at the suffering he had witnessed among textile workers in the north of England and his fears of violent protests should hardships continue. Unfortunately for the South, however, while distress among disfranchised mill hands was real, huge surpluses of both raw cotton and manufactured goods at the beginning of the Civil War and the development of alternative sources of supply in India, Egypt, and elsewhere enabled politically powerful mill owners to weather the storm with ease. Moreover, while the war brought hardship to some, it proved a boon to others: to steel-makers, munitions manufacturers, shipbuilders and shipowners, all of whom were perfectly happy to see the American quarrel drag on indefinitely. "We are as busy, as rich, and as fortunate in our trade as if the American war had never broken out and our trade with the states never been disturbed," the London *Times* noted in January 1864. "Cotton was no King, notwithstanding the prerogatives which had been loudly claimed for him."

The Confederates had also failed to reckon with the competing prerogatives of King Corn. Britain's trade of industrial products for American grain and foodstuffs had grown steadily during the 1850s and mushroomed once the Civil War began, thanks to poor English harvests, increased productivity on Middle Western farms, and surpluses made available for export by the closing of the Southern market. In the 1850s nearly a quarter of England's wheat, flour, and corn had come from the United States; in 1861 and 1862 the figure held steady at 45 percent before dipping to 37 percent in 1863. Sensitive to the historical relationship between the cost of bread and the incidence of popular uprisings, British officials were understandably chary of any step that would jeopardize England's supply of cheap American grains.

Once again, though, it was the Confederacy's failure to demonstrate military dominance that was most responsible for keeping Europe neutral. And just as Lee's retreat after Antietam had chilled interventionists in 1862, so the smashing Federal victories at Vicksburg and Gettysburg in July 1863 strengthened Great Britain's determination to grant the South only the most limited belligerent rights. Nowhere was this more apparent than in Lord John Russell's decision to seize the Laird rams.

Early in the Civil War the Confederates had been successful at buying a navy in Britain. Raiders such as the *Florida, Shenandoah,* and *Alabama* were built in British yards (by the Lairds among others) under the ruse that they were merchant vessels — even though, as in the case of the *Alabama,* their sides were pierced with gun ports. They were then taken to the Azores or elsewhere where they received Confederate crews and the armament befitting a man-of-war. In time these raiders destroyed some 250 Yankee merchantmen, doubling marine insurance rates in the North, forcing many vessels into foreign registry, in short, virtually driving the American merchant marine from the high seas.

Unlike the *Alabama*-class cruisers which preyed on enemy merchant vessels, the Laird rams were formidable armor-plated, steam-powered warships, with menacing underwater rams at the bow, designed to break the Federal blockade. The Union's wooden-hulled patrol force would have been easy prey for such ironclads. It was feared, moreover, that the rams' potent 9-inch rifled guns could reduce Northern seaports to rubble. To say, as one historian has, that "if the rams had put to sea, the South would probably have won its independence," may be something of an exaggeration. But the menace was nonetheless real. To the North's vast relief and to the South's crushing disappointment, therefore, the British government (not fooled by the fiction that these ships were intended for Emperor Napoleon or the Pasha of Egypt) on September 3, 1863, ordered Laird to hold the rams. Word of that decision cause Confederate bonds to drop fourteen points on the London market. While Minister Adams's son Henry gleefully tagged the outcome a "second Vicksburg," James M. Mason angrily abandoned his post in England and Secretary of State Judah P. Benjamin expelled all British consuls from the Confederacy.

Though obviously at the end of its diplomatic rope, the South made one last reckless bid for European assistance. In February 1865, as Sherman began his drive from Savannah back north through the Carolinas and Grant laid siege to Lee's army at Petersburg, Confederate agent Duncan F. Kenner arrived in Paris bearing an extraordinary proposition from Jefferson Davis. In exchange for recognition and aid from Britain and France, Kenner's instructions explained, the Confederacy would agree to abolish slavery. It seems wholly improbable that Southern planters would have permitted such an agreement to be carried out, but their reaction was never tested for Davis's desperate gambit came much too late. Palmerston refused to invest in a sinking ship and Napoleon III, as always, refused to move without British cooperation.

Early in the Civil War, then, the South found itself trapped in a vicious circle: military setbacks delayed foreign assistance, which in turn made new battle losses more likely. Lacking the kind of military and financial aid France had given to Americans during the Revolutionary War, Confederates saw chances of establishing their own independence fade with each passing year.

The War at Home

The outcome of the Civil War ultimately hinged on the actions and attitudes of those behind the lines. The policies of European governments, and, of course, the resourcefulness and courage of the blue and the gray armies, tipped the scales this way and that. Yet in the end it was the home front's willingness and ability to make the sacrifices necessary to sustain armed conflict that spelled the difference between victory and defeat. For four years, civilians North and South made those sacrifices, transforming their social and economic life in the process and accelerating the drift toward modern America. By 1865, however, the Southern people had lost the will to resist — and with it, the war.

I

The Civil War, needless to say, brought much pain, suffering, and heartbreak to the people of the North, as it did to those of the South. Casualties in Union armies exceeded enemy losses by roughly 40 percent and most Northern families knew at least one relative, friend, or neighbor who had marched off to war. Such sentimental songs as "Weeping, Sad and Lonely," "The Vacant Chair," and "Sleeping for the Flag" gained enormous popularity because they voiced widespread feelings of grief and anxiety. Not even the very young escaped. "I did not know what war meant," recalled a Wisconsin resident of his wartime boyhood, "except that it was something that made me afraid and then Ma cried every day and Pa was going to war." Grownups, he remembered, "went about with tense faces" and were "frantic for news" from the front.

For some groups, the war meant economic or social hardship as well. Many Northern workingmen, for instance, saw real earnings drop as wartime inflation raised prices faster than wages. By one reckoning, real wages in the North slipped from a base figure of 102 in January 1861 to 67 in January 1865. Some skilled workers, by means of successful strikes, managed to hold their own. Few laborers were organized, however, and those who were sometimes confronted Federal troops used as strikebreakers.

Black workers and their families in the North found the war years especially taxing, for in addition to the decline in purchasing power experienced by most wage earners they often encountered heightened discrimination, intimidation, and even violence at the hands of angry whites. In 1862 and 1863 antiblack feeling—fanned by job competition between the races, the employment of black strikebreakers, white fears that emancipation would depress wages by drawing hundreds of thousands of former slaves into Northern cities, and the hate-mongering of Democratic editors and politicians—erupted in a series of ugly race riots. The bloodiest of these occurred in New York City in mid-July 1863. Furious that the new conscription law had begun to snare working-class whites (3,000 of whom had recently been displaced by Negro strikebreakers) for service in an army of black liberation, a mob of mostly Irish workingmen and women raged through the metropolis. After destroying the recruiting station, the mob turned its wrath on the city's defenseless blacks. For four days, reported the *Christian Recorder,* New York City Negroes "were hunted like wolves." The Colored Orphan Asylum was burned to the ground and "many men were killed and thrown into the rivers, a great number hung to trees and lamp-posts, numbers shot down." By the time units of the Army of the Potomac, fresh from battle at Gettysburg, had restored order, well over a hundred lives had been lost (the bulk of them rioters) and many black homes and businesses had been destroyed by fire.

A great majority of Northerners enjoyed substantial prosperity during the Civil War years. Unlike the South, which went broke in a vain attempt to sustain its boys in gray, the North—largely untouched by invading armies and abundantly blessed with raw materials, technological know-how, literate, industrious workers, and ready capital—demonstrated an ability to provide both guns and butter. Its economic successes helped to uphold Northern morale even when Union armies suffered defeat after defeat in the field. It was much easier to keep one's chin up when employment was high, food relatively cheap and available, and most businesses recording fancy profits.

> Our people bear the burdens of the war without inconvenience [wrote one Northern business firm in the dark days of 1862], because they have an abundance of everything that supports war—men, money, food, clothing, and munitions of all kinds. All these can be had in the greatest profusion upon such terms

as the government offers. A similar strength, stability, and confidence displays itself in all the operations of society. Prices of property of all kinds are well maintained. There is no check to the progress of all useful enterprises that bid fair to be remunerative.

This prosperity was a bit slow to arrive, for the months during and immediately following the secession of Southern states were months of paralysis for many Northern business and financial firms. In addition to the shock that war or the threat of war always brings, Yankee merchants and bankers were suddenly faced with the loss of Southern markets, raw materials (especially cotton, sugar, and naval stores), and the repudiation of Southern debts. New England cotton textile mills operated at half their capacity throughout 1861 and remained in a depressed state for many years thereafter.

For the most part, however, the Northern economy not only recovered from the recession of 1861 but grew steadily more prosperous as the war progressed. In November 1863 Senator John Sherman of Ohio pointed to "the wonderful prosperity of all classes" as evidence that the North was but the latest "example of a people growing rich in a great war." And by March 1865 the *New York Sun* could declare: "There never was a time in the history of New York when business prosperity was more general, when the demand for goods was greater, and payments were prompt, than within the last two or three years." Giving credence to such glowing reports were a general rise in land values and bank records showing a decided increase in both the number and value of individual savings accounts.

In meeting the special demands of war both Northern industry and agriculture underwent profound and lasting change. The need to feed, clothe, arm, and equip an army and navy larger than any the world had ever seen, and at the same time provide for the wants of a burgeoning civilian population, led to increased innovation, consolidation, mechanization, and specialization in key sectors of the Northern economy. The shift already under way before the Civil War—from small shops to large factories, from primitive, labor-intensive farming to mechanized, scientific agriculture, and from production for local and regional markets to mass production for national and international markets—accelerated markedly in the North during the 1860s.

As might be expected, the drawing off of so much of the labor force into military service crimped commodity output; industrial and agricultural production in the loyal states grew more slowly during the 1860s than in any other decade in the nineteenth century. Yet that per capita output increased at all (in the South it plummeted by 39 percent) was, given the circumstances, remarkable. Production gains were most impressive in war-related industries such as canned food, meatpacking, shoes, woolens, ready-made clothing, shipbuilding, and munitions. Northern pig-iron production dipped during the first two years of the war but soared to a record level in 1863. Railroad construction proceeded at a slower pace than during the prewar decade but (in contrast to the dismantling of the South's rail system) proceeded nonetheless. Moreover, Northern railroads reaped substantial profits as for the first time their full carrying capacity was utilized. "At no former period," the *New York Tribune* asserted in 1864, "has the whole Northern railroad system been so prosperous."

Profits encouraged expansion and consolidation, not only in the railroad industry — where the Pennsylvania Railroad showed the way by establishing control over a network stretching west to St. Louis — but in numerous other enterprises. Chicago meatpackers, for example, more than tripled their production of pork, bacon, and lard, and with the opening of the Union Stock Yards in 1865 they christened their city the meatpacking capital of the world. The war gave rise to no striking technological advances, and some available discoveries (for instance, the Bessemer process of making steel) were adopted only after peace returned. The combination of scarce labor and unprecedented demand, however, led some industrialists to a new appreciation of labor-saving machinery. Clothing and shoe manufacturers, for example, challenged with supplying uniforms and shoes to some 2 million soldiers and sailors, turned increasingly to Howe and McKay sewing machines to perform operations once done by hand. Such innovations hastened the shift from piecework and home manufacture to more efficient, large-scale, factory production. Similarly, huge military orders for canned food called forth improvements in canning methods and machinery.

Many Northern businessmen found in the growth and restructuring of the Civil War economy opportunities for bountiful personal gain. Among those who amassed or consolidated great fortunes during these years were such rising captains of industry and finance as Andrew Carnegie, J. P. Morgan, John D. Rockefeller, Philip D. Armour, Gustavus Swift, Gail Borden, Charles Pillsbury, Collis P. Huntington, James J. Hill, George Pullman, Mark Hanna, Jay Gould, and Marshall Field. All managed to escape military service (several by hiring substitutes) and some openly disparaged those who preferred serving Mars over Mammon. When, for example, one of his sons proposed enlisting in the army, the Pittsburg banker Thomas Mellon rebuked him roundly:

I had hoped my boy was going to make a smart intelligent businessman and was not such a goose as to be *seduced from duty* by the declamations of buncombe speeches. It is only greenhorns who enlist. *You can learn nothing in the army.* . . . In time you will come to understand and believe that a man may be a patriot without risking his own life or sacrificing his health. There are plenty of other lives less valuable or ready to serve for the love of serving.

Clearly, Southern planters who exploited the "twenty Negro" loophole to shield draft-age sons from service had their counterparts in the North.

Northern farmers, profiting both from the military market at home and unprecedented demand from abroad (owing to three straight years of crop failure in England and one on the Continent), also survived the war in good shape. Harvests of wheat, corn, and oats remained bountiful, while livestock production — cattle, hogs, and especially sheep — advanced spectacularly during the 1860s. The wholesale price index of farm products rose from 77 in 1860 to 86 by the close of 1862, cresting at 162 in 1864. Only the recession year of 1861 caused setbacks for Northern farmers. Farm laborers as well as farm owners found the times propitious; some wages doubled over the course of the war, comfortably above the cost-of-living increase. "The farmers around here were never as well off . . . as they are at present," remarked one Michigan resident in 1862, "notwithstanding the war and its concomitant evils."

In responding to wartime demand for foodstuffs, livestock, and raw materials (especially wool), Yankee farmers made strides in transforming the character of agriculture. One significant development was a dramatic increase in the use of farm machinery. With so many young farmers now in uniform, the advantages of labor-saving, horse-drawn reapers, mowers, and threshers became apparent as never before. Even hidebound traditionalists rushed to buy the latest and best harvest rigs — McCormick's, Wood's, the Eureka, the Cayuga Chief, and others — and suppliers sometimes ran out of stock. "Over two hundred and fifty mowing machines have been sold in this town this season, and the demand was not fully met," a Pontiac, Michigan, farmer wrote in 1863. "Men are of no account now, except to vote — steam and horses do the work!" Between 1860 and 1865 the number of machines on Northern farms increased threefold and productivity per farm worker climbed 13 percent during the 1860s, more than in any decade before 1890.

Farming also became somewhat more specialized and scientific as a result of the war-bred need to do more with less. The factory production of butter and cheese, for instance, first begun in New York in 1851, spread as far as Illinois and Michigan in the mid-1860s. A Midwestern dairyman summed up the advantages of the factory system by saying, "I have found the manufacture of cheese to be very remunerative when made a primary business, and I might say very unprofitable when made secondary." Sheep raisers and sugar growers gave similar testimony. Despite wartime preoccupation with total output, and not with yield per acre (which fell throughout), a fair number of farmers heeded the commissioner of agriculture's call for "a more thorough knowledge and practice of agriculture as a science and as an art." Although the movement from extensive to intensive cultivation did not become general until later, the seeds for this development took root in the 1860s as farmers began to pay more attention to crop rotation, fertilization, and drainage. State boards of agriculture, county and township societies, a handful of agricultural colleges, state fairs, and the federal Department of Agriculture (established in 1861) all offered encouragement and instruction in more economical, scientific methods of farming.

As the creation of the Department of Agriculture indicates, the Republican government in Washington did its bit to foster economic growth, both in the economic reform program it enacted during the Civil War and in the implicit encouragement it gave to American entrepreneurs. Generous railroad subsidies (beginning with charters for the Union Pacific and Central Pacific in 1862), an inflationary monetary policy (built upon the issuance of $431 million in legal tender, "greenback" notes, and $2.5 billion in federal bonds), the national banking acts of 1863 and 1864 (which put an end to wildcat banking and established a sounder, more uniform currency), and perhaps also Civil War tariff and contract labor laws, not only offered tangible rewards, but, cumulatively, encouraged economic development by persuading businessmen that Washington had their interests at heart. (The Homestead Act, offering free 160-acre farms to actual settlers, and the Morrill Act, providing federal lands to states that built agricultural colleges, had much the same effect among Northern farmers.) Even those who stress the Civil War's retarding effect on industrialization admit the "possibility" that as a consequence of Northern victory and removal of the agrarian South from consideration "the atmosphere of government in Washington among members of both parties was more friendly to industrial enterprise and to northern-based national business operations than had formerly been the rule." In light of subsequent events, this would seem more than a mere "possibility." One need look only at the government's hostility to labor to gauge its friendliness toward business in the postwar years.

Buoyed by material well-being, Northerners found it unnecessary to make fundamental alterations in the pattern of their social and cultural lives. Higher education, for instance, was for a time disrupted as thousands of students, faculty, and even some college presidents marched off to war. Occasionally whole classes enlisted as a body, forcing cancellation of commencement exercises. Even high schools encountered enrollment problems as teenaged boys joined the army or skipped classes for jobs in business or industry. Yet, on balance the Civil War was a period of remarkable educational advancement throughout the North. With women teachers (all shockingly underpaid) filling in for male instructors who now shouldered muskets, public school enrollments made impressive gains. New York City counted 70,000 more elementary school pupils in 1865 than it had in 1861; in Chicago enrollment nearly doubled during the war years. Professional schools flourished, normal schools and teachers' institutes proliferated, college endowments ballooned, and fifteen new institutions of higher learning opened their doors — among them Cornell University, Swarthmore College, the Massachusetts Institute of Technology, and Vassar College, "the first institution of collegiate rank devoted exclusively to the interests of women."

The decline in real wages for many industrial workers led to a certain amount of labor unrest and occasionally violent confrontations between strikers and strikebreakers. Rightly or wrongly, many contemporaries also believed that the war served as "a school of violence and crime," and that acts of law breaking and licentiousness had become commonplace. Without question, prostitution grew in the large cities where soldiers gathered. "Fallen women" were said to constitute fully a quarter of Washington's civilian population; some 20,000 plied their trade in New York City; and even staid Boston, one visitor reported, "absolutely swarms with strumpets." Yet, once again, it was the relative lack of social conflict and disorder in the North that is most striking, the extent to which life outwardly continued much as before despite the strains of war.

Rural folk built their lives around seasonal chores and related rituals — barn raisings, husking and quilting bees, and the like — just as they had in time of peace. For companionship, entertainment, and release they turned, as always, to church services and socials, county fairs, neighborhood picnics, barn dances, and sundry sporting events: horse racing, sharpshooting, rope pulling, wrestling, footracing, horseshoe pitching, and baseball. Country towns and villages continued, now and then, to attract touring thespians, minstrel shows, and dog-and-pony acts. City dwellers, of course, enjoyed a much wider panoply of diversions: operas, concerts, fancy balls, theatricals, menageries, circuses, libraries, and museums, not to mention prizefights, bordellos, and saloons beyond number. Urban life not only moved in accustomed channels but, among the rich, it sometimes displayed a sybaritic quality which, critics charged, mocked the sacrifices of hard-pressed workers and brave soldiers.

> This war has entirely changed the American character [lamented the *New York Herald* in October 1863]. The lavish profusion in which the old Southern cotton aristocracy used to indulge is completely eclipsed by the dash, parade and magnificence of the new Northern shoddy aristocracy of this period. Ideas of cheapness and economy are thrown to the winds. The individual who makes the most money — no matter how — and spends the most money — no matter for what — is considered the greatest man. To be extravagant is to be fashionable. These facts sufficiently account for the immense and brilliant audiences at the opera and the theatres; and until the final crash comes such audiences will continue.

II

Three groups — Afro-Americans, white women, and immigrants — stand as exceptions to the rule of social continuity in the North. For each, the Civil War opened new opportunities for advancement, some quite temporary, others more lasting.

As already noted, Northern blacks found the war a time of pain as well as of gain. Racial prejudice still confined blacks to second-class citizenship, even, as we shall see, in the U.S. Army. Violent race conflict scarred not only New York City but Chicago, Detroit, Cleveland, Buffalo, Boston, and other cities. In some communities Negrophobia seems actually to have risen during the war. And yet for many Northern blacks the Civil War brought material gain, increased pride, and hope for the future. Job openings expanded and some blacks prospered as never before. "The blacks here are too comfortable to do anything more than talk about freedom," complained one Bostonian who wished that more would join the army. The bravery of those Afro-Americans who did enlist strengthened not only their own pride but that of the entire race. Civil equality would be hard to deny to a people who had fought for the flag. As Frederick Douglass pointed out, "Once let the black man get upon his person the brass letters U.S.; let him get an eagle on his button, and a musket on his shoulder, and bullets in his pocket, and there is no power on earth . . . which can deny that he has earned the right of citizenship in the United States." And, of course, the satisfaction of winning freedom for their slave cousins was incalculable.

The material gains of the war years rapidly eroded once peace returned and white servicemen reclaimed their old jobs. The road to political equality proved to be long and rocky, despite ratification soon after the war of the Fourteenth and Fifteenth Amendments. But the lift the war gave to black pride and self-confidence was never completely lost and helped to sustain the Afro-American community in the dark days ahead.

In the North, the Civil War also briefly enlarged the social and economic roles of another oppressed group, women. With so many of their menfolk at the front it was inevitable that Northern women would be called upon to perform tasks beyond the bounds of "woman's sphere." On the farm, women not only tended house and barnyard, but often lent a hand in the fields. The "Volunteer's Wife" in a popular wartime ditty urged her husband to

Take your gun and go, John,
   Take your gun and go,
For Ruth can drive the oxen, John,
   And I can use the hoe.

Often, in fact, farm wives turned not to hoes but to mowers or reapers. "We have seen, within the past few weeks," the *Merchants Magazine and Commercial Review* reported in 1863, "a stout matron whose sons are in the army, with her team cutting hay at seventy-five cents per acre, and she cut seven acres with ease in a day, riding leisurely upon her cutter." With the help of machines, the *Detroit Free Press* observed a year later, "A large portion of the corn in this state has been cultivated by women." Most women tilled only their own acres, but a few even hired out on neighboring farms.

City women in the North not only continued to fill occupations already open to their sex—maid, laundress, seamstress, boardinghouse keeper, and the like—but flocked to positions usually held by men. The war created over 100,000 new jobs for women in commerce and industry, greatly enhanced opportunities for female teachers and nurses, and for the first time opened federal government service to women. Thanks largely to the efforts of Francis Spinner, treasurer of the United

States, by 1865 the Treasury Department alone employed 447 women clerks, copyists, and currency counters.

While the Civil War undoubtedly promoted women's self-confidence and, perhaps, helped to weaken sexual stereotypes, most wartime advances proved illusory. Spinner's "government girls" weathered male gibes (could women be trusted with the *mail* without being tempted to pry?) and postwar demobilization, and women clerks and office workers became a (low-paid) fixture of the Washington scene. The ranks of female teachers continued to grow long after the war ended, if only because they too accepted substandard wages. But in business, industry, and even nursing, women found themselves shouldered aside once the crisis of war had passed and veterans reclaimed their old jobs. Perhaps the Civil War's chief contribution to the advancement of American women — greater even than the sense of solidarity and self-worth they gained through their labors in local soldiers' aid societies or the organizational stimulus of the National Woman's Loyal League (established in 1863 to support the war, emancipation, and, indirectly, women's rights) — was the "heroic myth" it spawned of great gains in woman's lot. The belief of Clara Barton and others that at the conflict's close "woman was at least fifty years in advance of the normal position which continued peace . . . would have assigned her" lent much-needed encouragement to American feminists.

The Civil War also left a special mark on American immigrants, most of whom settled in the loyal states. The onset of hostilities brought an abrupt decline in the number of newcomers (scarcely 92,000 came in each of the war's first two years, compared to nearly 154,000 in 1860), but in 1863 over 176,000 aliens reached the United States, more than in any year since the Panic of 1857. Still more arrived in 1864 and nearly a quarter of a million the following year.

Among the reasons for this resurgent wave of immigration were the manifest opportunities of a booming war economy and the Lincoln administration's skillful campaign to publicize those opportunities throughout Western Europe. Hoping to attract much-needed workers and fighting men, State Department representatives abroad advertised the United States as a land of boundless opportunity, of high wages, free farms, and easy naturalization. Congress cooperated in this venture, not only by making aliens eligible for lands under the terms of the Homestead Act of 1862 but by giving assurance that no one of foreign citizenship would be forced into military service in the United States. (Many a young German, Irishman, Briton, or Swede succumbed to the sweet talk of recruiting sergeants and the lure of enlistment bounties upon reaching American shores, however; in all, some half a million foreign-born men, many newly arrived, served in the Union army.) In 1864 Congress further facilitated immigration by permitting employers to enter into labor contracts with prospective emigrants in which money advanced for transportation to the United States would be repaid from future wages.

While by no means obliterating ethnic hostility, the Civil War does seem to have speeded the process of assimilation and (for the time being) tamed the virulent nativism of the 1850s. Except for organized labor, most Northerners welcomed the newcomers from Europe for the support they could give to the Union. Old political, religious, and social antagonisms faded. Massachusetts repealed its 1859 amendment barring immigrants from voting for two years after naturalization and overturned a law requiring Bible reading in the schools. Priests gained the right to attend to the spiritual needs of patients in Boston's City Hospital; Harvard University broke precedent by giving an honorary degree to an Irish Catholic bishop, J. B. Fitzpatrick; and Patrick Gilmore, composer of the immensely popular "Johnny Comes Marching Home," performed not only at Hibernian Hall but at parties and parades throughout Boston.

Increasingly, too, foreign-born Americans perceived themselves as an integral part of their adopted land, proudly embracing a new nationality. Thus Lars Dokken, a Norwegian private in a Wisconsin regiment, lying badly wounded on the Stone's River battlefield in Tennessee, was proud to hear the Confederates who found him say: "Here is a damn Yankee." Ethnic rivalry and exclusiveness remained—as the recruitment of purely Irish or German regiments attested—and malignant nativism would erupt again later in the century. For a time, however, the differences between native-born Americans and immigrants counted for less than those between the loyal and the disloyal. Rebels and Copperheads, not "wild Irishmen" or the Pope, now seemed the chief threat to the republic.

III

The vast majority of Northerners enthusiastically supported the Union war effort. Parents, wives, sweethearts, and friends applauded the decision of brave young men to risk their lives in a war that seemed both ghastly and grand. Inconveniences caused by the severance of trade with the South produced few complaints, and even workers whipsawed by inflation and taxation placed crushing the rebellion above immediate class interests. "One thing to which all else must assume a subordinate position," exclaimed Jonathan Fincher, president of the

Philadelphia Trades Assembly, in 1864, "is, the 'United States' must forever be a fact; we can tolerate no division." Besides, a Boston workingmen's newspaper added, the "oligarchy at the South" was "from the very nature of things, antagonistic to free labor" and must be overthrown. True to the spirit of their departed leader, Stephen A. Douglas, most Northern Democrats also joined Republicans in backing measures "to vindicate the honor, peace, and power of the [United States] Government."

Nonetheless, there was sufficient opposition in the North to the administration's war policies to cause Republicans many a sleepless night, force Lincoln into curtailment of civil liberties, and raise the real possibility of a Democratic victory in 1864. Except for those "Union" or "Loyal" Democrats who abandoned their party to vote for Lincoln in 1864, Democratic support of the Republican program was either qualified or nonexistent. Mainstream Democrats gave solid backing to calls for troops and measures to sustain them, but insisted that the war should be waged not to subjugate the South or to demolish its social order, but "simply to subdue, destroy, and scatter the rebel armies, leaving the rights of northern citizens and the property of Southern slaveholders just where the Constitution leaves them." Such men took issue with most of the Republican economic programs and viewed with horror not only the Emancipation Proclamation ("that masterpiece of folly and treachery") but the enlistment of black soldiers in the Union army.

Some so-called Copperhead Democrats—men like Clement L. Vallandigham, Thomas Seymour, and Fernando Wood—went further. Opposing the war altogether, they sought to discourage enlistments and called for an armistice and a negotiated peace. Strongest in the southern Middle West and among ethnic Catholics in cities of the Northeast, some (their numbers much inflated by Republicans for political effect) joined "dark lantern" orders like the Knights of the Golden Circle and dreamed of creating an independent "Northwest Confederacy" which would make peace with the South.

To keep disloyal activity in check, President Lincoln sometimes found it necessary to curtail civil liberties in a way that outraged Democrats and even some members of his own party. Twice, in September 1862 and again a year later, Lincoln suspended the writ of habeas corpus to permit the arbitrary arrest of "all Rebels and Insurgents, their aiders and abettors within the United States, and all persons discouraging volunteer enlistments, resisting militia drafts, or guilty of any disloyal practice." During the course of the war, federal authorities made at least 15,000 arrests, some for spying or sabotage, others for "disloyal" opinions. (Among this latter group was the outspoken Vallandigham, arrested in May 1863 on orders from General Ambrose E. Burnside for an antiwar speech at Mount Vernon, Ohio. Sentenced by a military tribunal to confinement in a Federal prison for the rest of the war, Valiant Val was instead banished to the Confederacy at the insistence of Lincoln who wished to avoid making him a martyr.) Federal officials also sometimes suppressed Democratic newspapers for publishing "disloyal and incendiary sentiments."

President Lincoln defended his record on civil liberties by reminding his critics that, especially in a civil war, an ounce of prevention was worth a pound of cure. The Confederates, he explained, had hoped "under cover of 'Liberty of speech' 'Liberty of the press' and *'Habeas corpus'* . . . to keep on foot amongst us a most efficient corps of spies, informers, suppliers [*sic*], and aiders and abettors of their cause in a thousand ways." Besides, he asked, "Must I shoot a simple-minded soldier boy who deserts, while I must not touch a hair of a wiley [*sic*] agitator who induces him to desert? . . . I think that in such a case, to silence the agitator, and save the boy, is not only constitutional, but, withal, a great mercy." In fact, Lincoln's abridgment of free expression was, given the circumstances, remarkably restrained. "You will only arrest individuals, and suppress assemblies, or newspapers, when they may be working *palpable* injury to the Military in your charge," he instructed General John M. Schofield in 1863; "and, in no other case will you interfere with the expression of opinion in any form, or allow it to be interfered with violently by others. In this you have a discretion to exercise with great caution, calmness, and forbearance." Accordingly, newspapers were rarely muzzled and most of those jailed for political reasons gained quick release. Nonetheless, something like 1 in every 1,500 Northerners *had* been arrested during the Civil War, and complaints of executive tyranny — together with grumbling over the administration's emancipation and reconstruction policies and growing war weariness — were among the burdens Republicans carried into the 1864 presidential campaign.

"Uncle Billy" Sherman's timely capture of Atlanta in September, a sharp drop in Grant's casualty count, and the backing of nearly four out of five Union soldiers who voted, permitted Lincoln to overcome these burdens and decisively defeat his Democratic opponent George B. McClellan. (Lincoln received 55 percent of the popular vote and carried every state but Kentucky, Delaware, and New Jersey.) Equally important to the well-being of the Republican party and the implementation of administration programs was the very partisanship which produced such hard-fought elections in the midst of civil war. Throughout the conflict the existence of a vital, disciplined, and for the most part loyal opposition paradoxically helped to unify the Northern war effort. While Democrats pulled no punches and sometimes were downright scurrilous in their attacks on Republicans (in 1864, for example, the La Crosse, Wisconsin, *Democrat* adorned its front page with a cartoon of Lincoln, captioned "The Widow-Maker of the 19th Century"), vigorous political competition kept Democratic criticism generally constructive and thwarted all attempts to hamper the energetic prosecution of the war. Democrats had no wish to play into the hands of Republicans only too eager to brand their opponents as the party of treason. At the same time, the need to hold the rival Democrats at bay kept the disparate elements of the Republic party pulling in harness. The presence of a common political enemy both heightened cooperation among Republicans in Congress and nurtured a relationship of mutual support between Republican state officials and the Lincoln administration in Washington. The kind of zealous concern for states' rights that plagued Confederate nationalists throughout the Civil War never blossomed in the North.

IV

Starting from a much weaker position than the North's in terms of manpower, resources, and industrial capacity, the South required far greater sacrifices from its people if its desperate bid for independence were to be successful. Hampered by problems peculiar to a slave society as well as the monumental obstacles in their way, the Confederates ultimately proved unequal to the task. Morale remained generally high during the first year of the war, thanks to a bountiful harvest in 1861, early battlefield triumphs, and hopes of European assistance. As early as 1862, however, the Southern outlook, though still resolute, had become more glum as a result of spiraling casualties and military reverses (especially in the West) and increasing hardship at home. "It is the hardeste times in olde Cobb I ever saw," a Georgia woman wrote to her soldier brother in February 1862, "lyeing, Swindling and a Speculation is all that is goinge on here now." By 1863 suffering had spread from the countryside to the city; bread riots erupted in Richmond, Atlanta, Mobile, and elsewhere; and everywhere what one historian has called "a quiet rebellion of the common people" was sapping the South's will and ability to remain at war.

Not that the Confederates did not try. Inevitably, some Southerners placed private gain above service to country, selfishly hoarding such scarce items as salt, bacon, molasses, whiskey, leather, and cotton cards in order to make a killing once prices had doubled or trebled. Others ran the Federal blockade for profits to be made in the sale of luxury goods, ignoring the Confederacy's pressing need for the munitions of war. Some even traded with the enemy. The "love of lucre," Jefferson Davis lamented in July 1863, had "eaten like a gangrene into the very heart of the land." Most Southerners, however, went to extraordinary lengths to support their boys in gray and prove to the world that a proud and independent people could never be conquered.

In the mistaken belief that by setting aside partisan loyalties a broader national loyalty might be strengthened, Southern politicians abandoned *party* politics for the war's duration. (As it turned out, the absence of a two-party system in the Confederacy simply made political battles more freewheeling and destructive than would otherwise have been the case and left President Davis particularly vulnerable to his critics.) Southern women not only prodded young men to enlist, forming "sulk and pout" clubs to shame unpatriotic foot-draggers, but themselves bolstered the war effort in countless ways. With most able-bodied white males in uniform, Confederate women, like their Yankee sisters, stepped out of customary roles to work farms; manage plantations; teach school; clerk in government offices; manufacture clothing, cartridges, and percussion caps; and engage in sundry commercial activities. Many wrapped bandages, sewed flags, or nursed sick or wounded soldiers. Some, like the celebrated Belle Boyd, acted as Confederate spies. Rumors insisted that some women actually fought in Rebel armies disguised as men. A pampered few escaped the war's sting completely. Most Southern women, however, bore staggering burdens, and with pardonable exaggeration South Carolina's Mary Chesnut observed in June 1862: "Grief and constant anxiety kill nearly as many women as men die on the battlefield."

Confederate women—plantation mistresses—were also largely responsible for overseeing the most sweeping economic transformation of the war: the shift from the cultivation of cotton to food production. Faced with the stoppage of foodstuffs from Northern farms, Southerners quickly perceived that their primary deficiency was not "the want of arms. IT IS THE WANT OF BREAD." The choice, warned one Southern newspaper, was "Plant Corn and Be Free, or plant cotton and be whipped." By the end of 1862, Texas and Louisiana were the only states without laws restricting the amount of cotton that might be grown, and local vigilante committees often joined state agents in enforcing compliance. In Calhoun County, Alabama, a band of forty women threatened to "pull up, cut up, and destroy" all the unsanctioned cotton they could find. A few obstreperous planters refused to be coerced. The imperious Robert Toombs, for example, defiantly planted 560 acres of cotton on his Georgia plantation and stormed at the committee of safety which censured him: "You may rob me in my absence, but you cannot intimidate me." Most planters willingly switched to the cultivation of food crops, however, if only because the market for cotton had dried up. Cotton production fell from 4.5 million bales in 1861 to 1.5 million bales in 1862 and 300,000 by 1864. Harvests of sugar and tobacco also plummeted as the shift to foodstuffs took hold.

The Confederates' determination and resourcefulness were also evident in their ingenuity in finding substitutes for hard-to-obtain manufactured goods and non-Southern-grown commodities. Coffee, universally popular in the Old South, became exceedingly scarce once the Union blockade took effect, but Southerners concocted "Confederate coffee" from parched peas and corn, okra and pumpkin seeds, chicory, acorns — almost anything "to color the water," grumbled one connoisseur. In place of Oriental tea, Southerners steeped sassafras roots and other herbs; parched peanuts took the place of chocolate; "Confederate needles" were fashioned from hawthorn bushes and "Confederate leather" from cotton cloth; wild indigo, bark, and walnut hulls provided colored dyes; Spanish moss furnished cord and rope; the plain side of colored wallpaper upon occasion served as newsprint. Everywhere homespun replaced store-bought clothes. Such resourcefulness and sacrifice drew mirthful taunts from Yankee invaders:

> The ladies down south they do not denigh
> They usted to drink the coffey and now they drink the rye
> The ladies in dixey they are quite in the dark
> They used to bye the indigo and now they bile the bark.

But Southern plain folk were rightfully proud of their ability to scrimp, save, and improvise.

The Confederate government in Richmond also took vigorous and innovative steps to maximize the South's limited resources. Accepting the necessity of drastic measures to overcome the Yankee juggernaut, Jefferson Davis and other Confederate nationalists often shelved limited government ideals in the name of national emergency, much to the displeasure of doctrinaire advocates of states' rights. An early step in this direction was, of course, military conscription, adopted in April 1862. Critics, led by Governor Joseph E. Brown of Georgia, denounced this act as an unconstitutional subversion of state sovereignty, "the very embodiment of Lincolnism, which our gallant armies are today resisting." President Davis, however, drawing on the same implied powers doctrine that Alexander Hamilton had used in justification of a national bank, defended conscription as a "necessary and proper" measure for raising armies and had the satisfaction of seeing Georgia's supreme court uphold its constitutionality.

An even earlier, and equally controversial, assertion of the central government's authority was the statute of February 27, 1862, giving Davis the power to suspend the writ of habeas corpus in regions threatened by invasion. Under the terms of this act, Confederate authorities not only jailed deserters, spies, and others suspected of disloyalty, but imposed martial law in and around such vulnerable places as Richmond, Atlanta, and Vicksburg. At Richmond, General John H. Winder imposed a passport system, ordered residents to hand over their firearms to the Confederate Ordnance Department, banned the sale of liquor, and even tried for a time to fix prices in the city's food markets. Though President Davis used the powers granted him with restraint and (unlike Lincoln) only with the prior approval of the Confederate Congress, he was labeled a tyrant, by Vice-President Stephens and others, for using them at all. Denouncing the writ's suspension as "a dangerous assault upon . . . the liberty of the people," the president's critics managed to restore full habeas corpus privileges in February 1863 and, except for a few months in 1864, to keep them in force for the remainder of the war. Conceived by nationalists as a measure to unify and strengthen the Confederacy by weeding out "deserters and traitors, skulkers and stragglers," suspension of habeas corpus proved instead a source of great internal dissension.

Confederate nationalists also acted forcefully to place the South's economy on a war footing. It may be too much to say, as one historian has, that "the national government all but nationalized the Confederate economy," but there can be no doubt that Jefferson Davis and his congressional supporters advanced wartime economic policies sharply at odds with traditional laissez-faire, free enterprise principles. When, for example, taxes and loans failed to net more than a third of what was needed to finance the war, the Richmond government not only printed mountains of paper currency ($1.5 billion in all), but authorized the impressment of supplies and equipment needed by Rebel armies. Initially an informal practice justified on grounds of military necessity, impressment received legal sanction in March 1863 when the Confederate Congress passed an elaborate law regulating the seizure of supplies and the fixing of prices. The system worked a great hardship on many, especially those on small farms (now often run by soldiers' wives), and stirred up protests that "too much Government is almost as bad as no Government." Even Jefferson Davis admitted that impressment was "so unequal in its operation, vexatious to the producer, injurious to the industrial interests, and productive of such discontent among the people as only to be justified by the existence of an absolute necessity." But the necessity being genuine, Confederate officials rigorously sustained impressment throughout the war, even including slaves in the catalog of "goods" which might be taken.

Necessity also prodded the Davis administration to assume a measure of control over the South's communication and transportation system that would have been unthinkable in peacetime. Scarcely a month after Fort Sumter, the Confederate Congress gave the president authority to control the Southern telegraph network and to construct new lines required for military operations. Congress was much slower to see the need for national regulation of Southern railroads and President Davis even slower to make use of the powers given him, with the result that the Confederacy depended throughout the Civil War upon a congeries of small, privately managed railroads for the transport of goods and persons. The government did, however, establish an Iron Commission to provide tracks for essential lines, build two railroads (one from Danville, Virginia, to Greensboro, North Carolina, the other between Meridian, Mississippi, and Selma, Alabama), and use draft exemptions to supply railroads with mechanics, switchmen, firemen, and engineers. It also appointed such capable men as William S. Ashe, William M. Wadley, and Frederick W. Sims to oversee the negotiation of military contracts and the enforcement of transportation priorities.

More forceful steps were taken to regulate foreign commerce. During the war's early years enterprising blockade runners often reaped fancy profits by importing European luxury goods — jewelry, furs, silks and satins, antiques, fine wines, and liquor — in exchange for coin and, in time, cotton. The rewards of blockade running were such that two successful voyages would more than offset the capture of a ship on a third. At first, Confederate authorities were content to let private companies and state governments (which chartered vessels or cargo space) monopolize this lucrative trade. By the fall of 1861, however, the Confederacy had begun to acquire a small fleet of its own to run military supplies through the Union blockade. And as the blockade tightened and the need of Rebel armies for foreign supplies increased, pressure mounted for more direct national control of all overseas commerce. In February 1864 the Confederate government virtually nationalized foreign trade by banning the importation of luxury goods and "the exportation of cotton, tobacco, military and naval stores, sugar, molasses and rice" without a special permit. Regulations published the following month required privately owned blockade runners to reserve at least half of their cargo space for Confederate shipments, and offered a premium rate to those who allotted two-thirds of their stowage to the government. Eventually Confederate agents assumed complete control over every phase of the blockade-running enterprise, from the collection and licensing of cotton and other exports to the purchase of essential supplies abroad.

Partly because Southerners were reluctant to admit the effectiveness of the Yankees' blockade, it never spurred private industrial activity in the South as the British blockade had accelerated manufacturing development in the Northeast during the War of 1812. As a result, the Confederate government found it necessary once again to scrap laissez-faire notions to insure that the South's industrial needs were met. No assistance was given to the manufacture of civilian wares, but the Confederacy entered into the production of essential military goods in many ways: by granting draft exemptions to workers in key industries, by making certain that railroads delivered raw materials, by tendering loans and inducements to coal and iron mines and firms making small arms. The army's Quartermaster Department founded tanneries as well as shoe and clothing factories, while the Ordnance Department, under the inspired leadership of Josiah Gorgas, established arsenals, foundries, and gunpowder works sufficient to keep Confederate soldiers amply supplied with arms and ammunition. The Confederacy operated its own salt works in Louisiana. It even assigned agents of its Nitre and Mining Bureau to collect nitrogenous refuse to obtain saltpeter, used in making gunpowder. The request of one such agent that the ladies of Selma, Alabama, preserve the contents of their chamberpots for this purpose prompted a salty piece of doggerel which closed,

> John Harralson, John Harralson, do pray invent a neater
> And somewhat less immodest mode of making your saltpeter:
> For 'tis an awful idea, John, gunpowdery and cranky
> That when a lady lifts her shift she's killing off a Yankee.

V

Unquestionably, then, the Confederates proved themselves willing to accept sacrifice and embrace drastic measures in pursuit of independence. Yet sadly for the South its sacrifices and adjustments were not enough. Policy errors, internal dissension, and military mistakes prevented the Confederates from making the most of their limited resources. No more mistake-prone — and certainly no less dedicated —

than the Yankees, Southerners simply had less room for schism and error. Unable to fight a near-perfect war, they fell before the superior resources of the enemy.

Many of the Confederacy's gravest problems were rooted in its planter-dominant social order. The planters themselves solidly supported the Confederacy—up to a point. Active Unionism among the planter class was practically unknown. Most accepted the need for drastic measures to win the war, and, as a class, slaveholding aristocrats saw more than their share of battle. Some, the sons of Robert E. Lee and P. G. T. Beauregard among them, volunteered as privates; most served with valor, many with distinction. Yet most planters gave primary allegiance not the Confederacy, which they viewed as simply a means, but to the end it had been designed to serve: plantation slavery.

Whenever governments took steps to secure Confederate independence that clashed with plantation interests, planters combined to resist them. Some, for example, like Mississippi's James Lusk Alcorn, defied pressures to grow food crops and filled their pockets by smuggling cotton to the enemy. A great many more resisted Confederate authorities who sought to impress supplies and, especially, slaves. "The patriotic planters," stated Senator Louis T. Wigfall of Texas, "would willingly put their own flesh and blood into the army, but when you asked them for a negro the matter approached the point of drawing an eye-tooth." Convinced that impressment struck at the very core of slavery by tampering with the master's authority, and upset that compensation was uncertain and slaves were often poorly treated, increasing numbers of planters simply ignored Confederate requisitions for their bondsmen. In South Carolina, a Confederate agent complained that planters had refused to comply with a request for "only one month's labor," and by 1864 as many as a quarter of the slaves claimed by Confederate officials in Virginia never left their masters' hands.

Like their masters, the slaves themselves were a source of both strength and weakness to the Confederacy. On the home front, black labor sustained the war effort in countless ways: by providing food and marketable staples; building and maintaining railroads; constructing fortifications; mining raw materials; manning riverboats; making shoes, harnesses, and munitions of war—above all by freeing white men for military service. "The institution of slavery in the South," the *Montgomery Advertiser* declared, "alone enables her to place in the field a force so much larger in proportion to her white population than the North, or indeed than any country which is dependent entirely on free labor." More directly, slaves served Rebel armies as cooks, body servants, teamsters, ambulance drivers, hospital helpers, musicians, and pick-and-shovel artists. At the same time, although great numbers of blacks remained faithful to their masters and white fears of a large-scale insurrection never materialized, the slave system created special problems for the Confederates. Theft, malingering, and open defiance increased under wartime conditions, especially when Union armies approached. Some blacks acted as Yankee spies and informants, or helped Union soldiers to escape from Confederate prisons. One, Robert Smalls, ran the Confederate steamer *Planter* out of Charleston harbor under cover of darkness and delivered it to the U.S. Navy. Many others stole themselves, fleeing at first opportunity to Union lines. Confederates found such actions not only damaging in a practical sense, but psychologically destructive as well. For they reminded white Southerners of the seething discontent inherent in human bondage, of the ever-present menace from an enemy within.

Besides depriving the Confederacy of much-needed labor, runaway slaves added to the military might of the North. Nearly four-fifths of the 179,000 black men to serve in the Union Army came from the slave states, many of them runaways. In the South, on the other hand, apprehensive planters successfully blocked proposals to arm slaves until it was too late. Suggestions that blacks be used as soldiers as well as military laborers surfaced as early as 1861. Some slaves, including those of Senator James Chesnut of South Carolina, offered to fight the Yankees if given arms, and by 1863, after the disasters at Vicksburg and Gettysburg, Chesnut's wife could report that "General Lee, Mr. Davis, &c &c—soldiers everywhere—want . . . [slaves] to be put in the army." Even a few planters came around to this view. "The element which has been the foundation of wealth should now be made the instrument of our salvation," one Mississippi slaveholder concluded. "Arm our slaves."

Yet arming slaves, a risky and radical measure which at least implied emancipation, was anathema to most planters. A Confederacy without slavery seemed to such men a contradiction in terms—as, indeed, did the very idea of slave soldiers. "You cannot make soldiers of slaves, nor slaves of soldiers," a prominent Georgia planter declared. "The day you make soldiers of them is the beginning of the end of the revolution. If slaves will make good soldiers our whole theory of slavery is wrong." Not until March 13, 1865, less than a month before Appomattox, did the Confederate Congress, acting at the behest of Jefferson Davis and Robert E. Lee, at last overcome planter resistance and authorize the enlistment of black soldiers. Even then, as a sop to the planters, the "Negro Soldier Law" left the question of freedom for slaves who signed up in the hands of the owners and the states. A few Negro companies were formed in the war's waning days, but much too late to see action. Reflecting upon the causes of Confederate defeat two weeks after Lee's surrender, Mary Chesnut ruefully noted in her journal: "We waited and hoped. They organized and worked like moles, with the riches of all the world at their backs. We talked of negro recruits. The Yankees used them. . . . The odds [were] too great."

Planter resistance to the taxation, as well as the impressment and military appropriation, of their slave property also created serious problems for the Confederacy. Throughout the war, planters saw to it that both their lands and slaves—the South's chief resources—remained virtually exempt from taxation. Moreover, a cotton export tax, which optimists predicted would raise $20 million, in fact netted the Confederacy less than $40,000, both because planters were able to keep the rate low (about 1.5 percent of cotton's specie value) and because most evaded it (only 5 percent of the cotton exported was taxed). In all, the Confederates raised barely 1 percent of their revenue from taxes (as against 23 percent by the Union government). The private sales of cotton to Europe by self-serving planters also undercut the Confederacy's campaign to sell bonds, convertible in cotton, abroad.

Lacking adequate tax and loan receipts, the government had little choice but to resort to impressment and a heavy reliance on paper currency. Fiat money eventually accounted for 60 percent of all Confederate revenues and helped to fuel an inflation that drove the price of a cup of coffee to $5, a lady's bonnet to $250, and a uniform coat to $2,000. Matters had come to such a pass, people said, that shoppers carried money to the market in a basket and brought their purchases home in a purse. Paper money was not the only cause for this inflationary spiral. The Federal blockade, declining productivity, military demand, and a compulsion to spend as a hedge against future inflation, all helped to force prices upward. Yet, more than anything else, it was the Confederacy's massive reliance on printing-press money that thrust prices up and the value of the dollar down, and saddled ordinary Southerners with more than their share of the war's costs.

This insensitivity to the plight of Southern yeomen and the apparent favoritism shown to planter aristocrats aroused latent class antagonism, undermined morale, and contributed powerfully to Confederate defeat. Complaints that the burden of war fell most heavily on humble farmers and workingmen appeared almost from the beginning. In May 1861 the South Carolina aristocrat James Chesnut pressed his son John and other young "gentlemen" to set an example by joining the army as enlisted men since poor, up-country farmers were saying that "this was a rich man's war—and the rich men would be officers and have an easy time and the poor ones be privates." Likewise, in September a north Georgia resident addressed a public letter to candidates for public office which asked: "Is it right that the poor man should be taxed for the support of the war, when the war was brought about on the slave question, and the slave at home accumulating for the benefit of his master, and the poor man's farm left uncultivated, and a chance for his wife to be a widow, and his children orphans? Now, in justice, would it not be right to levy a direct tax on that species of property that brought about the war, to support it?"

The failure to levy such a tax was but one of a long and growing list of grievances which Southern plain folk leveled against self-seeking planters and the government that coddled them. Common people complained bitterly at big slaveholders who hired substitutes or used the "twenty Negro" loophole to escape military service and then fattened their purses by trading with the enemy or by hoarding foodstuffs desperately needed by soldiers' families. The arrogance of men like Toombs who persisted in planting cotton when many stood at the edge of starvation was especially galling. Fewer and fewer planters displayed any generosity toward their less fortunate neighbors ("it seems that all harts is turned to gizards," bewailed a North Carolina woman), and attempts to excuse such hardheartedness only made matters worse. Few Southern farmers could have felt much empathy for the plantation mistress who sought to prove that both rich and poor suffered wartime privations by noting that "with five plantations we are restricted to the use of the proceeds from only the poorest."

Although it did make sporadic attempts to alleviate suffering, by assisting private relief agencies in the distribution of food, requiring that plantations seeking exemptions under the "twenty Negro" law provide foodstuffs to soldiers' families at fair prices, and on rare occasions exempting farmers in distressed areas from military service, the Confederate government all too often compounded the problems of the poor. Conscription was essential to replenish Confederate armies, but the failure to exempt nonslaveholding heads of families worked a terrible hardship upon ordinary Southerners, as did the government's failure to curb hoarding and speculation. Similarly, even some Confederate officials admitted that the government's impressment program and its 10 percent tax-in-kind on agricultural produce (imposed in April 1863) fell "harshly and oppressively on the poor." Collection agents were often arbitrary, capricious, and shortsighted, paying scant attention to the needs of their prey. "Women whose husbands are in the army," a Mississippian complained in 1864, "have thus lost the only horse they had for farm work." The depredations of Confederate troops — especially cavalry units — could be even worse. "If God Almighty had yet in store another plague worse than all others which he intended to have let loose on the Egyptians in case Pharoah still hardened his heart," cried North Carolina's governor Zebulon Vance, "I am sure it must have been a regiment or so of half-armed, half-disciplined Confederate cavalry."

Such grievances touched off no popular uprising and occasioned little overt disloyalty among Southern whites. Pockets of Unionism existed particularly along the Appalachian Highlands, from western Virginia and North Carolina, through east Tennessee, and into northern Georgia and Alabama. In 1863 the mostly slaveless counties of West Virginia broke from the Old Dominion and established themselves as a new Republican state. Similar movements reached the talking stage in east Tennessee and northern Alabama. Some Southern Unionists fought with the Federal army; a few served as spies and informants; others engaged in acts of sabotage or abetted Confederate deserters and draft dodgers. Such overt disloyalty was rare, however, even among Unionists. Most Southerners expressed their disillusionment with the war not by giving aid and comfort to the enemy but by yearning for peace. Even before Sherman cut a swath to the sea and Sheridan turned the Shenandoah Valley into a howling wilderness — and especially thereafter — hardship at home, together with bloody defeats on the battlefield and flagging faith in both political and military leaders had sapped the South's will to resist.

Letters from home swiftly carried the demoralization virus to those in the trenches. "Before God, Edward," implored one soldier's wife, "Unless you come home we must die. Last night I was aroused by little Eddie's crying. . . . He said 'Oh, mamma, I'm so hungry!' And Lucy, Edward, your darling Lucy, she never complains, but she is growing thinner and thinner every day." Less polished, but no less poignant — or potent — was the letter of a North Carolina woman to her soldier son in January 1865: "Tell theam all to s[t]op fiting and come home to live if you all wod put down you gouns and come home and let the Big men stae the fiting wod Soon Stop if you all Stae theaire you all will bee kild I want you all to come home."

As General Joseph E. Johnston observed, "Such a summons . . . was never unheeded." When asked "to choose between their military service and . . . their duties to their wives and children," most Confederate soldiers — often themselves ragged, shoeless, and underfed — "left the army and returned . . . to support their families." Desertions from Southern armies mounted alarmingly from the summer of 1863 onward. In November of that year Confederate Secretary of War James

Seddon estimated that a third of the Rebel army was absent without leave, and by the end of 1864 more than a half of all Confederate soldiers were for one reason or another missing from rank. After Sherman's capture of Atlanta, Jefferson Davis publicly lamented that "two-thirds of our men are absent—some sick, some wounded, but most of them without leave." By the spring of 1865 desertion had reached epidemic proportions. Lee lost 1,094 men to desertion within ten days in March. One brigade laid down its arms en masse. "Most of the desertions, lately," wrote a North Carolina captain from Petersburg, "have been caused by letters from home." Even soldiers who remained at their posts shared the despair of those who defected. Fraternization with the enemy soared and a fever for peace set in. "We want the ware stopt for the sake of our little ones at home," one Tar Heel soldier declared in the summer of 1864.

Defeatism on the home front having eroded the army's logistical base and infected its ranks, the stage was set for the simple ceremony at Appomattox Court House. Fittingly enough, that ceremony took place in the parlor of Wilmer McLean, a plain farmer who felt the war's hard hand both early and late. He had sold his farm near Manassas Junction after it became the storm center of the first major battle of the Civil War, and had resettled his family, so he believed, "where the sound of battle will never reach them." Much to his dismay, after Grant and Lee had finished their business, souvenir hunters plundered his household possessions. Even in peace the Southern people would know the pain of this cruel war.

The Blue and the Gray

The American Civil War was the first modern war. As a struggle for unlimited and uncompromisable objectives—independence versus reunion—it enlisted the energies of soldier and civilian alike. To an unprecedented degree, it was a war not of armed forces but of peoples. Mass armies of volunteers and conscripts as well as professional soldiers relied more extensively than ever before upon the logistical support of those who remained at home. And because Federal (and, to a lesser extent, Confederate) strategists learned to appreciate this fact, warfare was directed against the productive capacity and morale of civilians as well as against enemy armies. As William Tecumseh Sherman explained in December 1864, after his destructive march from Atlanta to the sea, "This war differs from European wars in this particular: we are not only fighting hostile armies, but a hostile people, and must make old and young, rich and poor, feel the hard hand of war." Earlier he had written: "If the people raise a howl against my barbarity and cruelty, I will answer that war is war, and not popularity-seeking. If they want peace, they and their relatives must stop the war." The Civil War, General Sherman was saying, was modern war because it was total war.

The war was also horribly modern in the free play it gave to new instruments of death and destruction. Not only the rifled musket, a weapon of vastly greater killing power than any used in previous conflicts, but rifled cannon, explosive shells, hand grenades, booby traps and land mines, wire entanglements, hydrogen balloons, the telegraph, armored ships and armored trains—even machine guns and a submarine—first appeared or received their first real test in the Civil War. So, too, did the use of conscription, mass armies, elaborate entrenchments, rail transportation, and (on the Union side) close cooperation between army and navy, cause the Civil War to resemble more nearly the military campaigns of the twentieth century than those of an earlier day. The sheer scale of this conflict was unprecedented, both in numbers involved and munitions expended. From the Wilderness and

Spotsylvania battlefields alone, Confederate ordnance officers salvaged for recasting over 120,000 pounds of lead, the residue, one authority estimates, of perhaps 19 million bullets fired in a single week of combat. "When," he asks rhetorically, "did Marlborough, or Wellington, or Napoleon face such a hail of projectiles?"

Not surprisingly, given these conditions and delays in adjusting traditional tactics to meet advances in weaponry, casualties on both sides were staggering. Union losses included 110,070 killed or mortally wounded in battle and 250,152 who died from disease (dysentery, typhoid, malaria) or accident. Another 275,175 survived battle wounds, many of them maimed for life. Confederate records, fragmentary at best, indicate that some 94,000 died from combat and at least 164,000 from sickness or other causes. Perhaps 190,000 Rebel soldiers received wounds but recovered. Total casualties thus exceeded a million, and nearly as many fighting men lost their lives in the Civil War as in all other American wars combined, including those of the twentieth century.

On the battlefield, the South's undoing was not simply that it had fewer lives to spend but that it failed to make the most of what military resources it did possess. Its powerful attachment to states' rights, for example, at times hindered the war effort. Historians no longer accept uncritically the long-fashionable thesis that the Confederacy "died of state rights." Most Southern governors did what they could to place their states' resources at the disposal of the Confederacy, and even those who resisted the Richmond government's "usurpations" acted vigorously to bolster civilian morale and local defenses. Yet obstreperous governors like Joseph E. Brown of Georgia and North Carolina's Zebulon Vance weakened conscription efforts by granting exemptions with a free hand and creating bogus militia units beyond the reach of Confederate officials. They also competed with the Richmond government for precious space in blockade runners, opposed impressment and the enlistment of black soldiers, insisted on the dispersal of troops throughout all parts of the Confederacy, and occasionally hoarded supplies desperately needed by Rebel armies. At a time when Lee's Army of Northern Virginia marched tattered and shoeless, Vance set aside 92,000 uniforms and great quantities of leather and blankets for the exclusive use of Tar Heel soldiers. He even prohibited Confederate agents from distilling "medicinal" whiskey within the bounds of his state.

Jefferson Davis, though by instinct and training an advocate of limited, decentralized government, perceived the need for central direction of the war effort and courageously espoused such nationalistic measures as conscription, impressment, martial law, and eventually emancipation. At times, however, his own Jacksonian states' rights preferences asserted themselves, to the detriment of the war effort. This was particularly true when it came to the regulation of Southern railways. Never did Davis seek authority to supervise rail traffic, and when in May 1863 Congress granted the president power to force cooperation among railroads and to insist on the primacy of military traffic, he made no use of its powers. Not until the final weeks of the war did the Confederate government establish complete control over private rail companies. All too often during the Civil War Southern soldiers and civilians went hungry while food surpluses rotted in distant warehouses waiting for shipment.

The strategic thinking of Davis—as, indeed, of his principal field commander, Robert E. Lee—was also to some extent shaped by states' rights pressures and the parochialism so characteristic of the plantation South. While not wholly rejecting the advice of such military experts as General P. G. T. Beauregard who preached the importance of rapid deployment and the concentration of Rebel armies against vulnerable enemy forces, Davis so dispersed Confederate troops that in April 1865 fewer than a third of the Southerners still under arms were deployed against Grant and Sherman. The rest were scattered among subsidiary units, fully 60,000 in General E. Kirby Smith's Trans-Mississippi Department alone. Rather than create a central command system like that of the North (which in 1864 appointed Grant commanding general and Henry Halleck chief of staff), President Davis divided the South into military departments, each departmental commander reporting directly and exclusively to Davis himself. Framed in response to political as well as military circumstances, this decentralized command system possessed certain merits. Besides reaffirming the Confederacy's determination to defend all parts of the South, it theoretically eased supply problems by making each department a self-sufficient unit. It also allowed for strategic flexibility, since boundaries could be altered to suit changed military and logistical conditions.

In practice, however, departmental organization worked imperfectly. The virtual autonomy of commanders often thwarted interdepartmental cooperation; departmental boundaries rarely conformed to strategic and logistical realities; the whole system was administratively top-heavy and wasteful of military talent. Yet because it fit so nicely with the principle of decentralization on which the Confederacy rested, the departmental command system remained in place throughout most of the war. Only in February 1865, much too late to have any effect on the war, did President Davis, his hand forced by the Southern Con-

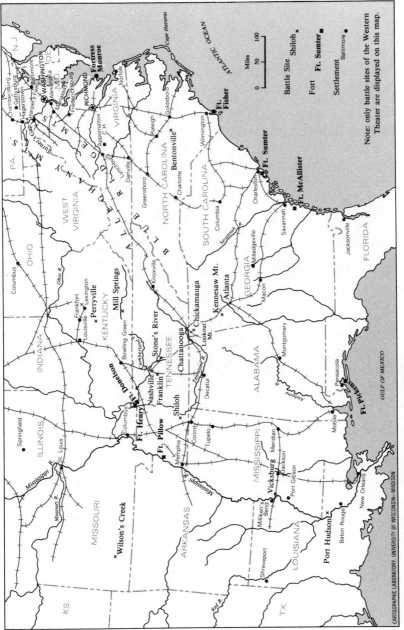

MAP 1. Theater of War, 1861–1865

CARTOGRAPHIC LABORATORY, UNIVERSITY OF WISCONSIN–MADISON

Note: only battle sites of the Western Theater are displayed on this map.

Battle Site   Shiloh×

Fort   Ft. Sumter■

Settlement   Baltimore●

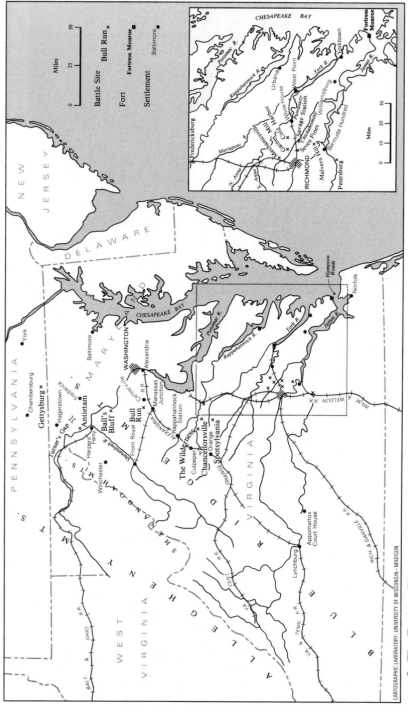

MAP 2. The Eastern Theater

CHESAPEAKE BAY

Potomac R.

Rappahannock R.

Fredericksburg

Mattaponi

Urbana

White House

West Point

York R.

Savage Station

Yorktown

James R.

Fortress Monroe

Mechanicsville

Gaines'
Mill

Cold Harbor

Chickahominy R.

Seven Pines

Williamsburg

RICHMOND

Malvern Hill

Bermuda Hundred

N. Anna

S. Anna

Petersburg

Miles

0   10   20   30

Battle Site   Bull Run ×

Fort   Fortress Monroe ■

Settlement   Baltimore ●

Miles

0   25   50

N E W

J E R S E Y

D E L A W A R E

C H E S A P E A K E   B A Y

Potomac R.

P E N N S Y L V A N I A

York ●

Chambersburg ●

Gettysburg ×

Hagerstown

Frederick ●

Baltimore ●

M A R Y L A N D

WASHINGTON

Alexandria ●

Turner's Gap ×

Antietam ×

Harpers
Ferry

Ball's
Bluff ×

B L U E

R I D G E

M T S.

Winchester ●

Front Royal

Manassas
Junction

Bull
Run ×

ALEXANDRIA R.R.

Rappahannock
Station

Shenandoah R.

Centreville

W E S T

V I R G I N I A

A L L E G H E N Y   M T S.

S H E N A N D O A H   V A L L E Y

The Wilderness ×

Culpeper ●

Chancellorsville ×

Orange

ORANGE & ALEXANDRIA R.R.

Spotsylvania ×

Rappahannock R.

York R.

James R.

Hampton
Roads

Norfolk ●

WELDON R.R.

WILM. R.R.

V I R G I N I A

VA. CENT. R.R.

Appomattox
Court House ●

Lynchburg ●

S O. SIDE R.R.

A. M. & O. R.R.

TENN. R.R.

RICH. & DANVILLE R.R.

BALT. & OHIO R.R.

B L U E   R I D G E

gress, appoint Robert E. Lee commander in chief of all Confederate armies.

In fact, had the move been made earlier, Lee would in all likelihood have proven unfit for the position, for although an often brilliant tactician he was never much of a strategist. The same attachment to place that drew him to the side of the Confederacy in the beginning clouded his understanding of affairs beyond his beloved Virginia. Throughout the war, Lee used his very considerable influence with President Davis to insist upon the primacy of the Virginia theater and to fend off any suggestion that troops from the Army of Northern Virginia be sent to reinforce beleaguered forces in the West. Not until 1864 did he recognize the importance of central Tennessee as an avenue of invasion to the Deep South. Never did he fully comprehend the strategic possibilities resting in the sheer size of the Confederacy. Such strategic parochialism also afflicted a good many other Southern leaders—Davis himself was slow to appreciate the vulnerability of the central South—and hindered the most advantageous allocation of the Confederacy's fighting forces.

II

In the beginning, however, Rebel armies scored a string of battlefield victories, mainly in the East, which sent Southern hopes soaring. The first of these came in mid-July 1861, near Manassas Junction, Virginia, about 25 miles southwest of Washington. Some 22,000 Confederate troops under the command of Brigadier General Beauregard had stationed themselves there, athwart the Orange and Alexandria Railroad, in order to menace the enemy's capital and defend their own. Another railroad, the Manassas Gap, linked Beauregard's army with General Joseph E. Johnston's Confederate force of 11,000 in the Shenandoah Valley. Hoping that a sudden thrust would scatter the Rebels, open the door to Richmond, and perhaps force an end to the war; aware that the three-month enlistments of many Union soldiers were about to expire; and eager to slake the public's thirst for aggressive action, Abraham Lincoln ordered Brigadier General Irvin McDowell, commanding 30,000 men encamped at Alexandria, to advance on Manassas. To McDowell's plea for more time to drill his raw recruits, Lincoln answered: "You are green, it is true; but they are green; you are all green alike." McDowell did receive assurances that if Johnston came to the support of Beauregard, General Robert Patterson and his Federal force of 15,000 near Harpers Ferry would follow "on his heels."

His apprehensions at least partially soothed, McDowell and his ill-trained army, with many regiments gaudily attired and some dressed in gray, set out for Manassas on July 16. Two days later they reached their destination and found Beauregard's infantry ranged along the far bank of a small stream, Bull Run. McDowell himself lacked field experience, but his plan of battle was well conceived. While part of his force feigned a frontal assault to hold the enemy in place, two of his five divisions were to cross Bull Run upstream and attack the enemy's left flank. It took two days for McDowell to make preparations, however, and by the time the battle occurred, on July 21, Beauregard had received strong reinforcements. Slipping away from the incompetent Patterson, General Johnston and most of his army arrived at Bull Run aboard the Manassas Gap Railroad during the afternoon and evening of July 20, and in the midst of battle next day. Gone was the Yankees' advantage.

Yet even so, the Union's raw recruits nearly carried the day. Beginning their flanking march by moonlight, hours before daybreak, they forded Bull Run in mid-morning and despite fierce resistance drove the Confederate left across the Warrenton Turnpike and onto high ground near Henry House, some 3 miles north of Manassas Junction. For a time it appeared that the Rebels would be routed. By mid-afternoon, Union volunteers, well supported by two regular army batteries, reached the crest of Henry House Hill and the Confederate line appeared to be wavering. But bolstered by the steadfastness of Thomas (henceforth Stonewall) Jackson's Virginians and the timely arrival of Johnston's last brigade from the Shenandoah Valley, the Confederates managed not only to hold their ground but to launch a counterattack. By late afternoon the Yankees were reeling in retreat, a retreat that turned into rout once the disorganized soldiers found their path to the rear choked with the buggies and carriages of civilian spectators who had come from Washington with picnic baskets, fine wines, and spyglasses to cheer the boys in blue. ("That is splendid," one lady had exclaimed after a particularly thunderous volley. "Oh, my! Is not that first-rate? I guess we will be in Richmond this time tomorrow.") Rumors that the Confederates' "Black Horse Cavalry" was in hot pursuit further increased the panic, and men who only hours earlier had fought with courage and discipline now rushed pell-mell to put Virginia behind them. "These are the times that try men's soles," one humorist gibed.

Although Stonewall Jackson boasted that with 10,000 fresh men "I would be in Washington tomorrow," the Confederates made no attempt to follow up their stunning victory. President Davis, who had traveled to Manassas in time to witness the Federal retreat, thought briefly of ordering a pursuit, but, after conferring with his generals, decided against it. There simply were not 10,000 fresh men, for one thing, and rations and ammunition were in short supply. By the morning of July 22 a steady downpour had turned northern Virginia's dirt roads into wagon-eating quagmires, making travel all but impossible. Fortifications around Washington were formidable, moreover, and the wide Potomac presented a daunting barrier to an army lacking adequate bridging equipment. What proved most decisive, however, was that, as General Johnston observed, the Confederate "army was more disorganized by victory than that of the United States by defeat." Believing that the invader had been dealt a mortal blow, many of his troops simply "left the army—not to return."

A good many Southerners, in the army and out, shared for a time this belief that the war was as good as won. "The recent triumph of our arms at Manassas," a Georgian exulted, was "a victory without parallel in the history of this western world, an engagement continental in its magnitude, a success whose influence must be felt and acknowledged not only within the limits of our own Confederacy and of the United States but also throughout the civilized world. Surely the God of Battles is with us." Even casualty figures which showed that more gray than blue soldiers had been hit were interpreted as proof of special Southern valor, as were those which revealed that hundreds of Yankees and hardly any Rebels had let themselves be captured. Realists worried that such euphoria was ill-founded and warned of trying days to come. "That victory did nothing but send us off into a fool's paradise of conceit," warned the wife of a presidential aide, "and it roused the manhood of the Northern people."

Indeed, First Bull Run had precisely that effect. At a stroke, the "grand debacle" taught Northerners that crushing the rebellion would be hard work, beyond the capabilities of ninety-day militiamen. Even as McDowell's broken army streamed back across the Potomac, President Lincoln signed legislation providing for half a million three-year volunteers, adding eleven regiments to the regular army, and greatly strengthening the navy. Now painfully aware of what a tough nut Richmond would be to crack, Lincoln also pondered more effective ways to use the military forces at his disposal. His July 23/27 "Memoranda of Military Policy Suggested by the Bull Run Defeat" contained his first proposal for simultaneous advances—"a joint movement from Cairo [Illinois] to Memphis; and from Cincinnati on East Tennessee"—as a way to maximize the North's numerical advantage. He seems also to have begun to understand, much sooner than most of his generals, that the true objective of Federal troops in the East should be the enemy's army, not his capital. To assist him in his strategical deliberations and to whip the Army of the Potomac into shape, Lincoln deposed McDowell and replaced him with General George B. McClellan, the self-proclaimed hero of minor Union victories in western Virginia. Three months later, upon the retirement of Winfield Scott, now "broken down by many particular hurts, besides the general infirmities of age," Lincoln added to McClellan's responsibilities by appointing him also general in chief of all Northern armies. "I can do it all," McClellan assured the president.

At first it seemed that he might. A superb administrator and fine trainer of troops, McClellan worked wonders in restoring the morale and fighting effectiveness of the Army of the Potomac. Though he drilled his men hard, "exacting the most rigid discipline and order," his obvious concern for their welfare and his dashing, charismatic manner made him enormously popular with all who served under him. Little Mac, as his troops affectionately dubbed him, also possessed a shrewd discernment of "the great advantages which are possessed by an army acting on the defensive and occupying strong positions." Though often called Young Napoleon by the press, he in fact eschewed Napoleon's fondness for offensive thrusts in quest of climactic victories, preferring instead flanking movements and a war of maneuver. If at all possible, he would gain "success by maneuvering rather than by fighting."

McClellan's strategic vision, despite an undue preoccupation with the capture of Richmond, was surprisingly acute for a man of thirty-four who had risen only to captain in the peacetime army. Having served as president of the Ohio and Mississippi Railroad before the war, he understood clearly that "the construction of railroads has introduced a new and very important element into war, by the great facilities thus given for concentrating at particular positions large masses of troops from remote sections, and by creating new strategic points and lines of operations." Hence, in addition to strikes down the Mississippi River and the Atlantic coast, as General Scott had proposed, McClellan recommended an advance into eastern Tennessee to support hill-country Unionists and to cut the railroads linking Memphis and the East. He also astutely perceived the need for close cooperation with the navy and the importance of logistics to military success.

Yet for all his virtues, McClellan possessed a number of shortcomings that greatly reduced his army's effectiveness and contributed to his personal downfall. His readiness to claim credit belonging to others and his penchant for dressing down subordinates in public cost him some support in the army, just as his arrogant, contemptuous attitude toward politicians—President Lincoln included—ruffled feathers in Washington. Republicans in particular grew to resent this Democratic general who scarcely concealed his disgust "with these wretched politicians." Many found distasteful his messianic complex ("Who would have thought," he wrote to his wife, "that I should so soon be called upon to save my country?"), which became a martyr complex once things turned sour. But his most crippling flaws by far were a paralyzing perfectionism, a chronic disposition to exaggerate the odds against him, and a pronounced reluctance to give battle.

Throughout the remainder of 1861, in fact, McClellan's troops remained encamped around Washington, despite increasing popular pressure for a southward advance to avenge the defeat at Bull Run. Although fair skies and mild temperatures made military operations feasible until the end of December, McClellan refused to budge, believing himself outnumbered when in fact his army was twice the size of the Confederate force in Virginia. Only minor amphibious operations which resulted in the capture of Fort Hatteras and Fort Clark on the North Carolina coast and occupation of the sea islands off South Carolina, and a bungled reconnaissance in force which cost the Federals nearly 1,000 men at Ball's Bluff, Virginia, broke the stillness in the East after Bull Run. "All Quiet Along the Potomac" became first a recurrent headline and then a popular song:

"All quiet along the Potomac," they say,
  "Except now and then a stray picket
Is shot, as he walks on his beat to and fro,
  By a rifleman hid in the thicket."

At first President Lincoln "stood up for McClellan's deliberateness." He had no wish to rush the general into action before he was ready. But prolonged inactivity in the West as well as in the East jeopardized Northern morale, and with it popular support for the war effort. By January 1862 Lincoln was fretting that "delay is ruining us." He, too, along with his new secretary of war Edwin M. Stanton, now joined the chorus of voices urging more aggressive action, especially against Joe Johnston's Rebel army still camped at Manassas. Finally, on January 27, the president ordered "a general movement of the Land and Naval forces of the United States against the insurgent forces," to commence on Washington's Birthday, February 22.

Western armies were on the move even before the twenty-second, but the Army of the Potomac fell behind schedule because of a disagreement between Lincoln and McClellan over what line of operations to take. Rather than repeat McDowell's direct, overland advance to Manassas and beyond, as the president preferred, McClellan developed a plan of his own designed to turn the enemy's flank and approach

Richmond from the east. By ferrying his army down Chesapeake Bay to a landing at Urbana on the lower Rappahannock he hoped to place himself between Richmond and the Confederate force at Manassas, either winning the race to the capital or forcing the Rebels "to beat us in a position selected by ourselves." Lincoln disliked this proposal, primarily because it appeared to leave Washington exposed to Confederate raiders. McClellan correctly perceived that the strong fortifications now ringing the District of Columbia and the threat his own army presented to Richmond made a Confederate attack on Washington improbable, but failed to grasp the *political* necessity of guarding the capital against even "danger and insult" lest public confidence in Lincoln and his generals be lost. Nevertheless, after requiring that Washington be left "entirely secure," and ordering operations to begin by March 18, the president reluctantly sanctioned McClellan's plan. To keep an eye on the Young Napoleon, however, and to ease suspicions that his sluggishness in mounting an offensive stemmed from an uncertain patriotism, Lincoln divided the Army of the Potomac into four corps, appointing good Republicans (including the recently demoted McDowell) to the command of each. Soon thereafter, he stripped McClellan of his authority as commanding general, ostensibly to permit him to concentrate his attention on the upcoming campaign in Virginia. For the time being the commander in chief would serve as his own general in chief.

On top of these gestures of mistrust in McClellan's generalship came word that the Confederates had withdrawn from Centerville near Bull Run to new lines south of the Rappahannock. In doing so, they knocked the Urbana scheme into a cocked hat and forced McClellan instead to advance on Richmond by way of the peninsula between the York and James rivers. President Lincoln's lingering apprehension for the safety of Washington again gave him pause, but after detaching McDowell's corps to hold Manassas and posting a strong force under General Nathaniel P. Banks in the Shenandoah Valley, he allowed the Peninsula campaign to go forward.

Forward McClellan went, but with maddening slowness. Moving swiftly, the Army of the Potomac might have used naval support to turn the enemy's position and reach Richmond's outskirts without great resistance. Even after the detachment of Banks and McDowell, McClellan enjoyed a two to one advantage over Johnston's army, and though still menaced by the Confederate ironclad *Virginia* (which on March 9 had fought its opposite number, the *Monitor,* to a draw), the Union navy assured him gunfire support and dependable lines of supply and transportation. When the last of his nearly 100,000 troops disembarked at Fortress Monroe on the tip of the Peninsula early in April, the only Confederate army in position to impede his advance was a force of some 11,000 commanded by Major General John B. Magruder at Yorktown. Upon reaching Magruder's lines, however, McClellan came to a dead halt. "No one but McClellan," Joe Johnston later observed, "would have hesitated to attack." But deceived by Magruder's stagecraft (the Confederate "strengthened" his defenses with fake cannons, or "Quaker guns," and paraded his men into and out of sight to give the appearance of greater numbers) and by his own habit of exaggerating the enemy's might, McClellan called for a siege. It took a full month to prepare this siege, and when at last McClellan's gunners were ready to unleash their barrage it was discovered that the Confederates had slipped safely out of Yorktown.

Not wishing to engage the Yankees so far from their main supply base, Richmond, for fear that McClellan would land a force in their rear, the Confederates (including Johnston's troops which had joined Magruder during the siege of Yorktown) withdrew up the Peninsula. McClellan followed, encountering only delaying actions until nearly in sight of Richmond's church spires. Here, with his army straddling the rain-swollen Chickahominy River, McClellan awaited reinforcement from McDowell's corps which in mid-May Lincoln had agreed to send by an overland route. Reinforcements never came, for in anticipation of this move the Confederate high command had beefed up Stonewall Jackson's "foot cavalry" and sent it surging down the Shenandoah Valley toward Washington. While Lincoln and his advisors doubted that Jackson's 17,000-man force posed a genuine threat to the capital, they reversed the decision to send McDowell to the Peninsula and ordered him instead to join Federal units in the Shenandoah Valley in an attempt to snare Jackson. Jackson, however, after striking the Federals hard at Front Royal and Winchester, eluded the trap. He, and not McDowell's exhausted corps, would soon reappear near Richmond.

Meanwhile, on May 31, as soon as he learned that McDowell had gone chasing after Jackson, Johnston pitched into McClellan. This Battle of Fair Oaks (or Seven Pines) ended inconclusively, except that Johnston himself was badly wounded and had to be relieved. In his place, Jefferson Davis named General Robert E. Lee, the president's chief military advisor and mastermind of Jackson's recent Shenandoah Valley campaign. It proved a wise choice, for the aristocratic Virginian, fifty-five years old at the time, was well suited to high command. The son of "Light Horse Harry" Lee, the famous Revolutionary War general, Lee had graduated second in his West Point class of 1829, served with distinction in the Mexican War and as superintendent of

West Point (1852–53), gained experience as an engineering and cavalry officer, and risen to the rank of colonel in the "old" army. Although opposed to both slavery and secession, he had declined sure appointment to high command in the Union Army to follow Virginia into the Confederacy, explaining that "a Union that can only be maintained by swords and bayonets . . . has no charm for me."

Lee possessed an insufficient appreciation of the war's political aspects (though he shared none of McClellan's arrogance toward politicians and managed to form a close relationship with the touchy President Davis), and his strategic vision went little beyond Virginia. But from the moment he replaced Johnston as commander of the Army of Northern Virginia, Lee showed himself a brave, resourceful, and daring — sometimes overly daring — field general. His essentially Napoleonic quest for a decisive, Austerlitz-like victory which would *annihilate* the enemy was doomed to fail, thanks to the resilience of mass armies equipped with rifles. Yet the triumphs he did win, staggering though the price often was, bolstered Southern morale and kept the North on edge.

To drive McClellan from Richmond's door, Lee conceived a brilliant plan. Rather than risk a frontal assault on heavily fortified Yankee positions, he proposed "to bring McClellan out" by threatening his line of supply. McClellan had left only Fitz John Porter's corps of 30,000 men north of the Chickahominy to guard communications with his base at White House Landing on the Pamunkey River, a tributary of the York. By concentrating his own forces against this exposed right wing of the enemy, Lee hoped to force McClellan either "to retreat or to give battle out of his entrenchments." In mid-June Jeb Stuart's cavalry sortie completely around McClellan's army confirmed the weakness of the Union right flank, and on the twenty-sixth Lee set his plan in motion.

Leaving barely 25,000 troops to fend off the main Federal body (70,000 strong), Lee ordered the remainder of his newly christened Army of Northern Virginia to assail McClellan's flank and rear. Counting Stonewall Jackson's command, which was to arrive by road and rail from the Shenandoah Valley, this attacking force would number 55,000 men — enough, Lee believed, to crush Porter, sever the Union supply line, and compel McClellan to fall back. His hopes were only partially realized. In the Seven Days' Battle which began at Mechanicsville on June 26 and ended at Malvern Hill on July 1, Lee's well-laid plans went often awry: Jackson reached the Peninsula a day late and was often tardy and confused once his troops did become engaged; faulty staff work and poor intelligence resulted in disjointed attacks against well-prepared Union positions. Only once, at Gaines' Mill, did the Confederates win what might be called a victory, and even then their casualties exceeded Union losses by nearly 2,000. At Malvern Hill, Lee's repeated assaults against well-protected Union lines left 5,000 Confederates (and 3,000 Yankees) dead or wounded. "It was not war," said one Rebel officer, "it was murder." Altogether, the Seven Days' campaign cost Lee 20,614 men and the Federals 15,849.

Thanks to McClellan's caution, however, Lee did at least succeed in driving the Yankees away from the Confederate capital. Had McClellan countered the Rebels' initial blow to his right flank by driving his main force straight for Richmond, as some of his lieutenants urged him to do, he might well have taken the city, or at least forced Lee to turn back to defend it. Instead, believing himself beset by a force of 200,000, the Union commander ordered a retreat to a new base on the James River and berated "the dolts in Washington" for failing to send reinforcements. "I have lost this battle because my force was too small," McClellan wired Secretary of War Stanton. "If I save this army now, I tell you plainly that I owe no thanks to you or to any other persons in Washington. You have done your best to sacrifice this army."

The telegraph supervisor in Washington prudently deleted these last two sentences, but even so Lincoln had grown weary of Little Mac's excessive caution, incessant pleas for reinforcement, and conspicuous lack of success. McClellan had withdrawn his army in good order to a safe haven at Harrison's Landing on the James River, preserving, he boasted, "our trains, our guns, our material, and above all, our honor." Even Robert E. Lee conceded that "under ordinary circumstances the Federal army should have been destroyed." But after visiting McClellan at Harrison's Landing on July 7, and querying corps commanders about the army's next step, Lincoln decided that changes were in order. The main task, he was now persuaded, was not the capture of Richmond—the difficulty of which was now fully apparent—but the defeat of Lee's army.

Lincoln had already created a rival to McClellan in the East by consolidating Federal forces south and west of Washington into a new Army of Virginia, under the command of Major General John Pope. Fresh from western victories at New Madrid, Missouri, and Island No. 10 in the Mississippi River, Pope was full of bluster and ineptitude; "if John Pope possessed a coat of arms," scoffed one detractor, "it would have been bombast rampant upon an expansive field of incompetence." Yet his appointment reflected not only Lincoln's eagerness to find generals who would fight, but a growing sense that tougher measures were needed to subdue the Southern people. McClellan, a Democrat with conservative views on slavery, was an advocate of "gentlemanly war," waged so as to facilitate reunion. "I have not come here to wage war upon the defenseless, upon non-combatants, upon private property, nor upon the domestic institutions of the land," he assured a Virginia planter upon whose lands the Army of the Potomac had camped. "I and the army I command are fighting to secure the Union and maintain its Constitution and laws, and for no other purpose." President Lincoln had initially shared such views. But military reverses, to which McClellan himself contributed, had persuaded the president that "war against armed forces and political organization" was not enough. Militarily, nothing signaled this turn more clearly than Lincoln's ratification of Pope's stern orders that his soldiers live off the country, reimburse only *loyal* citizens for requisitioned supplies, raze any house from which a Federal soldier was shot, and string up any Southerner within his lines found giving information to the enemy. Civil war was becoming total war.

After returning to Washington from Harrison's Landing, President Lincoln named another successful western soldier, Henry W. Halleck, to the vacant post of general in chief. He hoped that Halleck, whose study of military science (as well as his massive forehead) had earned him the nickname Old Brains, would take from his shoulders much of the responsibility for strategic planning and supervision of the Union's far-flung land forces. The bookish, bug-eyed, slow-moving Halleck soon disappointed these hopes by peevishly refusing to do more than offer advice on particular problems and help to carry out decisions made by the president and secretary of war. He did, however, participate fully in the decision to pull McClellan from the Peninsula by sea and to unite his army with Pope's new command in northern Virginia. Their combined forces, 140,000 strong, might then advance south of the Rappahannock toward Richmond. McClellan strenuously opposed this movement, insisting that "it is here on the banks of the James that the fate of the Union should be decided," and though Halleck urged him to hurry he proceeded northward with characteristic sluggishness.

Rather than encounter the combined Federal armies, Lee, counting on McClellan's pokiness, decided to strike Pope before he could be reinforced. Leaving a small force to safeguard Richmond, Lee moved north in mid-August with an army of 55,000 men. Using General James Longstreet's corps as a screen, Lee sent his second corps, under the hard-driving Stonewall Jackson, on a long sweep west and north of Pope, who was stationed near Rappahannock Station awaiting McClellan's arrival. On August 27 Jackson's troops poured through Thoroughfare Gap in the Bull Run mountains and attacked Pope's main supply depot at Manassas Junction, the "ragged and famished" soldiers gorging themselves on such delicacies as oysters, boned turkey, lobster salad, and Rhine wine, not to mention canned beef and whiskey, before turning countless tons of Federal supplies and munitions into a bonfire that "lighted up the country for miles."

Pope, augmented by advance units of McClellan's army, now turned back to strike Jackson's outmanned force which had dug in at the old Bull Run battleground. The Second Battle of Bull Run (or Second Manassas) began on August 29 and ended the next day in a resounding Union defeat after Longstreet's corps reached the scene and savagely counterattacked Pope's left flank. The rout of First Bull Run was not repeated, the Federals making an orderly withdrawal to the Confederates' old entrenchments at Centerville before falling back to Washington early in September. But the Union army had suffered heavy casualties (16,054 to the Confederates' 9,197) and Pope, who upon taking command in July had boasted, "I come to you from the West, where we have always seen the backs of our enemies," now stood disgraced. Two days after Second Bull Run Lincoln shunted Pope off to Indian duty in Minnesota and reluctantly restored McClellan to command of Pope's troops as well as his own. "Again I have been called upon to save the country," the Young Napoleon wrote his wife.

Lee gave McClellan little time to regroup. Before dawn on September 4, advance columns of the Army of Northern Virginia began splashing across the Potomac River and into Maryland, midway between Washington and Harpers Ferry. "They were," reported one witness, "the dirtiest men I ever saw, a most ragged, lean, and hungry set of wolves. . . . Yet there was a dash about them that northern men lacked." Lee's objectives in mounting this daring invasion of the North were both logistical and political. By crossing the Potomac he could feed his famished soldiers on the enemy's crops and protect the harvest on Virginia farms. If nothing else, his raid would keep the Yankees off balance and safely away from Richmond. With luck, moreover, he might exploit his position on Washington's flank to win a decisive victory which would demoralize the Northern people, strengthen the peace movement, and persuade European powers to intervene in support of the Confederacy.

At first, however, luck smiled not on Lee but on McClellan. For on September 13 near Frederick, Maryland, a private in the Twenty-Seventh Indiana Volunteers stumbled across a copy of Lee's Special Orders No. 191, wrapped around a few cigars. This document revealed that Lee had divided his forces to protect his line of communications as he advanced toward Pennsylvania. Half his army, under Stonewall Jackson, had marched off to capture the Federal garrison at Harpers Ferry and the rest was strung out between Turner's Gap and Hagerstown, Maryland. Acting quickly, Little Mac could gobble up Lee's scattered forces piecemeal. If he could not now "whip Bobby Lee," Mc-Clellan gloated, "I will be willing to go home."

Lee would have been well advised had he at this point retreated to safety below the Potomac. Instead, taking advantage of McClellan's slow-footed pursuit, he concentrated his troops at Sharpsburg, on Antietam Creek, some 17 miles north of Harpers Ferry. There, on September 17, the two armies clashed in what proved to be the bloodiest single-day battle of the Civil War. Both sides made tragic mistakes. Lee, though fighting on the defensive, failed to entrench; McClellan squandered his better than two to one numerical advantage by launching poorly coordinated frontal attacks and by holding 20,000 troops in reserve for use against a counterattack which never came. Day's end found both armies horribly mauled and the Confederates still in place. Although nearly a quarter of his brave soldiers lay dead or wounded, and McClellan's forces were now nearly three times the size of his own, Lee at first stubbornly refused to quit the field. "If McClellan wants to fight in the morning I will give him battle again," he told Longstreet and others who counseled retreat. When on the eighteenth the Union commander failed to resume combat, however, Lee abandoned his precarious position and, after sundown, led his proud but battered army back into Virginia. Not until October 26 did McClellan cross the Potomac in leisurely pursuit.

The Union "victory" at Antietam Creek chilled prospects of European intervention and allowed President Lincoln to issue his Preliminary Emancipation Proclamation (September 22) from a position of strength. It was not enough to save McClellan his job. Distressed that McClellan had let Lee slip so easily from his grasp and fed up with his endless excuses for inactivity ("He is an admirable engineer," the president concluded, "but he seems to have a special talent for a stationary engine"), Lincoln relieved Little Mac from command on November 7. In his place he appointed McClellan's second in command, Major General Ambrose E. Burnside, a big, dashing, bewhiskered West Pointer with a good fighting record who readily admitted his incompetence to lead a large army.

Burnside wasted no time in demonstrating that such self-doubts were fully merited. Assuming command of the Army of the Potomac at Warrenton, Virginia, just east of the Bull Run mountains, Burnside proposed to advance first to Fredericksburg on the south bank of the Rappahannock. From there he could strike south to Richmond, using the Richmond, Fredericksburg and Potomac Railroad as a supply route. President Lincoln preferred that Burnside forget Richmond (a well-nigh unobtainable objective, he had come to believe) and instead light into Lee's army, then divided between Longstreet's corps near Culpeper and Jackson's troops in the Shenandoah Valley. Nevertheless, Lincoln grudgingly "assented" to Burnside's plan. "He thinks that it will succeed if you move very rapidly," Halleck reported to Burnside; "otherwise not."

Burnside did move rapidly at first, his army covering 40 miles in two days. But upon reaching the Rappahannock, he hit a snag. Owing to Halleck's negligence, the pontoons needed to cross the river had not arrived. While Burnside waited for them anxiously, Lee collected his dispersed forces and dug in along Marye's Heights behind Fredericksburg. His army, well rested and in fighting trim, now numbered 75,000 men. Facing him from the opposite shore were half again that many Federals.

What followed was butchery. On December 11–12 Burnside's main force crossed the Rappahannock and on the thirteenth made repeated, futile assaults against the Rebels' well-prepared positions above Fredericksburg. Confederate artillery raked the open plain below and infantrymen, many of them shielded by a stone wall along the foot of Marye's Heights, laid down a murderous fire. One Union officer later recalled that

> the whole plain was covered with men, prostrate and dropping. . . . I had never before seen fighting like that—nothing approaching it in terrible uproar and destruction. There was no cheering on the part of the men, but a stubborn determination to obey orders and do their duty. . . . As they charged, the artillery fire would break their formation and they would get mixed. Then they would close up, go forward, receive the withering infantry fire, and . . . fight as best they could. And then the next brigade coming up in succession would do its duty, and melt like snow coming down on warm ground.

Never had the killing power of rifled weapons fired from entrenched positions been more apparent. Even the Confederates stood aghast at the carnage they had wreaked. "The Federals had fallen like the steady dripping of rain from the eaves of a house," General Longstreet remarked. The attackers' losses were more than twice those of the defenders.

Yet, incredibly, Burnside proposed to renew this suicidal assault the next morning. His senior commanders talked sense into him, however, and after taking two days to bury its 1,300 dead and attend to its 9,600 wounded, the still mighty but dispirited Army of the Potomac pulled back across the Rappahannock. Late in January of 1863, Burnside attempted to turn Lee's left flank by recrossing the river further upstream. This "Mud March," as it became known, ended in dismal failure when three days of torrential rain turned roads into impassible quagmires and forced the weary, wet, cold, and cursing army back to winter quarters opposite Fredericksburg. Both the army and the president had by now enough of Ambrose Burnside, and on January 26 Lincoln replaced him with "Fighting Joe" Hooker.

Lincoln knew full well Hooker's hot temper and oversized ego, his reputation for backbiting and intrigue. But he also judged Hooker "a brave and skillful soldier" and hoped that his fighting qualities would infuse new spirit in the downcast army. Hooker quickly set about to do just that, making certain that his troops got good food and decent lodgings, proper medical care, furloughs home, and a pat on the back. This was "the finest army on the planet," he bragged, and his men loved him for it. Even his reputed fondness for hard drink sat well: "Hooker is our leader," the soldiers sang; "he takes his whisky strong."

By spring, when the roads that stalled Burnside had dried, Hooker was ready to put his revitalized army to the test. His plan was a good one, if not, as he said, "perfect." Exploiting his two-to-one numerical advantage, Hooker proposed to hold Lee at Fredericksburg with 25,000 men under the command of General John Sedgwick. The bulk of his army, more than 70,000 strong, would cross the Rappahannock well upstream and fall upon Lee's left flank. At the same time, the Union cavalry would menace Lee's supply line to Richmond. Threatened from the front and flank, Lee would be forced to retreat or be caught in a vise. "The rebel Army . . . is now the legitimate property of the Army of the Potomac," Hooker boasted as his troops forded the Rappahannock late in April. "They may as well pack their haversacks and make for Richmond; and I shall be after them."

The Confederate commander had other ideas. Leaving 10,000 men under Jubal Early to hold the Confederate position at Marye's Heights, Lee with 50,000 seasoned troops moved east to meet Hooker's main force at Chancellorsville, a crossroads hamlet within a region of dense woods and tangled undergrowth known as the Wilderness. On May 2 he still further divided his forces, sending Stonewall Jackson and 28,000 men to attack Hooker's weakly fortified right flank while he occupied the Federals' front with barely 14,000 troops. Shortly before dusk Jackson's three divisions swept out of the woods and pitched into General O. O. Howard's Eleventh Corps, sending it reeling back toward Hooker's headquarters. Federal artillery and the onset of darkness, however, checked the Confederate advance and left Lee's forces divided. Worse yet for the Rebels, while reconnoitering the enemy's position Stonewall Jackson and his party were mistaken for Union cavalry and fired upon by an edgy North Carolina regiment. Old Jack fell mortally wounded. "I have lost my right arm," Lee noted sadly.

Strong action the next day might have saved Hooker, for his army greatly outnumbered the still-divided Confederates. But the general had lost his nerve; "I just lost confidence in Joe Hooker," he later admitted. By constricting his lines Hooker allowed the severed wings of Lee's command to reunite. After a blow to the head from a shell-struck porch column left him dazed and hurt, Hooker ordered a pullback to a new line around United States Ford on the Rappahannock. His hopes for salvation now rested on Sedgwick's troops which had driven Early from Fredericksburg and were marching on Chancellorsville. Yet, though Lee brazenly sent half of his force to head off Sedgwick, Hooker neither reinforced Sedgwick nor attacked the weakened Confederate line at Chancellorsville. As a result, the Virginian's gamble paid off: Sedgwick was forced to retreat and on the night of May 5, as Lee recklessly prepared to throw 35,000 tired soldiers against Hooker's 90,000-man, well-entrenched main force, the Army of the Potomac withdrew across the Rappahannock.

Owing to "the incomprehensible mental torpor of the Union commander," as one Yankee private put it, the Confederates had again sent their enemies reeling in defeat. "God! It is horrible—horrible!" Horace Greeley moaned, "130,000 magnificent soldiers so cut to pieces by less than 60,000 half-starved ragamuffins!" The South paid a steep price for this victory, however. Lee's losses, though numerically somewhat smaller than Hooker's, were proportionally 50 percent *higher.* And one casualty would be most sorely missed—the incomparable Stonewall Jackson.

Lee understood full well that Chancellorsville had been a costly and incomplete success, which is why he had contemplated what surely would have been a disastrous assault against Hooker's fortifications on the morning of May 6. Believing that time was running out and that only victories on the enemy's soil would secure Confederate independence, Lee began almost at once after Chancellorsville to prepare for a second invasion of the North. Some, including Lee's own corps commander James Longstreet, questioned the wisdom—or at least the timing of such a campaign. In the West, Union forces under General Ulysses S. Grant had Vicksburg in a hammerlock and William S. Rosecrans's Army of the Cumberland was pressing the Confederates hard in east Tennessee. Several of President Davis's advisors therefore urged that Lee forgo offensive operations and instead send reinforcements westward. Lee, however, argued that an eastern offensive would lessen Federal pressure on the Mississippi, and although Davis rejected *his* request for reinforcements Lee was allowed to proceed with his plans.

By now Union strategy was to accept military stalemate in the East while seeking victory in the West. So when in June Lee began moving north through the Shenandoah Valley toward Pennsylvania, Lincoln and Halleck rejected Hooker's proposal to take Richmond and ordered him instead to follow Lee "on the inside track, shortening your lines whilst he lengthens his." If the head of Lee's army was near Maryland and its tail between Fredericksburg and Chancellorsville, Lincoln noted, "the animal must be very slim somewhere. Could you not break him?" The president thought it unlikely that any mobile, rifle-equipped army could be annihilated, but there was always a chance that the Gray Fox would blunder. Lee's risky summer invasion held out hope that he might. Others might panic at reports of the Confederates' advance, but Abraham Lincoln did not. "I do not think the raid into Pennsylvania amounts to anything at all," he assured his wife in mid-June.

To improve chances of catching Lee in a mistake, on June 28 Lincoln replaced the contentious and error-prone Hooker with George Gordon Meade, a "damned old goggle-eyed snapping turtle" of a general whose unpretentious ways and steadiness in battle earned him the respect of his troops. That same day Lee, who had for some time been out of touch with his cavalry and hence unaware of the enemy's whereabouts, learned that the Union army had crossed the Potomac and was moving north from Frederick, Maryland. Immediately he ordered his scattered columns to rendezvous near Gettysburg, Pennsylvania, 10 miles north of the Mason-Dixon line. There, on the thirtieth, a Confederate brigade hunting for shoes stumbled across an advance contingent of Meade's force. Next morning the Rebels returned in force and for three days the two armies collided in the most savage battle of the Civil War.

At first all went well for the Confederates. Only two of Meade's seven corps (plus one cavalry division) were in place when Lee launched his attack on July 1, and after fierce fighting the Yankees were driven out of Gettysburg and back to the low hills south of town. By the second, however, Meade had arrived with the rest of his command. He deployed his troops in an inverted fishhook alignment, his right flank anchored at the barb on Culp's Hill southeast of town, his center running due south from Cemetery Hill along Cemetery Ridge, and his left flank securely placed on Big and Little Round Top, at the hook's eye. A sign on the arched gateway to the cemetery warned, "ALL PERSONS FOUND USING FIREARMS IN THESE GROUNDS WILL BE PROSECUTED WITH THE UTMOST RIGOR OF THE LAW." Holding so strong a position and enjoying now a decided edge in numbers, Meade hoped that Lee would attack. Lee, needing a quick, decisive victory, obliged him — twice — with disastrous results.

On the afternoon of July 2, Longstreet's corps charged the Federals' left flank and that evening Jackson's old corps, commanded now by General Richard S. Ewell, assailed their right. Longstreet drove back Northern units below the Round Tops and Ewell secured a lodgement part way up Culp's Hill. But the failure to coordinate these thrusts diminished their effectiveness, and nightfall found the Army of the Potomac firmly in place. Against the sensible advice of Longstreet, who urged Lee to find a strong position in Meade's rear and fight him on the defensive, Lee chose to make another assault the following day — this time at the Union center.

Lee apparently believed that troops from Cemetery Ridge had been siphoned off to strengthen the Federal flanks and that a sustained artillery barrage would wipe out many of those who remained, making a frontal assault feasible. The awful events of July 3 proved him sadly mistaken. Meade's center remained strongly manned and Rebel gunners, firing steadily for nearly two hours, constantly overshot their target. When, therefore, Major General George E. Pickett (who ranked last in the West Point class of 1846) and some 15,000 other brave Confederate soldiers marched in a mile-long line over open fields and surged up Cemetery Ridge they faced certain slaughter. Pounded by long-range artillery, smoothbore Napoleons firing grapeshot and canister, and a hail of rifle fire, Pickett's men fell as if cut by "the scythe of a mower." A very few managed to clamber past the stone wall atop the ridge and briefly to seize a Federal battery. The blue line held, however, and those Confederates who could do so fell back to the safety of their own lines. Fully 70 percent of Pickett's attack force — and all but one of his thirty-five officers above the rank of captain — had been killed, wounded, or captured. "Too bad! Too bad! Oh, too bad!" Lee lamented, rightly and honorably taking all blame upon himself. "I thought my men were invincible," he told Longstreet. In three days of battle Lee had lost 28,000 men — well over a third of his entire command. Never again would the Army of Northern Virginia be as strong as it was on the eve of Gettysburg.

Historians have offered various explanations for the penchant for attack which Robert E. Lee and most other Confederate commanders displayed throughout the war — a preference that increased casualties the South could ill afford. An "offensive-defensive" *strategy* may have been necessary as some have noted, to throw the North off balance and prevent it from applying pressure all along the Confederacy's rim, as well as to sustain Southern morale. Yet all too often, as at Gettysburg, the Rebel army squandered lives by taking the *tactical* offensive as well. Several scholars have explained this aggressiveness by reference to the tactical theories on which Civil War generals were weaned, notably those of Baron Henri Jomini, a Swiss student of Napoleon whose *Summary of the Art of War* preached the advantage of the offense and belittled the importance of earthworks and entrenchments. Yet none of Jomini's works appeared in English translation until 1854, the correspondence of Confederate generals rarely mentions them, and at least one Union commander, Grant, claimed "never [to have] looked at a copy of tactics from the time of my graduation." Dennis Hart Mahan taught Jominian doctrines at West Point, but he emphasized the value of entrenchments more than frontal attacks. Besides, Lee and others had already graduated before Mahan arrived.

It may be that the lessons of the Mexican War were far more influential than those of the Napoleonic War. Lee, Braxton Bragg, Beauregard, Jackson, Hooker, Grant, and many others had served with Winfield Scott and Zachary Taylor in Mexico, witnessing firsthand the success of assault tactics in a conflict fought with premodern weapons. Understandably, many were slow to adapt to the tactical demands of rifle warfare. Some military specialists, among them General Scott, himself a Southerner, contend that "the greater impetuosity of the Southern temperament" led the Rebels to attack, and Lee's most recent biographer suggests that deep feelings of inadequacy and insecurity underlay his recklessness in battle. One might also speculate, then, that the paranoia and siege mentality of the Old South found surcease by substituting offensive for defensive military actions in the Civil War. The North, it should be noted, attacked more often than did the South. But the North was better able to sustain losses than the undermanned Confederacy.

General Meade, who had suffered 23,000 casualties of his own at Gettysburg (roughly one-quarter of the men on hand) chose not to counterattack. When Lee headed back to Virginia on July 5, Meade pursued cautiously, content simply "to drive from our soil every vestige . . . of the invader." By mid-month the Confederates were safely across the Potomac. For the rest of the year the two armies watched one another warily while public attention shifted westward.

III

From the beginning, Union forces in the West had enjoyed greater success than those in the East, and Lincoln had early decided that there the war would be won. Once it had secured the neutrality of Kentucky and Missouri, a task largely completed by the end of 1861, the North's prime strategic objectives in the West were (1) to split the Confederacy by gaining control of the Mississippi River and (2) to liberate east Tennessee Unionists, sever the main railroad between Memphis and Richmond, and seize a region rich in resources by invading east and central Tennessee. In November 1861 Lincoln gave organizational definition to these twin objectives by dividing western land forces into two departments, the first under Henry Halleck, who kept his headquarters at St. Louis, and the second commanded by General Don Carlos Buell at Louisville. Facing both of these armies stood some 70,000 widely dispersed Confederates led by General Albert Sidney Johnston. By holding a line through southwestern Kentucky from Bowling Green to Columbus, Johnston could stymie Federal advances along the Cumberland, Tennessee, and Mississippi rivers and safeguard an extensive rail network linking Tennessee to the rest of the eastern Confederacy.

In keeping with Lincoln's developing strategy of simultaneous advances, Halleck and Buell began to strike south early in the new year. On January 19, 1862, Buell's men, led by Brigadier General George H. Thomas, dealt the Confederates their first real defeat of the war at Mill Springs, Kentucky. Soon thereafter Halleck dispatched Brigadier General Ulysses S. Grant, 15,000 men, and seven gunboats controlled by Flag Officer Andrew H. Foote to capture Fort Henry on the Tennessee River, just below Kentucky. Weakly defended and poorly positioned, Fort Henry fell to Foote's naval bombardment on February 6, even before Grant arrived. Grant thereupon marched quickly to the Cumberland River where, after a stiffer fight, on February 14 he captured Fort Donelson and nearly 15,000 prisoners. It was the Union's first major victory and earned Grant a new nickname as well as the plaudits of the Northern people. When the Confederate commander Simon Bolivar Buckner asked to discuss "terms of capitulation," Grant had replied: "No terms except unconditional and immediate surrender can be accepted. I propose to move immediately upon your works." Overnight "Unconditional Surrender" Grant became a new national hero and Lincoln promptly promoted him to major general.

Little in Ulysses Grant's early career suggested the renown he would achieve in the Civil War. Born at Point Pleasant, Ohio, the son of a thrifty tanner, Grant graduated from West Point in 1839 near the middle of his class, distinguished only for his horsemanship. In the Mexican War he displayed a cool-headed courage that others admired ("Ulysses don't scare worth a damn," one soldier later remarked), but afterward languished at a godforsaken post in California. There, lonely and despondent over low pay, he took to drink. Run-ins with his superior touched off his resignation in 1854, promptly accepted by Secretary of War Jefferson Davis. Grant then drifted unsuccessfully through a series of civilian occupations: farmer, real estate agent, custom house clerk. He was clerking in his father's leathergoods store at Galena, Illinois, when the war broke out. In June 1861 Governor Richard Yates appointed him colonel of the Twenty-First Illinois Volunteers.

The fall of Forts Henry and Donelson opened central Tennessee to invasion along the Tennessee and Cumberland rivers, threatened to isolate the Confederate flanks, and compelled Johnston to pull back to a new line from Memphis to Chattanooga. While Halleck, now in command of all western land forces, sent troops to take New Madrid and Island No. 10 on the Mississippi and ordered Grant and Buell to push into southwestern Tennessee, Johnston concentrated his army at Corinth, Mississippi, and prepared a counterattack. On April 6, before Buell could get there, Johnston's gray columns caught Grant unawares near Shiloh Church and Pittsburg Landing, Tennessee, some 20 miles north of Corinth. That the attack came as a surprise was itself a surprise, for the Confederate advance had been anything but stealthy: soldiers practiced bugle calls, took potshots at wild game, and rehearsed Rebel yells. Yet many Federals were still sipping their breakfast coffee when the enemy swept forward and overran their outlying camps.

Grant's army had camped, without making entrenchments, with its back to Pittsburg Landing. So sudden and strong was the Confederate offensive that Johnston at first appeared correct when he told his staff, "Tonight we will water our horses in the Tennessee River." Once they steadied themselves, however, the Yankees put up a fierce resistance. Fighting was especially vicious in a peach orchard on the Union left where bullets sent blossoms falling like snow, and in the "Hornet's Nest" nearer the center where Benjamin Prentiss's division drove back eleven Rebel assaults before finally being overwhelmed. Johnston himself was among those killed near the peach orchard, and although his successor, P. G. T. Beauregard, claimed "a complete victory" for the South, Grant still held a tightly drawn line around Pittsburg Landing when darkness fell. Night brought heavy rain (which added to the suffering of the untended wounded) and reinforcements for Grant: a fresh division under Lew Wallace and 20,000 men from Buell's Army of the Ohio. When fighting resumed the next morning it was the Federals who took the offensive. Outmanned and exhausted from the previous day's combat, the Confederates broke off fighting late in the afternoon and retreated to Corinth.

Shiloh was easily the bloodiest battle yet fought, one full of lessons and omens for the future. Killed and wounded numbered almost 20,000, evenly divided between the two sides. Even Grant was appalled. "I saw an open field," he recalled, "over which the Confederates had made repeated charges . . . , so covered with dead that it would have been possible to walk across the clearing, in any direction, stepping on dead bodies, without a foot touching the ground." The awful toll of casualties showed not only Grant's dereliction in failing to entrench his army, but the risks of assaulting rifle-armed defenders, even when they were unentrenched. At the same time, the South's very willingness to attack awakened the North to the magnitude of the task before it. As Grant remarked after the war:

> Up to the battle of Shiloh I, as well as thousands of other citizens, believed that the rebellion against the Government would collapse suddenly and soon, if a decisive victory could be gained over any of its armies. [Forts] Donelson and Henry were such victories. An army of more than 21,000 men was captured and destroyed. . . . But when Confederate armies were collected which not only attempted to hold a line farther south . . . , but assumed the offensive and made such a gallant effort to regain what had been lost, then, indeed, I gave up all idea of saving the Union except by complete conquest.

While Grant and Buell were engaged in southwestern Tennessee, other Federal forces were active in opening the Mississippi River. In April, Flag Officer David Farragut's fleet transported 18,000 troops commanded by General Benjamin F. Butler up the river and captured New Orleans; by mid-May he had taken Baton Rouge as well. Meanwhile, Union forces had swept aside Southern defenses on the upper Mississippi all the way to Memphis. By August only the 150-mile stretch between Vicksburg, Mississippi, and Port Hudson, Louisiana, remained in Confederate hands.

In the wake of Shiloh, General Halleck took personal command of his combined forces and followed the Confederates to Corinth. Averaging less than a mile a day, owning to muddy roads and Halleck's decision to entrench at every stop, the 120,000-man army occupied this important rail center late in May, taking 2,000 prisoners. At this point, however, Halleck let all the steam out of the Federals' western offensive by scattering his forces and wasting the talents of his best general,

Ulysses Grant. The aggressive Grant was assigned to hold Memphis and western Tennessee while the cautious Buell received orders to advance on Chattanooga, repairing the Memphis and Charleston Railroad as he went.

While Grant stood still and Buell crawled eastward, the Confederates seized the initiative. Late in July, General Braxton Bragg, the new commander of the Army of Tennessee, transferred 35,000 troops from Mississippi to Chattanooga by railroad, outflanking the slow-moving Buell. From there he struck north into Kentucky. Together with a smaller Confederate force under Major General Edmund Kirby Smith, Bragg hoped to cut Buell's supply line to Louisville, force him back to the Ohio River, and into a fight on Bragg's terms. It was a well-conceived plan, made all the stronger by Buell's tardiness in realizing that Bragg's objective was Kentucky and not Nashville. Yet though Kirby Smith captured Lexington and Frankfurt early in September and Bragg occupied Munfordsville, athwart Buell's rail link to Louisville, two weeks later, the Confederate offensive quickly unraveled. Enjoying independent departmental commands, Kirby Smith and Bragg cooperated imperfectly, and a tactical blunder by Bragg permitted Buell to slip past him to Louisville. On October 8 the Federals pitched into Bragg's army at Perryville. Although the outcome was essentially a draw, Bragg afterward retreated into middle Tennessee. There (December 31, 1862 to January 2, 1863), at Stone's River near Murfreesboro, he fought an equally indecisive but much bloodier battle against Buell's successor William S. Rosecrans and the renamed Army of the Cumberland. Casualties exceeded even those at Shiloh and months would pass before either army saw action again. By assuming the tactical offensive and failing to entrench his troops, Bragg threw away lives that might have been saved—lives the South now found it nearly impossible to replace. "Our maximum strength has been mobilized," Jefferson Davis worried, "while the enemy is just beginning to put forth his might."

Grant, meanwhile, had resumed offensive operations designed to give the United States complete control of the Mississippi River, cutting the South in two. The Union blockade was now becoming effective, and, it was believed, if the eastern Confederacy could be isolated from its trans-Mississippi sources of supply its ability to wage war would be seriously curtailed. Grant's primary objective was Vicksburg, dubbed the "Gibraltar of the West" because of its commanding position atop high bluffs overlooking the Mississippi. At first all went badly. Grant's own attempt to approach Vicksburg from the east had to be aborted when in December Rebel cavalry ripped up rail lines in Tennessee and destroyed his main supply depot at Holly Springs, Mississippi. (The

Holly Springs raid netted a distinguished prisoner, Mrs. Grant, whom the Confederates quickly and courteously released.) Soon afterward the Confederates savagely repulsed what was to have been a coordinated assault by William Tecumseh Sherman's troops at Chickasaw Bayou, just north of Vicksburg.

Grant nonetheless persevered. After joining forces with Sherman at Milliken's Bend on the west bank of the river some 12 miles above Vicksburg, he rethought the question of how best to reach his objective. Conventional wisdom said that he should return to Memphis, fortify it as his base of supply, and move south again by railroad. But ever since he was a boy Grant had preferred roundabout hikes to turning back; there would be no turning back now. A withdrawal to Memphis, he reasoned, would demoralize the North. "There was nothing left to be done but to *go forward to a decisive victory.*" All winter Grant experimented with ways to get below Vicksburg "without an apparent retreat." A canal across a bend in the Mississippi, a channel to the Red River, two expeditions to the upper Yazoo River—all failed to get him where he wanted to be: on high ground east of the river.

By April of 1863, however, Grant had readied a brilliant new plan which secured his reputation as the most daring, dogged, and resourceful general in the Union army. Marching his troops down the swampy western shore of the Mississippi, he sent Admiral David Dixon Porter's fleet of ironclad gunboats and three cargo steamers past Vicksburg's batteries on the night of April 16–17. Simultaneously, Colonel Benjamin Grierson began a diversionary cavalry raid through the length of Mississippi which thoroughly distracted the Confederates and disrupted their communications. On April 30 Porter's ships ferried Grant's troops across the Mississippi, some 35 miles below Vicksburg. With lightning swiftness, Grant then struck inland. In less than three weeks, living off the land, his army marched 200 miles, fought and won five battles, prevented attempts to reinforce Vicksburg's defenders, and placed the city under siege. In the process it inflicted half again as many casualties upon the enemy as it suffered itself. On July 4, after six weeks of siege — during which those in the bombarded city burrowed like moles into the earth and came to subsist on mule steak, stewed cats, and even cooked rats—the Confederate commander John C. Pemberton surrendered Vicksburg, nearly 30,000 men, 172 cannon, more than 50,000 rifles and muskets, and huge quantities of ammunition. Four days later Port Hudson fell to Federal forces under Major General Nathaniel P. Banks. "The Father of Waters," Abraham Lincoln rejoiced, "again goes unvexed to the sea."

To the Confederates, the practical consequences of losing control of the Mississippi counted for less than Pemberton's loss of men and materiel. For a year or more the two halves of the Confederacy had functioned largely independently of one another, with regard to both logistical and strategic interaction. It has even been suggested that "except for psychological and domestic political advantages, the conquest of the Mississippi proved almost a white elephant," since it meant "more territory to be guarded." The loss of Pemberton's entire army, on the other hand, coming on top of Lee's 28,000 casualties at Gettysburg, represented an almost insurmountable setback for the South.

Having accomplished one of its major objectives in the West—the opening of the Mississippi—the North shifted its attention to east Tennessee. Lincoln's hopes for the liberation of that region and its use as a sally port for an invasion of the lower South had thus far come to naught. For six months following his bloody victory at Stone's River, Rosecrans remained at Murfreesboro, refusing to budge even when Halleck urged an advance to relieve pressure on Grant in Mississippi. When at last he did break camp, however, Old Rosy moved rapidly and with considerable finesse. With only minuscule casualties he managed to maneuver Bragg's army out of middle Tennessee and, on September 9, to occupy Chattanooga. A week earlier Federal troops under the resilient Ambrose Burnside took possession of Knoxville.

Although Union hopes soared, the Confederates had no intention of abandoning Tennessee without a fight. Instead, in one of the few successful interdepartmental concentrations of the war, elements of General Longstreet's corps—traveling by train from Virginia—and detachments from two western armies reinforced Bragg in northern Georgia and prepared a counterblow. When Rosecrans pressed southward, the Confederates furiously attacked him at Chickamauga Creek on September 19-20. Possessing for once numerical advantage over the enemy, the gray army crushed the Union right flank and sent it streaming toward Chattanooga. Only the stiff resistance of George H. Thomas's corps averted a wholesale rout, and under cover of darkness it too fell back. Chickamauga (an Indian term meaning "river of death") proved an inconclusive and costly victory for the South. Confederate casualties in this, the war's bloodiest two-day battle, totaled 18,434—more than a quarter of those engaged—and escaping Yankee prisoners reported "rebel soldiers as saying that a few more such battles will kill them all off." Bragg himself seemed unnerved by his losses, and to the disgust of several subordinate commanders allowed the fruits of this "sanguinary victory to pass from him by the most criminal negligence." Rather than risk assault against a still-dangerous enemy, Bragg occupied strong positions on Missionary Ridge and Lookout Mountain overlooking Chattanooga and placed the city under siege.

Worse for the Confederates than Bragg's understandable restraint in pursuing his victory was the shake-up Chickamauga produced within Union ranks. Jarred into an awareness of the vulnerability of dispersed, independent armies, in October Lincoln and Halleck placed Ulysses Grant in command of a new Military Division of the Mississippi, comprising the Armies of the Ohio, the Cumberland, and the Tennessee. Grant at once named General Thomas to replace Rosecrans (who, said Lincoln, had become "confused and stunned like a duck hit on the head") and hastened to Chattanooga to break Bragg's hammerlock. He was joined there by two corps from the Army of the Potomac, led by Joseph Hooker, and four divisions from his old Army of the Tennessee, under its new commander William T. Sherman. By October 27 the Federals had cleared a "cracker line" to supply the beleaguered city and on November 24–25 they stormed up Lookout Mountain and Missionary Ridge, driving the Rebels back into Georgia. Soon afterward, General Longstreet abandoned his brief investment of Knoxville. The back door to the Confederacy stood wide open.

IV

Abraham Lincoln had long held Grant in high esteem. "I can't spare this man," the president had declared after the Battle of Shiloh, "he fights." The Vicksburg campaign ("one of the most brilliant in the world," Lincoln called it) and the triumph at Chattanooga raised Grant's stock higher still, throughout the North. In March 1864, therefore, the president promoted Grant to the newly revived rank of lieutenant general and named him commander in chief of all Union armies. Sherman took Grant's place in the West and Halleck dutifully accepted the new position of chief of staff, mediating between Grant and his civilian superiors (Lincoln and Stanton) above and field commanders below.

With a reorganized command structure and a shrewd, hard-driving commanding general in place, the North was at last prepared to make the most of its superior resources. Grant's grand strategy was like the man himself: simple, direct, and, in the end, overpowering. Riding herd on Meade's Army of the Potomac, he would constantly assail Lee — wearing down his army and preventing him from sending reinforcements to the West. "Lee's army will be your objective point," he instructed Meade. "Wherever Lee goes, there you will go also." At the same time, western armies would swing through the Deep South, hitting the enemy, cutting railroads, destroying war resources, and demoralizing the Southern people. In keeping with the concept of taxing the Confederacy's limited resources by applying pressure at many points, Grant proposed "a simultaneous movement all along the line" on May 5, 1864. The primary advances, by Meade in Virginia and Sherman in Georgia, were to be supported by three collateral offensives. Nathaniel Banks was to lead 30,000 men against Mobile and thence inland; Benjamin F. Butler was to approach Richmond below the York-James peninsula; and Franz Sigel was to strike up the Shenandoah Valley, "covering the North from an invasion through the channel" and seizing or destroying supplies needed by Lee. As Lincoln, delighted at finding his own ideas embedded in this plan, observed, "Those not skinning can hold a leg."

Although the leg-holders botched their assignments, the skinning went pretty much as planned. Banks became embroiled in an expedition up the Red River and never got started to Mobile. Butler's incompetence soon had his army pinned between the James and Appomattox rivers, "as completely shut off from further operations directly against Richmond," fumed Grant, "as if it had been in a bottle strongly corked." And not until "Fighting Phil" Sheridan replaced the inept Sigel did the Federals in the Shenandoah Valley become an effective force. Between the tough and well-fought armies of Grant and Sherman, however, the North had all it needed to win the war.

The turning point in the East came early. Crossing the Rapidan on May 4, Grant hoped to maneuver Lee out of his entrenchments by slipping around his right flank. Before he could do so, however, Lee surprised him in the Wilderness. There dense, dank woods and matted undergrowth negated the Union's numerical advantage, rendered its artillery all but useless, and enabled the Confederates to stop the Yankees cold. After two days (May 5-6) of some of the most desperate, often hand-to-hand, fighting of the war Grant had lost nearly 18,000 men, more than double the Confederates' total. It was a depressing situation, all too familiar to the courageous soldiers in the Army of the Potomac. Most expected yet another retreat. But Grant was no Hooker, Burnside, Pope, or McClellan, and when on the seventh of May the army reached the crossroads at Chancellorsville it turned not northward but to the South—toward Spotsylvania Court House and Richmond beyond. "Our spirits rose," one private recalled. "We . . . began to sing. . . . That night we were happy."

For the next five weeks Billy Yank and Johnny Reb fought almost continuously—at Spotsylvania, North Anna, Totopotomy Creek, and Cold Harbor—as Grant sought repeatedly to turn the enemy's right wing and place his army between Lee and Richmond. Desperately and skillfully, Lee fought him off. "We must destroy this army of Grant's before he gets to the James River," he declared. "If he gets there, it will become a siege, and then it will be a mere question of time." Yet though the Confederates inflicted hideous casualties upon the Federals (especially at Cold Harbor where Grant's ill-advised frontal assault left 12,000 killed or wounded, with 7,000 falling in less than an hour), Lee was unable to prevent Grant from crossing the James and laying siege to Petersburg, a vital railway junction south of Richmond. Moreover, Lee's own losses in the campaign from the Wilderness to Petersburg had been heavy—in fact, proportionally heavier—than Grant's. As Grant justifiably remarked afterward, "Lee had to fight as much as I did, . . . every blow I struck weakened him, and when at last he was forced into Richmond it was a far different army from that which menaced Washington and invaded Maryland and Pennsylvania. It was no longer an invading army. The Wilderness campaign was necessary to the destruction of the Southern Confederacy."

Meanwhile, Sherman's army of 100,000 battle-tested Westerners moved out of Chattanooga and advanced along the Western and Atlantic Railroad toward Atlanta. Facing them were some 60,000 Confederate troops, commanded now by Joseph E. Johnston, a master of defensive tactics. Sherman, a relentless but careful fighter, preferred a campaign of maneuver to one of direct confrontation and Johnston was only too glad to oblige. As Sherman repeatedly turned the Confederates' flank and threatened their supply line southward, Johnston fell back from one prepared position to the next, husbanding his army's strength and waiting for the right moment to strike a punishing blow. Only once, when he attacked the Rebel breastworks at Kennesaw Mountain on June 27 at a cost of 2,000 dead and wounded, did Sherman play into Johnston's hand, and it was not nearly enough to stem the Yankee invasion. By early July Sherman's army had reached the outskirts of Atlanta.

Unhappy at Johnston's reluctance to give battle or even to reveal his plans, Jefferson Davis now replaced him with John Bell Hood. A sad-eyed, battle-scarred West Pointer, Hood was famous for his reckless courage, his eagerness to attack. "All lion, none of the fox," was Robert E. Lee's estimation of him. True to his reputation, Hood at once lashed out at the Federals. In three battles fought at the end of July—Peachtree Creek, Atlanta, and Ezra Church—Hood threw his troops against well-entrenched Union lines, without success and with casualties double those of the enemy. Davis thereupon instructed Hood to avoid further life-squandering assaults and the Confederates withdrew to Atlanta. (One Rebel soldier fleeing to the rear was accosted by a

Georgia officer who asked, "What are you running for?" Without breaking stride the soldier replied, "Bekase I kaint fly!") A month later, Sherman destroyed the Confederates' rail communications to the south and, fearful of being trapped, Hood abandoned Atlanta on the night of September 1–2. Next day the Stars and Stripes flew in this vitally important Southern city and Sherman proudly telegraphed Washington: "Atlanta is ours, and fairly won."

The stage was now set for the most daring operation of the war. After chasing Hood in northern Georgia for a month, Sherman hit upon a more promising plan of action. Leaving General Thomas at Nashville with enough troops to defend the Tennessee River line against Hood, he proposed marching his army through Georgia to the sea. "Until we can repopulate Georgia, it is useless for us to occupy it," he explained to Grant, "but the utter destruction of its [rail]roads, houses, and people, will cripple their military resources. . . . I can make this march, and make Georgia howl!" Such a raid promised psychological dividends as well. In marching "a well-appointed army" through the very heart of Rebeldom, carrying off slaves and laying waste to the countryside, the Federals would demoralize Southerners, Sherman declared, by giving the lie to their government's "promise of protection."

Grant at first reacted coolly to Sherman's proposal, thinking it better "to entirely ruin" Hood before striking south. Lincoln, too, confessed himself "anxious, if not fearful" over the risky venture. Once assured that Thomas could take care of Hood, however, they let Sherman put his plan in motion. On the morning of November 15, after setting Atlanta ablaze, Sherman's men moved out, 62,000 strong, bound for the Atlantic coast. Foraging "liberally on the country" and encountering meager opposition, the high-spirited Yankees reached Savannah a month later, having cut a swath of destruction 60 miles wide through previously untouched, harvest-rich Georgia. Hood, meanwhile, obliged the Yankees by launching a suicidal assault against a powerful, dug-in Union detachment at Franklin, Tennessee, on November 30. Though his losses (which included five generals killed, one captured, and six wounded) were thrice those of the Federals, he rashly pressed onward, laying nominal siege to Thomas's army at Nashville. With 50,000 men to Hood's 23,000, Thomas was in little danger. On December 15–16 he attacked and sent the Army of Tennessee reeling in defeat, no longer an effective fighting force. By the time it found sanctuary in Mississippi, Hood's once-proud legion of 51,000 had withered away to barely 15,000 tattered, pinch-cheeked survivors—a ruinous decline to which his own tactical errors had contributed much.

Having ransacked a goodly portion of Georgia and presented

Savannah to Lincoln "as a Christmas gift," Sherman paused long enough to rest his troops and stockpile supplies. By February 1865 he was off again, following Grant's instructions to "break up the railroads in South and North Carolina, and join the armies operating against Richmond." Moving swiftly and deceptively, avoiding battle when possible, Sherman swept northward "like a full developed cyclone," a Confederate cavalry officer remembered, "leaving behind him a track of desolation and ashes fifty miles wide. In front of them was terror and dismay." On February 17 the Federals reached and burned Columbia, South Carolina. By mid-March, having crushed the Confederates' last-ditch counterattack at Bentonville, North Carolina, Sherman's "dirty, ragged, and saucy" Westerners stood between Raleigh and the coast, ready to join Grant's army in the trenches around Petersburg and Richmond.

Before that could happen, however, Lee had bowed to the inevitable and surrendered his ragged army to Grant at Appomattox Court House on April 9, 1865. Grant's siege, the destruction or interdiction of essential supplies by Sherman and Sheridan, and the closing in January of Wilmington, North Carolina, the Confederacy's last open port, had all put heavy pressure on Lee's army. Disease, desertion, and Lee's reckless assault of Fort Stedman on Grant's right flank (March 25) had thinned already depleted ranks. Morale sank, especially in units from regions plundered by Sherman's army, and many anticipated their commander in resigning themselves to defeat. "There are a good many of us who believe this shooting match has been carried on long enough," one soldier asserted in January. "A government that has run out of rations can't expect to do much more fighting, and to keep on in a reckless and wanton expenditure of human life." Persuaded that the Confederacy's last chance lay in uniting his forces with those opposing Sherman in North Carolina, Lee abandoned Richmond and Petersburg on the night of April 2–3 and headed west. He counted on the Richmond and Danville Railroad to make his escape, but Grant blocked that line of retreat. At last, his tatterdemalion army all but surrounded, Lee met Grant in Wilmer McLean's parlor and signed articles of surrender. Other Rebel armies would soon follow suit.

Five days later, on April 14, Major General Robert Anderson and a shipload of Northern dignitaries, including William Lloyd Garrison and Henry Ward Beecher, gathered at Fort Sumter to commemorate the war's beginning and celebrate its triumphant end. As the distinguished guests and some 4,000 others looked on, Anderson proudly raised the same "weather-beaten, frayed, and shell-torn old flag" he had lowered in defeat exactly four year earlier. "When the flag reached the apex," Garrison reported, "the whole bay thundered with such a volley of cannon from ship and shore, that one might imagine the old battle of the Monitors renewed again. Then we grasped hands, shouted, embraced, and wept for joy." Yet the rejoicing was soon tempered with sadness. That very evening, as he sat in Ford's Theater watching Laura Keene in *Our American Cousin,* Abraham Lincoln was fatally shot — as much a casualty of war as those who fell on the field of battle.

The Destruction
of Slavery

"If . . . [the South] pushes matters to a bloody issue," Senator James R. Doolittle of Wisconsin had predicted not long before the shots on Fort Sumter, "the disunion question and the slavery question may all find their solution & their end together." Events would prove Doolittle a sound prophet. Yet only gradually did the war to preserve the Union also become a war to free the slave. Northern Democrats made it clear from the start that "we are not fighting for negro freedom or negro abolition" but simply to restore the Union. Even most Republicans were at first reluctant to espouse emancipation in Southern states. It was only after military disasters like First Bull Run convinced Northerners that winning the war would require extraordinary measures, and after the loyalty of the border slave states was secure, that Republicans took steps to destroy slavery in the South.

Many doubtless hoped—even expected—that the war would somehow lead to emancipation, but at first both Congress and President Lincoln acted with a caution that radical abolitionists found maddening. In a letter to representatives of the Virginia secession convention written on the day Fort Sumter fell, Lincoln reaffirmed his earlier pledge that "I have no purpose, directly or indirectly, to interfere with the institution of slavery in the States where it exists. I believe I have no lawful right to do so, and I have no inclination to do so." Likewise, when at the emergency session of Congress in July 1861 Representative John J. Crittenden of Kentucky and Senator Andrew Johnson of Tennessee introduced resolutions disclaiming any intention of meddling with "the rights or established institutions" of the South, Republicans gave overwhelming approval. In the Senate the vote was 30 to 5, with Charles Sumner abstaining; in the House only Pennsylvania's Thaddeus Stevens dissented. Typical, even of radical Republican opinion at this time, was the speech of Senator John P. Hale of New Hampshire. "I, for one," he told his colleagues, "have . . . repeatedly avowed my sentiments to be that the Government had . . . no more legal or constitutional authority to interfere with slavery in the States than they had to interfere with the condition of the serfs in Russia, or the rights and wrongs of the laboring classes in England."

By the time the first regular session of the Civil War Congress convened in December 1861, however, Hale and most other Republican congressmen had embraced the need for a tougher stand against slavery. The House of Representatives gave an early indication of its growing radicalism by refusing to reaffirm Crittenden's disclaimer resolution; the Senate neglected even to discuss it. To Wisconsin's Timothy Howe it seemed that a powerful faction was already forming whose watchword was "Emancipation—the utter extinction of slavery." "The old Chiefs of Abolition," he observed in mid-December, "are in the very midsummer of a rich revenge."

Behind this heightened hostility toward slavery lay a sharper recognition of slavery's practical consequences. Experience was teaching that although one might in theory distinguish between a war to preserve the Union and a war to eradicate slavery, in practice the distinction soon blurred. Northern military officers quickly discovered that whether they liked it or not there was no way to dodge the slavery issue. As Yankee forces moved south, freedom-hungry bondsmen flocked into their camps or sought sanctuary aboard Federal naval vessels. What was to be done with these runaways—many of them engaged in erecting Confederate batteries and earthworks, and all at least indirectly buttressing the Southern war effort? Were they to be treated as contraband property, confiscated, and perhaps in time set free? Or were they to be denied asylum, even returned to their masters? Recognizing the question to be "one of very serious magnitude," Union commanders improvised often conflicting policies and sought guidance from their civilian superiors. Secretary of War Simon Cameron developed instructions which somewhat ambiguously opened Federal lines to black refugees, but in September President Lincoln countermanded General John C. Frémont's overly zealous proclamation which "declared freemen" all slaves of disloyal Missouri masters. It was inevitable that Congress should speak its mind as well.

Shaping the response of Congress to the problem of slavery and war were the battlefield disasters of 1861 and early 1862. A bloody Union defeat at Ball's Bluff, Virginia, on October 21, 1861—in which Colonel Edward Baker, a former senator and a friend of Lincoln, lost his life—coming so soon after the debacle at Bull Run, offered proof not only of bungling Northern generalship but of Southern spunk and resourcefulness. To crush the rebellion the North would need to do more than just flex its muscle. Already some were suggesting that one sure way to wreck the Confederate war machine was to strike hard at the institution of slavery. "It is often said that war will make an end of Slavery," Charles Sumner told the Republican state convention at Worcester, Massachusetts, on October 1. "This is probable. But it is surer still that overthrow of Slavery will make an end of the war." Similarly, another radical Republican later maintained that

> when the rebellion commenced, Mr. Lincoln and the Republican party and all those that undertook to defend the country . . . were sincere, honest, and earnest in their professions to leave existing things as they found them. But, sir, they could not do it. They found as the war progressed that slavery was the giant that stood in their way. They saw that slavery obstructed their efforts to preserve, maintain, and defend the nation's life, and they said, "If that is the alternative and it comes to this, that slavery or the nation must die, let slavery die."

Thus, beginning early in 1862 and continuing for the rest of the war there poured from the Capitol a stream of measures designed to cripple and eventually to crush slavery throughout the land. One of the first was an article of war, enacted in March 1862, forbidding the use of Union soldiers in the return of fugitive slaves. Aimed especially at Democratic generals such as Alexander McCook, who was so obliging in returning runaways that he received praise from the Confederate press, and at Henry Halleck's recent order denying fugitives sanctuary within his lines, this law freed no slaves, but it was clear that this was its intent. "It is an invitation to all such people to resort to the lines of the army as a harbor of refuge, a place of asylum, a spot where they can be safe from the operation of the undoubted legal rights of the owner," complained Senator James A. Pearce of Maryland. "It is not an act of emancipation in its terms; but . . . it leads directly to that result." The resounding defeat of an amendment exempting the slaves of border state masters from the terms of this article revealed the broad antislavery commitment of its sponsors. Yet while the measure strengthened the hand of those disposed to shelter runaway slaves, some military commanders managed to circumvent its spirit. One estimate puts at 20,000 the number of fugitives "either driven back or turned over to the rebels."

Congress struck a more direct blow against slavery the following month. Despite the caterwauling of slaveholders and the Washington city council's warning that emancipation would turn the capital "into an asylum for free negroes, a population undesirable in every american community," early in April Congress passed a bill abolishing slavery in the District of Columbia. In keeping with President Lincoln's known preferences, provision was made to compensate masters and to support the voluntary colonization of freedmen in Haiti or Liberia. Though pleased at these features and at the bill's objective (having himself proposed emancipation in the District, during his single term in Congress), Lincoln harbored small misgivings, notably over the failure to obtain Maryland's consent. For two days the bill lay on his desk unsigned, making him, said Sumner, "the largest slave-*holder* in this country." On April 16, however, the president set aside his doubts and signed this measure which, crowed the *National Anti-Slavery Standard,* marked "the Beginning of the End of Slavery."

Other antislavery legislation soon followed, legislation that revealed both a practical interest in crushing the rebellion and a humanitarian concern for the rights of black Americans. In May Congress provided for the education of black children in the District of Columbia. In June, again along nearly straight party lines, it abolished slavery in the territories—the basic tenet of political abolitionists for more than a generation. July brought even more radical and potentially far-reaching measures. The Militia Act of July 17 opened the door to the enlistment of black soldiers for the first time since the War of 1812 by authorizing the use of former slaves in "any military or naval service for which they may be found competent." At the time, Lincoln chose to interpret this authorization narrowly, permitting merely the employment of contrabands as laborers. But the act did set "forever free" the families of freedmen, formerly belonging to disloyal masters, who served the United States; and before long blacks would be welcomed as fighting men, thereby guaranteeing their freedom and strengthening the claims of their race to national citizenship.

Paired with the Militia Act and adopted on the same day was a drastic new law providing for the confiscation of Confederate property, including slaves. An earlier such statute, passed in August 1861, had merely confiscated (without setting free) those "chattels" actually employed in support of the rebellion. The Second Confiscation Act of July 17, 1862, went much further. Appealing to the "laws of war" and the power of Congress to punish treason, it proclaimed that all slaves of disloyal masters were to be "forever free of their servitude." Fugitives were guaranteed sanctuary within Union lines and the president again received authority to employ "persons of African descent" in any capacity deemed "necessary and proper for the suppression of this rebellion."

Although Democrats denounced its vindictive spirit, some antislavery advocates complained that the new confiscation act did not go far enough. Abolitionists protested the act's failure to touch the slaves of loyal masters and the slow, piecemeal legal proceedings required to obtain the freedom even of those belonging to disloyal owners. It was, Maria Weston Chapman grumbled, "an Emancipation bill with clogs on."

II

Abraham Lincoln's failure to enforce the new confiscation law vigorously and his insistence that it include provision for the voluntary colonization of freedmen outside the United States also upset radical abolitionists. "Stumbling, halting, prevaricating, irresolute, weak, besotted," William Lloyd Garrison said of the president's policy in a *Liberator* editorial on July 25. Yet although he kept it a secret — at first even from his cabinet — Lincoln had already decided to issue an executive proclamation emancipating all slaves in rebellious parts of the South.

The president had come to this momentous step slowly and deliberately, driven alike by changing circumstances and his own sense of moral and constitutional propriety. Certain that slavery was "a moral, social and political evil," a "monstrous injustice" which mocked the Declaration of Independence's promise of equality, Lincoln was only too willing to take a hand in its destruction. He as much as anyone had been responsible for the emphasis prewar Republicans gave to the *evil,* as well as the undesirability, of slavery and had considered free soil a legitimate way to bring about its "ultimate extinction." Although he shared much of the radical prejudice common among nineteenth-century whites, Lincoln displayed no personal repugnance for blacks and repeatedly expressed a willingness to accord them the inalienable rights guaranteed to all men by the Declaration of Independence.

As chief executive, however, facing first secession and then civil war, Lincoln felt constrained to move cautiously with regard to the South's peculiar institution. His first inaugural message not only disclaimed any intention of interfering with slavery in the states but announced his determination to enforce the Fugitive Slave Law. "We gather no comfort from the inauguration of Abraham Lincoln," noted one Negro newspaper. Even after Fort Sumter and the secession of the upper South, Lincoln's concern to hold border slave states in the Union and his respect for constitutional restraints on federal power inclined him to moderation. When, for example, on August 30, 1861, John C. Frémont boldly freed the slaves of all Confederate sympathizers in Missouri, Lincoln swiftly countermanded his order lest it "alarm our

Southern Union friends, and turn them against us." Likewise, when in May 1862 General David Hunter on his own hook set "forever free" slaves on the Union-occupied sea islands of South Carolina, the president promptly overruled him. He, too, wished "that all men everywhere, could be free." But, said Lincoln, it remained solely his responsibility to decide when, if ever, emancipation became essential "to the maintenance of the government." To his mind, the time had not yet come.

In revoking the actions of Frémont and Hunter, and in repudiating Secretary of War Cameron's recommendation in December 1861 that black "contrabands" be armed as soldiers, Lincoln courted censure from abolitionists and many radical Republicans. "Shame and confusion to the President for his halting, shuffling, backward policy!" Garrison stormed after the annulment of Hunter's edict. Already, however, Lincoln had initiated his own antislavery policy, one designed to reach the radicals' basic goals by less constitutionally assailable means.

His first step was to send Congress, on March 6, 1862, a request that financial compensation be given to "any state which may adopt gradual abolishment of slavery." Calling his proposition a "most efficient means of self-preservation," Lincoln argued that it would materially shorten the war by dashing Southern hopes that border slave states might eventually join the Confederacy. *Gradual* emancipation, he remarked without elaboration, was "better for all," and by leaving states "perfectly free" to accept or reject it Congress could avoid constitutional challenges. *Compensated* emancipation would enhance the plan's appeal to slaveholders and, by curtailing the war, prove itself cost-effective. While some antislavery extremists agreed with Thaddeus Stevens that it was "the most diluted, milk-and-water gruel proposition that was ever given to the American nation," most Republicans and even a few Democrats reacted warmly to Lincoln's proposal. Even so radical an abolitionist as Wendell Phillips at first thought well of it and a leading black newspaper praised its "half silent evidence of power and will to blast the institution of slavery at any moment."

Congress swiftly approved Lincoln's scheme for gradual, compensated emancipation, but the nearly solid opposition of border state representatives foretold trouble. Repeatedly during the spring and summer of 1862 the president urged citizens of the loyal slave states to accept the federal government's offer and set in motion some plan of emancipation. Failure to do so, he warned, would not only needlessly prolong the war, but risk the loss of slave property "by mere friction and abrasion," with "nothing valuable in lieu of it." To allay fears of emancipation, Lincoln offered assurances that change "would come gently as the dews of heaven, not rending or wrecking anything." Besides, he noted, the voluntary colonization of free Negroes in South America offered at least a partial solution to racial problems, for "when numbers shall be large enough to be company and encouragement for one another, the freed people will not be so reluctant to go." Much to the president's disappointment, however, the border South refused to implement emancipation on any terms. Rebuffed, Lincoln felt himself "driven," as he later explained, "to the alternative of either surrendering the Union, and with it, the Constitution, or of laying [a] strong hand upon the colored element. I chose the latter."

There were other reasons as well for Lincoln's decision in the summer of 1862 to lay a "strong hand" upon the South's peculiar institution. In the first place, the allegiance of the border states—Maryland, Delaware, Kentucky, and Missouri—was by then secure beyond doubt. Moreover, pressure from radical Republicans for a more aggressive emancipation policy had mounted steadily, and Lincoln was reluctant to alienate so powerful an element "whose support the country can not afford to lose," particularly since he personally favored its antislavery goal. Equally important, battlefield reverses—notably McClellan's failed Peninsula campaign—reinforced the argument that emancipation was justified as a war measure, a way of weakening the Confederacy and bolstering the North's manpower reserves. Finally, Lincoln wished to keep control of the slavery question as much in his own hands as possible, for he quite rightly understood that the manner of its handling would influence both the conduct of the war and the shape of the peace to come.

The president first revealed his decision to issue an emancipation proclamation in a supper-table conversation with Vice-President Hannibal Hamlin on June 18, 1862. In mid-July Lincoln broke the news to Secretary of State Seward and Secretary of the Navy Welles, and on July 22 he presented his Preliminary Emancipation Proclamation to the entire cabinet. Except for Seward and Welles, all were astonished at Lincoln's bold pronouncement. "The measure goes beyond anything I have recommended," Secretary of War Stanton noted. Treasury Secretary Salmon P. Chase preferred that military commanders make the announcement of freedom so as to reduce the likelihood of slave insurrections, but all except Postmaster General Montgomery Blair, who feared that the proclamation would hurt Republican candidates in the fall elections, expressed approval of Lincoln's message. Seward, now something of a conservative where slavery was concerned, offered the most practical suggestion. Repeated military disasters, he reminded the president, had so depressed "the public mind" that the issuance of so revolutionary a pronouncement at present might appear to be an act of desperation born of weakness — "the last *shriek* on our retreat." Much better, Seward said, to await military success before releasing the message. Lincoln agreed and for the moment returned it to his desk, now and then "touching it up . . . , anxiously watching the progress of events."

In the meantime, Lincoln kept his intentions secret from all but his cabinet despite the solicitations of conservatives who cautioned against interference with slavery and of radicals who sought emancipation. To a group of Chicago church leaders who presented him with a memorial asking for an end to slavery, the president replied with the words of a man whose mind was not yet made up. Admitting his right as commander in chief "to take any measure which may best subdue the enemy," and conceding that emancipation "would weaken the rebels by drawing off their laborers" and "help us in Europe," Lincoln nonetheless questioned the effectiveness of an executive proclamation against slavery. "Would *my word* free the slaves," he asked, "when I cannot even enforce the Constitution in the rebel States?" Would not an executive proclamation of emancipation be as ineffective as "the Pope's bull against the comet?" he asked. Not even Horace Greeley's thunderous editorial, "The Prayer of Twenty Millions," berating the president for his lackadaisical enforcement of the new confiscation act and demanding harsher antislavery action, moved Lincoln to reveal his plan. Though he reiterated his "oft-expressed *personal* wish that all men every where could be free," Lincoln replied to Greeley that his "*official* duty" was neither to save nor to destroy slavery, but to preserve the Union. "If I could save the Union without freeing *any* slave I would do it," he wrote, "and if I could save it be freeing *all* the slaves I would do it; and if I could save it by freeing some and leaving others alone I would also do that."

Such noncommital — even dissembling — statements served an educational purpose, for threaded cleverly through them ran a strong justification of the revolutionary step Lincoln was about to take. Emancipation, when it came, would rest on the firm constitutional ground of military necessity and preservation of the Union. And it would carry with it tangible gains as well as certain risks. Meanwhile, events — particularly Pope's defeat at Second Bull Run and Bragg's invasion of Kentucky — broadened support for emancipation throughout the North.

At last, McClellan's repulse of Lee at Antietam Creek gave the president the victory he was waiting for. On September 22, just four days after Lee's army retreated across the Potomac, Lincoln summoned his cabinet to the White House. He began what was for the most part a solemn occasion by reading aloud from the humorist Artemus Ward's

A High Handed Outrage at Utica. Lincoln chuckled, Chase managed a sickly smile, Stanton sat stone-faced. Having relieved the tension (or so he thought) the president then announced that although Antietam was not quite the victory he had hoped for, it nonetheless gave promise of better things to come. He therefore planned to go ahead and issue the Emancipation Proclamation in preliminary form, that is, as a warning to the Confederates that on January 1, 1863, all slaves in states or regions still "in rebellion against the United States shall be then, thenceforward, and forever free." Carelessly, Lincoln ordered military and naval authorities to do nothing to repress slaves in Confederate states "in any efforts they may make for their actual freedom." Meant simply to announce the government's unwillingness to enforce the Fugitive Slave Act, this passage could easily be construed as an invitation to servile insurrection and was dropped from the final proclamation of January 1, 1863.

By implication, the peculiar institution would be left untouched in states that returned to the Union before 1863, as well as in the loyal slave states. Lincoln did, however, vow to pursue a program of federal assistance to states that voluntarily adopted "immediate or gradual abolishment of slavery," together with efforts "to colonize persons of African descent" abroad. Despite the misgivings of some, Lincoln's advisors encouraged him to carry through with his brave new policy. Next morning, September 23, the Preliminary Emancipation Proclamation appeared in newspapers across the land.

Reaction to the president's manifesto was predictably mixed. At home, most Republicans and many abolitionists applauded it warmly. No one was more delighted than Lincoln's recent critic Horace Greeley. "It is the beginning of the end of the rebellion; the beginning of the new life of the nation," he cheered. "God bless Abraham Lincoln." Charles Sumner spoke for most congressional Republicans when he rejoiced: "Thank God, the skies are brighter and the air is purer, now that slavery has been handed over to judgment." David Tod, the Democratic governor of Ohio, hailed "every word and syllable of it," and even those who thought it too narrow saw the proclamation as a step in the right direction. "How decent Abe grows," declared Wendell Phillips. Northern blacks rarely quibbled over the manifesto's shortcomings—its restriction to rebellious states, hundred-day grace period, and talk of gradual, compensated emancipation in the loyal South—preferring instead to applaud its promise of freedom. "We shout for joy that we live to record this righteous decree," Frederick Douglass proclaimed. The war, he wrote, was now "invested with sanctity."

Precisely because it added a new, humanitarian dimension to the war, the Emancipation Proclamation provoked angry dissent from most Democrats and some conservative Republicans. Lincoln himself acknowledged resistance to it in a letter ("Strictly private") to Vice-President Hamlin on September 28. "It is six days old," he observed, "and while commendation in newspapers and by distinguished individuals is all that a vain man could wish, the stocks have declined, and troops come forward more slowly than ever. . . . The North responds to the proclamation sufficiently in breath; but breath alone kills no rebels."

Northern Democrats denounced Lincoln's pronouncement in often violent language and made it the central issue in the forthcoming congressional elections. The president's new policy, they charged, unfairly and unconstitutionally changed the war's object from reunion to abolition. In its misguided solicitude for the rights of Southern blacks, the proclamation trampled on the liberties of white Americans. By menacing the South's social system and "inaugurating servile war," it was bound to stiffen Confederate resistance and thus prolong the fighting. Some, like Congressman S. S. Cox of Ohio, played upon racial fears, warning that Yankee soldiers might lose heart if their sacrifices resulted in a northerly migration of "millions of blacks." The virulence of the racial and political hatred that fueled Democratic castigation of the Emancipation Proclamation is apparent in a "Lincoln Epitaph," published in Ohio's *Logan County Gazette* and reprinted throughout the Confederacy:

> Beneath this stone, corrupt and stinking,
> Repose the bones of Abraham Lincoln.
> He freed the niggers, and for his pains
> His own old soul is now in chains.

Although by no means a clear-cut referendum on Lincoln's antislavery program — military reverses, tax hikes, inflation, and curtailment of civil liberties also influenced voters' choices — the results of the fall elections in 1862 suggested that the Emancipation Proclamation had as many Northern critics as friends. In New York, Pennsylvania, Ohio, Indiana, and Illinois — all states carried by Lincoln in 1860 — Democrats polled popular majorities and captured a majority of congressional seats. New Jersey again went Democratic and Wisconsin sent an equal number of Democrats and Republicans to Congress. Although the proclamation may have helped Republican candidates in New England, northern Ohio, and Michigan, it appears to have hurt them elsewhere. "Of Lincoln's emancipation . . . one still sees no effect up to the present," the German socialist Karl Marx noted in mid-November, "save that from fear of a Negro inundation the Northwest has voted Democratic." Lincoln, admitting that his edict contributed to the election outcome, took this setback in stride. He felt, he said, like a boy who had stubbed his toe: too big to cry but too pained to laugh.

The Confederates, of course, although pleased at the dissension the Emancipation Proclamation produced in Northern ranks, were outraged at its terms. It was, they roared, an "Insurrection Proclamation," "a most infamous attempt to incite flight, murder, and rapine on the part of our slave population." Before long such fears subsided, as overt uprisings failed to materialize. The manifesto "is causing some trouble among the bad . . . [ones]," a Louisiana planter wrote in May 1863, "but there is no alarm." At the time, however, the Confederate Senate entertained a resolution providing that captured Federal soldiers should be assumed to have come "with intent to incite insurrection and abet murder" and, unless they could prove otherwise, put to death. Nothing came of this proposal, nor did anything come of President Davis's promise to hand over captured Union officers to the states for indictment under statutes "for the punishment of criminals engaged in exciting servile insurrection." But both responses showed the depths of Southern fury and an acceptance of desperate measures to survive a total war.

Abroad, the effect of the proclamation was less positive than Lincoln had hoped and Southerners had feared. Though his overriding aim had been to shape domestic rather than foreign policy, the president expected that emancipation would curry favor with Europeans by convincing "them that we are incited by something more than ambition." Some did applaud Lincoln's "bold humanitarian act." But in the circles that counted—especially the British government—the initial reaction proved decidedly downbeat. Prime Minister Lord Palmerston scoffed that this "singular manifesto . . . could scarcely be treated seriously. It is not easy to estimate," he said, "how utterly powerless and contemptible a government must have become which could sanction . . . such trash." Lord John Russell, the foreign secretary, was but one of many who believed that the Emancipation Proclamation placed "a premium . . . [on] acts of plunder, of incendiarism, and of revenge."

In light of all the criticism and political backlash attending the proclamation, some wondered whether when New Year's Day came President Lincoln would fulfill his promise to make it final. He had scarcely mentioned it in his annual message to Congress on December 1, dwelling instead upon his recommendation that the Constitution be amended to permit congressional remuneration to all states that abolished slavery at any time before 1900 or provided for the voluntary colonization of free Negroes outside the United States. "If the President means to carry out his edict of freedom on the New Year, what is all this stuff about gradual emancipation?" fretted one abolitionist editor. In private interviews, however, Lincoln made plain his resolve. He "would rather die than take back a word of the Proclamation of Freedom," the president told a delegation of Kentucky Unionists. "There is no hope," conservative Republican Senator Orville H. Browning of Illinois lamented on December 31. "The proclamation will come."

True to his word, on New Year's Day, 1863, Abraham Lincoln proclaimed the freedom of all slaves in rebellious regions. Union-occupied parts of Louisiana and Virginia, the entire state of Tennessee, and all loyal slave states were exempted from this "fit and necessary war measure." Where the proclamation's writ did apply Lincoln urged slaves "to abstain from all violence, unless in necessary self-defense." At the same time, he not only called on the army and navy to protect the rights of those made free, but, by welcoming freedmen "into the armed service of the United States," gave blacks an active role in the liberation of their race. "I never, in my life, felt more certain that I was doing right than I do in signing this paper," Lincoln remarked in affixing his name to the document.

In a sense, it was true, as William Seward observed at the time, that the Emancipation Proclamation freed slaves beyond its compass and left them in chains where it might have had effect. At the moment of its issuance it liberated not a single slave. Yet Lincoln had cause to be proud of his handiwork and abolitionists to give it their blessing. Henceforth every foot of Confederate soil conquered by Federal armies would be soil forever closed to human bondage. And once slavery had toppled in the Cotton Kingdom, how could it possible survive in the border states? Besides, notwithstanding its prosaic language (fitting, Lincoln believed, for a decree issued in the name of military expediency), the Emancipation Proclamation inevitably added a moral dimension to the conflict. The Lincoln administration now stood securely "on the side of freedom, justice, and sound policy," James Russell Lowell noted happily:

> Thet's wut we want, — we want to know
> The folks on our side hez the bravery
> To b'lieve ez hard, come weal, come woe
> In Freedom ez Jeff doos in Slavery.

Without question, those most directly affected — the slaves — rejoiced as word of Lincoln's Freedom Proclamation reached them from advancing Yankee armies, angry Southern whites, or along the slave "grapevine." Thomas Wentworth Higginson, the white colonel of the first black regiment in the Union Army, the First South Carolina Volunteers, captured as well as anyone the meaning of emancipation to those enslaved in his account of events at Beaufort, South Carolina, on New Year's Day, 1863. Beaufort and other parts of the South Carolina sea islands had been occupied by Federal forces since the end of 1861, and on the day the Emancipation Proclamation took effect the Yankee invaders and sea island blacks gathered to mark the occasion. As Higginson recorded in his diary that evening, after William H. Brisbane, an antislavery emigré from South Carolina, had read the president's proclamation and the colors had been presented, there

> followed an incident so simple, so touching, so utterly unexpected and startling, that I can scarcely believe it on recalling, though it gave the keynote to the whole day. The very moment the speaker had ceased, and just as I took and waved the flag, which now for the first time meant anything to these poor people, there suddenly arose, close beside the platform, a strong male voice (but rather cracked and elderly), into which two women's voices instantly blended, singing, as if by an impulse that could no more be repressed than the morning note of the song-sparrow —
> "My Country, 'tis of thee,
> Sweet land of liberty,
>   Of thee I sing!"
> . . . Firmly and irrepressibly the quavering voices sang on, verse after verse; others of the colored people joined in . . . I never saw anything so electric; it made all other words cheap; it seemed the choked voice of a race at last unloosed. . . . When they stopped, there was nothing to do for it but to speak, and I went on; but the life of the whole day was in those unknown people's song.

The day of Jubilee had arrived.

During the course of the war an estimated 500,000 slaves swarmed into the lines of approaching Union armies, eager for the freedom — and unaware of the prejudice — that awaited them there. Even among those who for one reason or another remained on the "home place," deference and diligence waned while malingering, theft, and petty acts of insubordination mounted. "Slavery did not explode," concludes one historian; "it disintegrated."

III

With the promise of freedom came new challenges, responsibilities, and burdens for a race long enslaved. For black males of military age, Northern and Southern alike, the decision to recruit Negro soldiers and sailors created opportunities for personal advancement and service both to race and country—as well as hardship and danger.

Recruitment of black soldiers in fact preceded the authorization given in the Emancipation Proclamation. During the summer of 1862 military commanders in South Carolina, Louisiana, and Kansas formed black regiments from the slaves and free Negroes in their districts. For many reasons, however, the Lincoln administration at first overruled these actions. The military necessity of mustering in blacks had yet to be demonstrated, and the president's lingering fear of alienating loyal slave states made him doubly cautious. When on August 4, 1862, a deputation from Indiana called at the White House to offer two black regiments, Lincoln politely declined on the grounds "that to arm the negroes would turn 50,000 bayonets from the loyal Border States against us that were for us."

Many, including President Lincoln, at first doubted that blacks would made good soldiers. "Negroes—plantation negroes, at least— will never make soldiers in one generation," a Northern missionary in the sea islands of South Carolina contended in May 1862. "Five white men could put a regiment to flight." And in his meeting with western church leaders in September, Lincoln himself speculated that if freedmen were armed, "I fear that in a few weeks the arms would be in the hands of the rebels." Still others worried that the mustering of black men into the Union army would promote not only emancipation but an undesirable racial equality. A high-caliber black soldier was as much to be feared as a wretched one. "If you make him the instrument by which your battles are fought, the means by which your victories are won," cautioned one Ohio Democrat, "you must treat him as a victor is entitled to be treated, with all decent and becoming respect." That prospect a majority of Northerners, both Democrats and Republicans, found decidedly unappealing.

Yet it was not long before arguments in favor of black enlistments shouldered such views aside. Most decisive was the same dawning awareness of the North's military predicament which lay behind the Emancipation Proclamation proper. As battlefield setbacks followed thick and fast, as casualty lists mounted, desertions soared, and enlistments fell off, opposition to a black soldiery waned. "I wish that *loyal slaves might be armed for the conflict,*" wrote a Syracuse minister who had lost a son in the Peninsula campaign. "I am a known friend of the coloured people, but I am not such *'a negro worshiper'* as to wish to keep *them* out of all danger, when the interests of a common humanity demand that they should stand side by side with us—their white brethren." Even bitter racists grew to appreciate the utility of putting blacks in uniform. "If a bob-tail dog can stick a bayonet on his tail, and back up against a rebel and kill him, I will take the dog and sleep with him" said one Federal officer, "and if a nigger will do the same, I'll do the same by him. I'll sleep with any thing that will kill a rebel." The unwelcome Conscription Act of March 1863 added support for the proposition that a black man could stop a bullet as well as any white. As "Private Miles O'Reilly" explained in "Sambo's Right to be Kilt," a widely popular song by the Irish-American poet, journalist, and army officer Charles G. Halpine:

> Some tell us 'tis a burnin shame
> To make the naygers fight;
> An' that the thrade of bein' kilt
> Belongs but to the white;
> But as for me, upon my soul!
> So liberal are we here,
> I'll let Sambo be murthered instead of myself
> On every day in the year.

In time the proficiency of black troops in combat confirmed for all but the most bigoted the wisdom of giving them arms.

Reflecting this shift in popular sentiment, the Lincoln administration set about to recruit black soldiers, haltingly at first (beginning in the sea islands of South Carolina), more efficiently and wholeheartedly after the spring of 1863. From the start this enterprise had the enthusiastic backing of most black leaders in the North. No sooner had Fort Sumter fallen than Frederick Douglass proposed formation of *"a liberating army"* of *"slaves and free colored people"* to bring the war to a swift conclusion. Ten thousand black soldiers might easily be assembled in a month, he maintained, and throughout the North black spokesmen sought the government's permission to raise regiments from among their people. By 1863 black recruiters, including Martin R. Delany, Henry Highland Garnet, John Mercer Langston, and Douglass himself, blanketed the North, heartened by Negro conventions like the one in New York which resolved that "more effective remedies ought now to be *thoroughly* tried, in the shape of warm lead and cold steel, duly administered by two hundred thousand black doctors."

Black participation was important, such men insisted, not just to strengthen the Union war effort but to bolster racial confidence and pride. "Liberty won by white men would lose half its luster," Frederick Douglass advised potential black recruits. "You owe it to yourself and your race," he told them, "to rise from your social debasement and take your place among the soldiers of your country, a man among men. . . . You will stand more erect, walk more assured, feel more at ease, and be less liable to insult than you ever were before. He who fights the battles of America may claim America as his country—and have that claim respected." Military service also offered instruction in the use of arms—valuable in defense of person and race, and in exacting vengeance against slaveholders.

Although Northern blacks responded enthusiastically to such appeals, the free states' pool of roughly 46,000 military-age black males was much too small to satisfy the Union's manpower needs. Early in 1863, therefore, Secretary of War Stanton augmented recruiting efforts already under way in South Carolina's sea islands by assigning three Federal generals to supervise slave enlistments in Louisiana, coastal North Carolina, and the upper Mississippi Valley, and by stepping up recruitment within the border states.

Since the Emancipation Proclamation had no effect beyond the Confederacy, slaves in Delaware, Maryland, Kentucky, and Missouri readily perceived that military service offered the quickest, surest path to freedom, and despite the risks involved large numbers ran off to enlist. Slaveholders, understandably distressed at this threat to their labor force, used both carrot and stick to keep blacks at home. Some offered wages or share-crop privileges to keep bondsmen content; others sought to discourage enlistments by making flight difficult (for example, by locking up clothing at night) and by whipping, harassing, and even selling, the families of those who did enlist. In the end, the slaves' desire for freedom and the Union's needs for troops won out over the slaveholders' claims to their chattels—partly because nonslaveholding whites backed black enlistments as a painless way to meet Federal draft quotas. Maryland abolished slavery in October 1864 and Missouri followed suit early the following year. Well before then, however, black enlistment had undermined slavery in all the border states.

In the Confederacy (except for Tennessee) freedom came with the arrival of blue-clad armies and offered no inducement to slave enlistment. As a result, recruiters in the Deep South found it hard to meet their quotas. Not infrequently press gangs—sometimes made up of black soldiers—descended on plantations without warning and carried off to the army every able-bodied male slave they could find. A Virginia black, himself forcibly recruited by "a number of colored soldiers, armed," told of other men "being obliged to 'tote' balls" or "being confined in the guard house on hard bread & water" because they refused to enlist. A good many bondsmen in the lower South, of course, needed no special incentive to join Mr. Lincoln's army and were only too happy to play the role of black liberator. One such was Sergeant Prince Rivers of the First South Carolina Volunteers who proudly exclaimed in November 1863, "Now we sogers are men—men de first time in our lives. Now we can look our old masters in de face. They used to sell and whip us, and we did not dare say one word. Now we ain't afraid, if they meet us, to run the bayonet through them."

In one way or another, and for one reason or another, Afro-Americans contributed significantly to the Union combat forces. As early as the summer of 1863 more than thirty black regiments were under arms, fourteen of them battle-ready; by October fifty-eight regiments had been mustered in; and by war's end 179,000 black soldiers (nearly 10 percent of the Union total) had donned the Yankee blue. Of these, some 33,000 had come from the free states, 42,000 from the loyal slave states, and nearly all the rest from the Confederacy. Confederate slave recruits, of course, represented a double bonus: a strengthening of the Northern army and a corresponding deterioration of Southern might.

Black recruits who expected equality in the ranks were most certainly disappointed. Though they faced the same danger, disease, loneliness, and boredom as their white comrades-in-arms, black soldiers encountered racial discrimination wherever they turned. Segregated in all-black regiments, they took their orders from white officers; with rare exceptions, the only blacks to obtain commissions were chaplains and surgeons. Although thousands of whites received commissions for having raised companies or regiments, or merely for being popular with the troops, the government declined to make an officer of even so prominent a black leader—and valuable recruiter—as Frederick Douglass.

Even more galling to black soldiers and their abolitionist allies was the pay differential between white and black troops. Despite the assurances of many recruiters that they would receive the same wages, rations, equipment, and bounties as other volunteers, black enlistees soon discovered that while white privates pulled down $13 a month *plus* clothing, all black soldiers regardless of rank were paid $10 a month, *minus* $3 for clothing—the rate established for military laborers by the Militia Act of 1862. Black fighting men understandably viewed this discriminatory wage policy, which paid white buck privates nearly twice as much as the most high-ranking black officers, as a gross injustice, and some went without pay rather than acquiesce in unequal treatment.

Their protests were vehement, continual, and, on at least two occasions, fatal. When some two dozen members of the black Fourteenth Rhode Island Heavy Artillery were sentenced to imprisonment at hard labor for refusing to accept their inferior pay, a confrontation occurred between a white lieutenant and a black enlisted man in which the officer killed the soldier on the spot. Likewise, a sergeant in the Third South Carolina Volunteers was "shot to death by musketry" after a court-martial found him guilty of inciting mutiny for persuading his company of former slaves to lay down their arms until they received equal pay. White humanitarians, including some army commanders, joined blacks in the fight against pay discrimination, and in mid-June 1864 Congress at last provided impartial compensation to all Union soldiers.

The tardy equalization of pay by no means ended discrimination against black soldiers. Besides the ban on Afro-American officers, black troops still had to contend with patronizing interference in their personal lives from white liberals and ridicule and harsh punishment at the hands of more bigoted superiors. Throughout the conflict they found themselves excluded from military academies, denied representation in court-martial proceedings, and placed in frightful peril as prisoners of war. Confederate authorities considered black soldiers insurrectionists and angrily refused to so much as report their capture. Most black captives were placed in stockades, released to civilian authorities, or set to work on entrenchments and fortifications. But some were executed or enslaved, and not until the closing months of the war were black soldiers included in exchanges for Rebels held in Northern prisons.

Rather than deal with black prisoners at all, some Confederates made certain that none were taken. The most notorious of these was General Nathan Bedford Forrest, who on April 12, 1864, led an attack on Fort Pillow, Tennessee, in which hundreds of black soldiers were slaughtered as they tried to surrender. Afterward, Forrest boasted that the Mississippi River, which flowed beside the fort, "was dyed with the blood of the slaughtered for two hundred yards." The massacre, he trusted, would "demonstrate to the Northern people that negro soldiers cannot cope with Southerners." In July 1863 President Lincoln had pledged that for every Federal soldier killed "in violation of the laws of war" a Rebel prisoner would be executed, and that for every one enslaved a Confederate would be placed at hard labor. The difficulty, Lincoln confessed following the Fort Pillow bloodbath, lay "not in stating the principle, but in practically applying it," and neither then nor at any other time was retaliation taken. The Lincoln administration did, however, stop all prisoner exchanges in 1863 because of the Confederate government's refusal to include black soldiers in such swaps, and it may be that the mere threat of retaliation softened the South's treatment of black prisoners.

Discrimination against black soldiers, especially former slaves, also helped to shape the assignments they drew. Although yearning for an opportunity to display their courage and fighting spirit — their manhood — on the field of battle, black recruits commonly found themselves saddled with the most menial tasks. Admittedly, any soldier who entered the army after 1863 faced a greater likelihood of pulling guard or garrison duty, defending railroad junctions, bridges, and telegraph lines, digging trenches and constructing earthworks, or shielding contraband camps, than one who served early in the Civil War. Federal penetration of the South and the changing character of the war guaranteed that. Yet white doubts about the fighting capability of allegedly docile and servile "Africans" unquestionably resulted in a disproportionate assignment of black troops to noncombat duties. "Instead of the musket It is the spad and the Whelbarrow and the Axe," one black soldier complained in 1864.

Increasingly, however, the Union's pressing need for front-line troops offset white prejudices and gave black soldiers a chance to prove their mettle under fire. Most impartial observers seem to have agreed with President Lincoln that when tested they showed themselves to be "as good soldiers as any." In raids along the Carolina coast, in assaults on Fort Wagner near Charleston and on Port Hudson, Louisiana, in fierce action at Milliken's Bend, in General Banks's ill-fated Red River campaign, in Grant's bloody battles with Lee, and elsewhere, black troops displayed fighting qualities which won the respect even of many skeptics. "I never believed in niggers before," admitted one Wisconsin cavalry officer, "but by Jasus, they are hell for fighting." On occasion, the Rebels themselves offered grudging praise of black warriors. Following the battle at Milliken's Bend, Confederates reported that black soldiers had opposed their attack "with considerable obstinacy, while the white or true Yankee portion ran like whipped curs." Like white recruits, some blacks quailed under fire or even cut and ran. Most, however, stood their ground and some fought with a gallantry that earned them the nation's highest honor. Seventeen black soldiers and four black sailors received Congressional Medals of Honor.

The price of honor and respect was, of course, dear. Casualties among black troops totaled 68,178 — well over a third of those in uniform. But with the awful cost came substantial gain, not just for those who shouldered arms but for the entire black race. Military service carried with it the assumption of American citizenship, and pointed the way to such basic civic rights as the vote. President Lincoln admitted as much when in 1864 he recommended to the first free state governor of Louisiana that "some of the colored people . . . , especially those who have fought gallantly in our ranks," be given the right to vote. Once free to exercise their civic prerogatives, moreover, black veterans might draw on practical experience gained in the army. For petitions and protests against such abuses as unequal pay and discriminatory promotion policies not only schooled former slaves in the techniques of self-government but imparted something of the essence of democracy itself. And in those who had fought for the liberation of their race — especially the corporals and sergeants who had mediated between black privates and a predominantly white officer corps — Afro-Americans would find admired and experienced leaders for the struggles ahead. Former slaves also gained from military service rudimentary knowledge of the legal process, valuable lessons in coping with a money economy, and — usually for the first time — access to the three R's.

Above all, the enlistment of blacks in the U.S. Army and Navy gave a mighty fillip to the confidence and pride of a long-oppressed people. By joining in the overthrow of the slave Confederacy, by shedding their blood to free those in chains, black soldiers heightened the self-esteem of all black Americans. No one spoke more eloquently of this fact than Private Thomas Long, a former slave and lay chaplain in the First South Carolina Volunteers.

> We can remember, when we fust enlisted, [he reminded the regiment late in the war] it was hardly safe for we to pass by de camps to Beaufort and back, lest we went in a mob and carried sidearms. But we whipped down all dat — not by going into de white camps for whip um; we didn't tote our bayonets for whip um; but we lived it down by our naturally manhood; and now de white sojers take us by de hand and say Broder Sojer. Dats what dis regiment did for de Epiopian race.
>
> If we handn't become sojers, all might have gone back as it was before; our freedom might have slipped through de two houses of Congress and President Linkum's four years might have passed by and notin' been done for us. But now tings can neber go back, because we have showed our energy and our courage and our naturally manhood.
>
> Anoder ting is, suppose you had kept your freedom witout enlisting in dis army; your chilen might have grown up free and been well cultivated so as to be equal to any business, but it would have been always flung in dere faces — "Your fader never fought for he own freedom" — and what could dey answer? Never can say that to dis African Race any more.

IV

The Emancipation Proclamation by no means ended the Republican antislavery program. Attempts to extend the bounds of freedom and render it secure continued throughout the war and beyond. In loyal slave states untouched by Lincoln's liberating decree, Republicans kept up pressure for emancipation "in some substantial form." Lincoln's own hopes for gradual, compensated emancipation ran afoul of planter resistance, and by 1864 (after the failure of colonies established in Haiti and Central America) he had "sloughed off the idea of colonization" as an inducement to manumission. But the "friction and abrasion" of war—especially the flight of bondsmen to army lines and the recruitment of black soldiers—both weakened the peculiar institution and emboldened its border state critics. Even in Kentucky, which like Delaware withstood emancipation until the Thirteenth Amendment forced its hand, slavery lost vitality long before the Civil War had ended. The same corrosive forces also ate away at slavery in Tennessee and other portions of the Confederacy excluded from the Emancipation Proclamation.

During the war antislavery advocates also developed policies and programs designed to prepare former slaves for freedom and to demonstrate to the world that blacks could and would work outside the slave system. In the South Carolina sea islands, southern Louisiana, the Mississippi Valley, and elsewhere, Federal authorities put contrabands to work for wages. Some served the army and navy as cooks, laundresses, nurses, road builders, teamsters, woodchoppers, pilots, scouts, and the like. Most, however, continued to labor in the fields of abandoned and confiscated plantations, raising cotton or some other staple under the close supervision of white lessees or, on government-held lands, managers provided by Northern freedmen's aid societies. In the rarest of instances, the freedmen leased lands themselves. The best known and most successful such arrangement came at Davis Bend, Mississippi, where former slaves secured leases to six large plantations, including those of Jefferson Davis and his older brother Joseph.

Army commanders who set contraband policy were invariably more concerned with military efficiency than with the plight of the freedmen. Especially on the lands of profit-hungry private lessees, the transition from slave labor to free labor was often more apparent than real. Not only were wages often pitifully low ($7 a month for men and $5 a month for women was the going rate for agricultural workers in the lower Mississippi Valley in 1863) but deductions for clothing, sick time, and medical care left little for freedmen to spend as they wished. "The difference between working for nothing as a slave, and working for the same wages under the Yankees," one fair-minded white Northerner remarked, "was not always perceptible to the unsophisticated negro." Labor contracts, once signed, were to be honored for a full season; illness could lead to a loss of rations or pay; a worker needed a pass to leave his or her plantation; and provost marshals stood ready to compel "continuous and faithful service, respectful deportment, correct discipline and perfect subordination." Such a system, many abolitionists complained, substituted "serfdom for slavery."

Yet despite their shortcomings, abuses, and overt paternalism, wartime attempts to introduce former slaves to the workings of a free labor economy were sufficiently progressive to win the approval even of some radical abolitionists, among them William Lloyd Garrison. Gone, at least, was that hated symbol of servitude, the lash (and, often, gang labor). Skilled workers frequently commanded good wages, and if field hands were required to contract their services for a year at a stretch, they at least enjoyed the freedom to choose their employer. Paltry wages were an insult, but the allocation of substantial garden plots to black families offered some compensation. Likewise, provision for the schooling of black children was a welcome change, as indeed, was the very concept of voluntary, written, labor contracts.

In the Port Royal region off the coast of South Carolina the government undertook a still more radical experiment in black free enterprise. During the first planting season after the Union occupation of these sea islands in November 1861, former slaves worked the abandoned cotton plantations under the supervision of Yankee managers. Each received an extremely small wage—about $9 a year—and some also received small garden plots on which to grow food for themselves. After the 1862 harvest, however, the federal government decided that these lands would be sold in forfeiture of taxes left unpaid by their former, Rebel, owners. Some, among them the islands' military governor, General Rufus B. Saxton, and the Northern band of "Gideonites" who had gone to Port Royal to help the freedmen, urged that the lands be sold exclusively to blacks at nominal prices, payable in installments. Others contended that the freedmen were not yet ready for independent ownership and ought for a while longer to work as wage laborers under qualified, white supervisors.

Eventually, a compromise of sorts was reached. At the tax land sale which occurred in March 1863 some 60,000 acres were set aside by the government "for charitable purposes"—meaning for the future use of freedmen. Of the roughly 16,000 acres sold at auction (at an average price of $1 per acre) some 600 acres were bought by individual blacks and another 2,000 acres by groups of freedmen who had pooled their savings; the remaining 14,000 acres went to Northern interests, some of which subsequently passed into black hands.

Sea island blacks also gained small plots of their own under the terms of the Freedmen's Bureau Act of 1865 which permitted former slaves to preempt confiscated or abandoned lands, rent them cheaply for three years, and purchase them at any time within this period at a fair price. Still others gained small farms along the coast thanks to William Tecumseh Sherman's need to relieve his army of the thousands of black refugees who fled with it through Georgia. Taking the advice of black leaders in Savannah who told him that "the way we can best take care of ourselves is to have land," Sherman issued a special field order in January 1865 which set aside for the exclusive settlement of freedmen the Georgia–South Carolina sea islands and the coastal strip from Charleston to Jacksonville, Florida, extending 30 miles inland. Black families were permitted to claim 40 acres in that region under "possessory titles," pending congressional confirmation. By June some 40,000 blacks had colonized the region. Although Lincoln's successor, Andrew Johnson, soon scuttled land distribution under the Freedmen's Bureau and Sherman plans, a surprisingly large number of sea island blacks gained permanent title to small farms of their own during the Civil War. And with landownership came a degree of independence and, as best one can tell, contentment, far greater than that enjoyed by other blacks in the postwar South.

That land reform came to so little, during the war and after, was perhaps regrettable but hardly surprising. Even many abolitionists and radical Republicans (to say nothing of Democrats eager to charge Republicans with "partiality" toward blacks) doubted the propriety and constitutionality of taking lands from whites and giving them to blacks at anything less than fair market price. Such charity was not only misguided—encouraging dependency and sloth instead of thrift and diligence—but, antislavery spokesmen had long insisted, unnecessary.

> We are in danger of *too much* northern managing for the Negro [Henry Ward Beecher declared in March 1865]. The black man is just like the white in this—that he should be left, and obliged, to take *care* of himself and suffer and enjoy, according as he creates the means of either. He needs to be extricated from slavery, to be guarded from imposition, to have the means of Education, and to have, in the case of plantation slaves, a small *start* in tools, seed etc. Beyond this, I think nursing will only pauperize him.

Despite the insistence of some radicals that to give blacks "only freedom, without the land, is to give them only the mockery of freedom which the English or the Irish peasant has," the public sided heavily with Beecher, making idle all talk of "forty acres and a mule."

The same laissez-faire, self-help ideals which militated against the distribution of land to freedmen also stood in the way of legislation to help blacks make the transition from slavery to freedom. "Are they free men or not," asked Iowa's Republican senator James W. Grimes during debates on the Freedmen's Bureau Bill in 1864. "If they are free men, why not let them stand as free men?" But as Henry Ward Beecher's remarks indicate, many admitted the need and propriety of limited, temporary assistance to a long-oppressed people suddenly having to make their own way in the world. To offer such aid, and at the same time to help loyal *white* refugees in the South, Congress created in March 1865 the Bureau of Refugees, Freedmen, and Abandoned Lands. An agency of the War Department, the Freedmen's Bureau was charged with providing food, clothing, and fuel, and distributing abandoned lands to impoverished white refugees and former slaves. As a relief agency, the Freedmen's Bureau offered invaluable aid to destitute Southerners of both races. Moreover, in making it possible for blacks as well as whites to purchase land—however temporary their title may have been—the Freedmen's Bureau Act tacitly repudiated the "serfdom" of the contract system and gave sharper recognition of the former slaves' standing as freemen.

The crowning arch in the North's antislavery program was, of course, the Thirteenth Amendment. For until a prohibition against slavery was chiseled into the U.S. Constitution, it remained possible that the Emancipation Proclamation and the confiscation acts might be overturned. Some contended that as a war measure the Emancipation Proclamation would lose its validity once peace returned, and others maintained that emancipating slaves did not necessarily abolish laws upholding slavery. If the government confiscated all the horses in Massachusetts, William Whiting argued in *The War Powers of the President* (1863), it "would change the legal title to these horses," but neither "alter the laws of Massachusetts as to personal property; nor . . . deprive our citizens of the legal right to purchase and use *other* horses." Even as matters stood, both the border slave states and a sizable portion of the Confederacy (including all of Tennessee) remained unaffected by Lincoln's liberating decree. The prospect of a Democratic presidential victory in 1864—and with it a peace that left slave laws intact—frightened many antislavery men and women, including President Lincoln. As late as mid-summer 1864, Frederick

Douglass thought slavery "only wounded and crippled, not disabled and killed."

Pressure for a constitutional amendment abolishing slavery throughout the United States began late in 1863. By December the measure had been introduced in Congress, and abolitionists launched a massive petition campaign which collected nearly 400,000 signatures in support of its passage. The Senate overwhelmingly approved the proposed amendment in April 1864, by a vote of 38 to 6. But Democrats, contending that the measure was an unconstitutional use of the amending power to control the domestic institutions of Southern states, prevented it from receiving the requisite two-thirds when it came to a vote in the House on June 15.

At this point President Lincoln took charge. His first move was to urge the Republican national convention, which met at Baltimore in June, "to put into the platform as the key-stone" a plank endorsing the emancipation amendment. Subsequently he thanked the delegates in a public letter for having honored his request, declaring that only such an amendment could "meet and cover all cavils." After the fall elections, which he rightly interpreted as a mandate for his antislavery program, Lincoln redoubled his efforts to secure congressional approval of the proposed amendment. He made a strong pitch for it in his annual message to Congress in December, joined other Republicans to lobby lame-duck Democrats, and dangled promises of patronage before representatives whose votes might be decisive. These efforts bore fruit when on January 31, 1865, the House approved the Thirteenth Amendment by the required margin and sent it along to the states for ratification. The final vote was witnessed by a packed gallery that included several senators, five Supreme Court justices, various other dignitaries and government workers, and a smattering of Washington blacks. When the Speaker of the House announced the outcome, a ten-minute demonstration erupted which, the *New York Times* reported, "was grand and impressive beyond description."

No one rejoiced more than Abraham Lincoln. Though not required to do so, he proudly signed the original copy of the amendment, "Approved, February 1, 1865. A. Lincoln." And to a crowd that gathered at the White House to serenade his triumph, the president pronounced the amendment, "a King's cure for all the evils. It winds the whole thing up."

Looking Ahead: Wartime Reconstruction

As historians commonly use the term, "Reconstruction" refers to the process by which Republicans sought both to restore the Union and to replace the backward customs and beliefs of the Old South with the more modern, egalitarian ways of the North. Though it is most often associated with the period of Republican rule in the South following the Civil War, Reconstruction in fact began well before the war had ended and, in the protracted struggle for racial equality, continues still.

I

Abraham Lincoln's early attention to Reconstruction derived both from his hope that appealing terms of reconciliation might undermine the Confederate war effort by rekindling Southern Unionism, and from his awareness of Reconstruction's bearing on emancipation. Nothing would more surely guarantee the destruction of slavery in the seceded states, he perceived, than for those states to frame antislavery constitutions before readmission to the Union. As early as the spring of 1863, therefore, Lincoln began to use his influence to insure that as soon as conditions permitted loyal governments committed to the abolition of slavery were established throughout the South. At first the president worked behind the scenes to strengthen the hand of antislavery Unionists in states occupied by Federal armies, using personal appeals, patronage, and military pressure to do so. Typical was his letter in September 1863 to Andrew Johnson, war governor of occupied Tennessee.

Observing that it was "the nick of time" for creating a loyal government in the Volunteer State, Lincoln reminded Johnson that the "whole struggle for Tennessee will have been profitless to both State and Nation" if it ended in disloyalists returning to power. "Let the reconstruction be the work of such men only as can be trusted for the Union," he advised. "Exclude all others, and trust that your government, so organized, will be recognized here, as being the one of republican form."

Praising Johnson for his recent declaration in favor of emancipation, the president added: "Get emancipation into your new State government — Constitution — and there will be no such word as fail for your case."

Uncertain of his reelection as president, and fearful that a Democratic victory would produce a negotiated peace settlement protecting slavery in the South, Lincoln wished to move quickly, to bring within the Union as many *free* states as possible while he still held office. To that end, he publicly set forth his preferred plan of reunification in the Proclamation of Amnesty and Reconstruction, dated December 8, 1863, and in his third annual message to Congress, given that same day. Believing Reconstruction to be essentially the president's responsibility, and finding in his power to pardon an instrument of compliance, Lincoln offered full pardons and restoration of "all rights of property, except as to slaves" to those Rebels willing to take an oath to uphold the Constitution, the Union, and all laws and proclamations affecting slavery. Only high-ranking Confederate civil and military officers, persons who had left Congress or resigned commissions in the U.S. armed forces to aid the rebellion, and persons who had mistreated captive black soldiers, sailors, or their officers were excluded from these benefits.

Whenever in any state a number of adult males equal to at least 10 percent of those who voted in the 1860 presidential election had taken the loyalty oath and reestablished a "republican" government, that government would "be recognized as the true government of the State." Lincoln left little doubt that a republican government was necessarily an antislavery government, and he asked that freedmen be protected in their liberty and provided an opportunity for education. But although he favored labor contracts as the simplest and most flexible way to establish a new relationship between the races, Lincoln expressed a willingness to approve a temporary system of black apprenticeship. Likewise, though he personally no longer objected to the enfranchisement of freeborn Afro-Americans, his plan excluded blacks from every phase of Reconstruction — oath taking, voting, officeholding.

It should be noted that in his urgent desire to create free states as swiftly as possible, Lincoln was willing to argue that republican government need not rest upon the will of the majority. His aim, he explained to Congress, was to provide "a rallying point — a plan of action" which might speed the work of restoration. If others could devise a better plan, he would willingly entertain it, but it was important that the task of creating loyal free states in the South proceed with dispatch. Clearly, requiring the participation of a majority of Southern voters would mean shelving Reconstruction until the war was over.

Under the terms of Lincoln's proclamation, loyal state governments were established before the war ended in Louisiana, Tennessee, and Arkansas. In portions of those states occupied by Federal troops, loyal voters took the required oath, elected governors and other state officials, and selected delegates to a constitutional convention. These conventions then framed new constitutions which repudiated secession and the Confederate debt, abolished slavery, and introduced a variety of other reforms. In Louisiana, for instance, delegates acting under pressure from Governor Michael Hahn and General Nathaniel P. Banks (who in turn took their instructions from President Lincoln) established free public school for *all* children, opened all courts and militia service to blacks and whites alike, altered the basis for representation in the state legislature to lessen planter domination, and extended protection of basic civil rights belonging to all citizens. Suffrage was for the time being reserved to white males only, but the revised constitution did authorize the legislature to grant voting privileges to nonwhites who met military service, taxpaying, or literacy requirements. Except for restrictions on voting and officeholding, the Louisiana constitution of 1864 contained no distinctions based on color. Having revised their constitutions, the "reconstructed" states elected state and national representatives and applied for admission to Congress. Neither the House nor Senate would admit the validity of presidential Reconstruction, however, and when representatives from Louisiana, Arkansas, and Tennessee arrived in Washington, Congress refused to admit them.

From the beginning, in fact, there had been strong opposition from many quarters to Lincoln's design for Reconstruction. Abolitionists pounced on the president's "wrong-headed" toleration of apprenticeship schemes, denounced his failure to insist upon black suffrage, and questioned the trust he placed in Southern Unionists. In the states being reconstructed, radical Unionists themselves criticized Lincoln and his local followers for stopping short of universal suffrage and neglecting other safeguards against a restoration of planter dominance. Louisiana's free Negroes, especially those in New Orleans who had for generations formed a sizable, prosperous, and literate part of the community, were particularly critical of their disfranchisement. The black *New Orleans Tribune* went still further, adding to manhood suffrage a call for property confiscation and land reform. "It is enough for the republic to spare the life of the rebels, without restoring to them their plantations and palaces," the *Tribune* editorialized. "The whole world will applaud the wisdom of the principle: amnesty for the persons, no amnesty for the property."

Ultimately fatal to Lincoln's hopes for a rapid, harmonious restoration of the Union was the hostility of congressional Republicans toward the blueprint he had drafted. Some, it must be said, objected less to the president's plan than to the manner of its introduction. While he explicitly admitted the legislature's constitutional right to determine "whether members sent to Congress from any State shall be admitted to seats," Lincoln had in a sense presented Congress with a fait accompli. As one scholar observes, "Much annoyance and misunderstanding would have been averted had the President consulted congressional leaders before giving a promise which without their co-operation he would be unable to fulfill." Jealous of their own prerogatives, many legislators thought that Congress ought to have a much stronger voice in setting Reconstruction policy than Lincoln proposed to give it. This constitutional question of just whose business it was to oversee Reconstruction also underlay the fight between Congress and Lincoln's successor.

More serious, there were those in Congress, including some of the most influential, who sincerely doubted that the governments established under presidential Reconstruction would adequately protect the rights of black and white Unionists. Certain Republicans, among them Charles Sumner, believed that the failure of Lincoln's plan to insist on black suffrage was a serious flaw. "If all whites vote, then must all blacks," Sumner contended. "Without them the old enemy will reappear, and . . . in alliance with the Northern . . . [Democratic party] put us all in peril again." Interestingly enough, even so deep-dyed a radical as Thaddeus Stevens came hesitantly to the support of black suffrage in the South (not until 1867 would he give that measure his unqualified support); but Stevens and many others agreed with Sumner that Lincoln's program would play into the hands of Democrats, North and South, and precipitate the overthrow of the Republican party and all it stood for.

Finally, there were some who, like Stevens, argued that more was required than simply emancipation and the resumption of normal political relationships. "The whole fabric of Southern society *must* be changed," Stevens would soon be saying, "and it can never be done if this opportunity is lost. The Southern states have been despotisms, not governments of the people. It is impossible that any practical equality of rights can exist where a few thousand men monopolize the whole landed property. . . . If the South is ever to be made a safe republic let her lands be cultivated by the toil of the owners or the free labor of intelligent citizens. This must be done even though it drive her nobility into exile. If they go, all the better."

The differences between President Lincoln's Reconstruction policies and those of his radical critics were, in fact, narrower than most contemporary observers—and historians since—have admitted. At first many Republican ultras as well as conservatives had applauded the Reconstruction Proclamation, for they approved of its commitment to emancipation, its determination to place power solely in the hands of loyal antislavery men, and its apparent flexibility. Even Sumner initially pronounced himself "fully and perfectly satisfied" with Lincoln's proposals. Moreover, the president not only agreed that Congress had a perfect right to grant or deny representation to reconstructed states, but that it might set conditions for their readmission to the Union. On the suffrage question, he was at least as liberal as most in his party. Even when it came to the treatment of Southern whites, Lincoln stood closer to the radicals than is sometimes thought. His misgivings about the severity of the Second Confiscation Bill, for example, arose not from any soft-hearted desire to protect the property of traitors—a position he labeled "absurd"—but from his sense that the "severest justice may not always be the best policy" and concern that it would be hard to apply confiscation fairly.

Once the process of presidential Reconstruction was under way, however, conflict between Lincoln and Republican radicals rapidly escalated. Reports from disgruntled antislavery Unionists in Louisiana that Lincoln's agents, especially Governor Hahn and General Banks, used military influence to sway elections, opposed black suffrage, and supported a contract-labor system little different from slavery, persuaded many that presidential Reconstruction was a sham. The 10 percent provision in Lincoln's plan also received mounting criticism, even though more than twice that many voted in the first Louisiana and Arkansas elections. "We may conquer rebels and hold them in subjection," a grim Thad Stevens lectured the House of Representatives, but it was a "mere mockery" of the democratic process to say that a tenth of the citizens of a conquered state could govern for the rest because they were "more holy or more loyal than the others." "When the doctrine that the *quality* and not the *number* of voters is to decide the right to govern," he added, "then we no longer have a republic, but the worst form of despotism." Increasingly, too, radical Republican congressmen protested the president's "usurpation" of business rightfully belonging to the legislative branch.

To support their contention that Congress rather than the president had authority to superintend Reconstruction, and at the same time to justify a more stringent policy toward the South, congressional radicals produced a number of constitutional theories which had been percolating since early in the war. Whether by committing "state suicide" or becoming "conquered provinces," men like Charles Sumner and Thaddeus Stevens contended, the seceded states had effectively forfeited their place in the Union and had reverted to the status of unorganized territories. Since Congress was empowered to "make all needful Rules and Regulations" for the territories, the defeated Confederate states fell under its control, and Congress might presumably keep them in a state of suspended animation, without governments of their own, so long as it wished. Moreover, because the United States guaranteed to "every State in this Union a Republican form of Government," and because Congress possessed the power to admit new states or not, as it saw fit, the national legislature might rightfully impose conditions on reconstructed states prior to their readmission—including black suffrage, disfranchisement of Rebel leaders, civil rights guarantees, and the like.

On the eve of the adjournment of Congress in July 1864, radical Republicans secured passage of the Wade-Davis Bill which embodied a substitute for presidential Reconstruction. This measure, mainly the work of Representative Henry Winter Davis of Maryland and sponsored in the Senate by Ohio's Benjamin Wade, differed from Lincoln's plan in several respects. Most conspicuously, it required a *majority* of registered white male citizens, not just 10 percent, to take a loyalty oath before Reconstruction could begin. This majority had to pledge merely future loyalty to the United States, but participation in the revision and ratification of new state constitutions was restricted to those who could swear to past loyalty as well. Lincoln's plan relied on Southern adherence to the confiscation acts and the Emancipation Proclamation, along with the prospect of an antislavery constitutional amendment, to abolish slavery in the South, leaving somewhat ambiguous the status of slaves in regions not touched by the Emancipation Proclamation. Sponsors of the Wade-Davis Bill, however—less confident of the Thirteenth Amendment's passage, mistrustful of Southern whites, and skeptical even of Lincoln's antislavery resolve—attacked slavery directly. As a condition of readmission to the Union, all seceded states were required to abolish slavery forever. In addition to disfranchising high-ranking Confederates, as the president had done, the Wade-Davis Bill sternly revoked the American citizenship of Rebel leaders who continued to hold office after July 1864.

Yet, for all their differences, the two Reconstruction plans were in fundamental ways quite similar. First and foremost both the president and Congress sought to place the reorganization of Southern state governments exclusively in the hands of trustworthy, antislavery Unionists. While Congress insisted that Reconstruction might begin only after a majority of voters had renounced the Confederacy — effectively postponing reorganization until after the war — it nonetheless reserved to a small minority of the consistently loyal the right to draft and ratify new "republican" constitutions. Likewise, in its practical effect the congressional requirement for an oath of *past* loyalty *after* the war would be little different from Lincoln's demand for a pledge of *present* loyalty *during* the war. The two plans were also alike in what they left out. Neither, to the disgruntlement of ultras like Stevens, treated the seceded states as territories; neither, for political reasons, gave the vote to blacks.

Had it not been for his belief that Congress lacked authority to prohibit slavery in the South and his reluctance to jettison the governments already established in Louisiana and Arkansas, President Lincoln might have gone along with Republican congressmen who overwhelmingly approved the Wade-Davis Bill. Instead, he pocket vetoed the bill despite warnings that by doing so he would damage Republican chances in the fall elections. The new government in Louisiana might only be "as the egg is to the fowl," Lincoln would later suggest, but "we shall sooner have the fowl by hatching the egg than by smashing it." He therefore let the bill die rather than be a party to the destruction of his own Reconstruction program. Yet in his proclamation explaining the veto he commended the Wade-Davis Bill "as one very proper plan" and pledged his assistance to "the loyal people of any State choosing to adopt it."

If Lincoln hoped by such expressions of flexibility and open-mindedness to placate Republican radicals and unify his party before the presidential campaign, he was sorely disappointed. His proclamation seems to have mollified few and exasperated many. Some, Old Thad Stevens among them, urged radicals to "condemn privately and applaud publicly." Others, like Senator Sumner, kept their peace altogether, lest Democrats make political capital of Republican divisions. Wade and Davis, however, were unwilling to paper over their dispute with the president. Furious at Lincoln's veto and his attempt to justify it, the bill's sponsors published in the *New York Tribune* on August 5 a manifesto that criticized the president in blistering language. "A more studied outrage on the legislative authority of the people has never been perpetrated," the two radicals charged. By his "rash and fatal act," the president had struck "a blow at the friends of his administration, at the rights of humanity, and at the principles of republican government." It was time for Lincoln to understand, they said, "that our support is of a cause, and not of a man; that the authority of Congress is paramount, and must be respected; . . . and that, if he wishes our support, he must confine himself to his executive duties—to obey and execute—not to make the laws; to suppress by arms armed rebellion, and leave political reorganization to Congress."

Public reaction to the Wade-Davis manifesto was generally unfavorable. Its framers had been unable to get anyone else to sign their "protest" and the *Tribune,* which printed it, withheld its endorsement. Even most radical Republicans thought the manifesto "ill-timed, ill-tempered, and ill-advised." Wade was roundly condemned by Republican conventions in the Western Reserve and Davis paid for his authorship by losing his bid for renomination to the House of Representatives. Though understandably displeased at being "wounded in the house of one's friends," President Lincoln took the affair in stride. It reminded him, he said, "of an old acquaintance who, having a son of a scientific turn, bought him a microscope. The boy went around, experimenting with his glass upon everything that came in his way. One day, at the dinner table, the father took up a piece of cheese. 'Don't eat that, father,' said the boy; 'it is full of wrigglers.' 'My son,' replied the old gentleman, taking, at the same time, a huge bite, 'let 'em *wriggle*; I can stand it if they can!'"

Broad condemnation of the Wade-Davis manifesto and the strong support Lincoln received from Republicans of all stripes in his campaign for reelection (in the end even Wade and Davis stumped for the Union ticket) revealed that cooperation was still possible between the president and Congress in shaping a Reconstruction program. In December 1864 Lincoln and Republican leaders in the House agreed to a compromise by which Congress would recognize the governments of Louisiana and Arkansas in exchange for presidential support of Reconstruction elsewhere on terms similar to those in the Wade-Davis Bill. This understanding came a cropper when House Republicans fell to quarreling over provision for black suffrage and Senate Democrats joined Republican radicals to prevent recognition of Louisiana's reorganized government. But in his last public address, on April 11, 1865, Lincoln not only repeated his willingness to be flexible, disclaiming again any notion that his was the only acceptable plan of Reconstruction and expressing a willingness to repudiate the Louisiana regime if convinced that "the public interest" required it, but for the first time he publicly endorsed the enfranchisement of Southern blacks, at least "the very intelligent, and . . . those who serve our cause as soldiers." Hopes for cooperation in the development of a Reconstruction program sensitive to the needs of Southern whites yet protective of the rights of the freedmen were shattered, however, by an assassin's bullet and the succession of a Tennessee president who shared neither Lincoln's political savvy nor his determination to secure the emancipationist goals of the Civil War.

II

The path of Reconstruction was, of course, shaped by the war's effects on the South as well as on the North. The emergence of emancipation as a war aim produced a rising Northern concern (among Republicans, at least) to guarantee black civil rights. In the South it triggered a revolution in race relations which left freedmen in many ways more vulnerable than ever before. Well before emancipation, in fact, old patterns of racial accommodation had begun to break down. Not only the introduction of wage labor in regions under Union control, but the intransigence of slaves everywhere, eroded the paternalistic element in black servitude and heightened the probability of racial antagonism during Reconstruction and afterward. In their growing hurt and rage at the "ingratitude" of slaves who shirked or ran away, planters altered the very language they used when speaking of their chattels. Before the war and for some months thereafter slaveholders usually referred to their bondsmen as "servants," "laborers," or even "my people," "my black family," or some other such euphemism. By the war's last years, however, planters most often spoke bluntly of their "slaves" or "niggers." Because Southern whites had always viewed slaves ambivalently, as both dutiful children and potential insurrectionaries, this ominous shift in attitude came swiftly and easily.

The "loss of mastery" planters experienced during the war also strengthened their conviction that blacks were inherently lazy and insolent, requiring some system of coercion and subordination to make them fruitful members of society. The restrictive Black Codes of Reconstruction and the Jim Crow laws that followed would build upon this persistent belief.

Emancipation, far from erasing a pervasive sense of the necessity of white superiority, created new dangers — as well as welcome opportunity — for Southern blacks. As one student of the Southern mind observed long ago:

> So long as the Negro had been property, worth from five hundred dollars up, he had been taboo — safer from rope and faggot than any common white man, and perhaps even safer than his

master himself. But with the abolition of legal slavery his immunity vanished. The economic interest of his former protectors, the master class, now stood the other way about—required that he should be promptly disabused of any illusion that his liberty was real, and confirmed in his ancient docility. And so the road stood all but wide open to the ignoble hate and cruel itch to take him in hand which for so long had been festering impotently in the poor whites.

Another legacy of the Civil War that would bedevil the task of reconciliation and Reconstruction was the bitterness and hatred it spawned in many Southern whites toward the Yankee invader. Billy Yank and Johnny Reb occasionally did swap coffee, tobacco, and small talk during lulls in the fighting, and some Southerners welcomed reunion with an alacrity and good feeling that revealed their lukewarm attachment to the Confederacy. Yet four years of killing, cruelty, and devastation could not help but yield a bitter harvest, and for many Southerners "DamnYankee" would remain a single word, never to be forgotten. Such feelings seem to have been particularly strong among noncombatants, as if those who did the fighting gained a certain respect for the brave foe whose dread experience they shared. "Day by day and hour by hour does the deep seated enmity I have always had . . . for the accursed Yankee nation increase & burn higher," wrote one young planter in 1864. "They have slaughtered our kindred, . . . destroyed our prosperity as a people & filled our whole land with sorrow. . . . I have vowed that if I should have children—the first ingredient of the first principle of their education shall be uncompromising hatred & contempt of the Yankee." Rather than live in the slaveless world the enemy had forced upon them, some whites (perhaps as many as 10,000 by one reckoning) left the South altogether, settling for a time in Mexico, Brazil, or some other more congenial land.

For old Edmund Ruffin, the Virginia fire-eater whose honor it had been to open the firing on Fort Sumter in 1861, the Confederacy's collapse made life itself seem pointless. Wishing no more than to be wrapped in a blanket and "buried as usually were our brave soldiers who were slain in battle," Ruffin sat at his desk and on June 17, 1865, proclaimed in his diary his "unmitigated hatred to Yankee rule—to all political, social and business connections with Yankees, and the perfidious, malignant and vile Yankee race." This done, he cocked his pistol and put a bullet through his brain. The man who fired the first shot of the Civil War had become its final casualty.

III

The "dark and bloody ground" of postwar Reconstruction falls beyond the scope of this book. It may be appropriate to note, however, that although Southerners lost the Civil War, and with it both slavery and political independence, they soon proved themselves anything but a vanquished people. While Northerners congratulated one another on having saved the Union, strengthened federal authority, liberated 4 million slaves, and established legal and constitutional safeguards of black rights, Southern whites launched a guerrilla-like counteroffensive to salvage what they could from the "Lost Cause." By 1877, proud, defiant, sometimes violent former Confederates had "redeemed" control of state governments from Republican regimes and forced the withdrawal of federal troops from every Southern state. And with Northern acquiescence in Southern home rule came the return of white supremacy — notwithstanding Reconstruction acts, civil rights and freedmen's bureau acts, and the Fourteenth and Fifteenth Amendments — and a sense of Southern honor preserved. "The South surrendered at Appomattox," one Republican carpetbagger lamented, but "the North has been surrendering ever since." So far as American blacks were concerned, this reversal of the fortunes of war would continue well into the twentieth century.

Bibliographical Essay

The literature on the American Civil War is vast, and the works mentioned here may be taken as a mere sampler of one of the richest fields of American historiography. My intention has been to list merely those books and articles most helpful in the writing of this volume. Students wishing a more detailed catalog should consult Allan Nevins et al., eds., *Civil War Books: A Critical Bibliography,* 2 vols. (1967–69); and the extensive, up-to-date bibliography in James M. McPherson, *Ordeal by Fire: The Civil War and Reconstruction* (1982).

GENERAL WORKS

The fullest general treatment of the Civil War era is Allan Nevins's magisterial *Ordeal of the Union,* 8 vols. (1947–71). Based extensively on primary sources, it gives close attention to social and cultural, as well as political, economic, diplomatic, and military aspects of the period. Among the better single-volume studies of these years are James McPherson's *Ordeal by Fire* (1982), which emphasizes sectional disparities in the pace of modernization; J. G. Randall and David Donald, *The Civil War and Reconstruction* (1961); Peter J. Parish, *The American Civil War* (1975); David Potter, *Division and the Stresses of Reunion* (1973); William R. Brock, *Conflict and Transformation: The United States, 1844–1877* (1973); William L. Barney, *Flawed Victory: A New Perspective on the Civil War* (1975); and David Herbert Donald, *Liberty and Union* (1978). Still valuable on the social developments of the period is Arthur C. Cole, *The Irrepressible Conflict, 1850–1865* (1934).

ANTHOLOGIES

Several excellent anthologies conveniently gather important essays on various aspects of the mid-nineteenth century. Especially useful for my purposes were Bertram Wyatt-Brown's brilliant *Yankee Saints and Southern Sinners* (1985), which includes a thoughtful new essay entitled "Honor and Secession"; Kenneth M. Stampp, *The Imperiled Union: Essays on the Background of the Civil War* (1980), containing particularly provocative explorations of the causes of the war and of Confederate defeat; Eric Foner, *Politics and Ideology in the*

Age of the Civil War (1980), especially the essay on "The Causes of the Civil War: Recent Interpretations and New Directions"; David M. Potter, *The South and the Sectional Conflict* (1968); and George M. Fredrickson, ed., *A Nation Divided: Problems and Issues of the Civil War* (1975). Fredrickson's own contribution to this last volume, an essay arguing that "the South lost the war primarily because it had fewer sources of cohesion than the North and less aptitude for innovation," merits special attention. Other helpful collections are David Donald, *Lincoln Reconsidered: Essays on the Civil War Era* (1961); Donald, ed., *Why the North Won the Civil War* (1960); Edmund Wilson, *Patriotic Gore: Studies in the Literature of the American Civil War* (1962); Charles G. Sellers, Jr., ed., *The Southerner as American* (1960); Grady McWhiney, *Southerners and Other Americans* (1973); Robert H. Abzug and Stephen E. Maizlish, eds., *New Perspectives on Race and Slavery in America: Essays in Honor of Kenneth M. Stampp* (1986); and William J. Cooper, Jr. et al., eds., *A Master's Due: Essays in Honor of David Herbert Donald* (1986).

BIOGRAPHIES

One of the best ways to break through the surface of events to a deeper understanding of nineteenth-century actions and ideas is through biography. Fortunately there exist any number of first-rate biographies of prominent, and not so prominent, members of the Civil War generation. For some reason, except for military men, Northerners have been better served by historians than have their Southern counterparts. There are, however, exceptions to this rule, among them Drew Gilpin Faust's superb *James Henry Hammond and the Old South: A Design for Mastery* (1982); Theodore Rosengarten, *Tombee: Portrait of a Cotton Planter* (1986), a marvelous reconstruction of the world of a South Carolina sea island planter before, during, and after the Civil War; Robert E. May, *John A. Quitman: Old South Crusader* (1985); and Avery Craven, *Edmund Ruffin, Southerner* (1932). Also worthwhile are Clement Eaton, *Jefferson Davis* (1977), the best of a number of indifferent biographies of the Confederate president; William B. McCash, *Thomas R. R. Cobb: The Making of a Southern Nationalist* (1983); Craig M. Simpson, *A Good Southerner: The Life of Henry A. Wise of Virginia* (1985); James B. Ranck, *Albert Gallatin Brown, Radical Southern Nationalist* (1937); Gerald S. Henig, *Henry Winter Davis: Antebellum and Civil War Congressman from Maryland* (1973); and Laura A. White, *Robert Barnwell Rhett: Father of Secession* (1931). Elisabeth Muhlenfeld, *Mary Boykin Chesnut: A Biography* (1981), captures the life of the Confederacy's leading diarist. Chesnut's sparkling, candid, and insightful journals, and the book that emerged from them, have been handsomely edited by C. Vann Woodward and Elisabeth Muhlenfeld in *The Private Mary Chesnut: The Unpublished Diaries* (1984), and by Woodward in *Mary Chesnut's Civil War* (1981).

Among the best biographies of Northern public figures are David Donald's Pulitzer Prize-winning *Charles Sumner and the Coming of the Civil War* (1960) and *Charles Sumner and the Rights of Man* (1970); Robert W. Johannsen,

Stephen A. Douglas (1973); Richard N. Current, *Old Thad Stevens: A Story of Ambition* (1942); John Niven, *Gideon Welles, Lincoln's Secretary of the Navy* (1973); Benjamin P. Thomas and Harold M. Hyman, *Stanton: The Life and Times of Lincoln's Secretary of War* (1962); Glyndon G. Van Deusen, *William Henry Seward* (1967); Martin Duberman, *Charles Francis Adams, 1807–1886* (1961) and *James Russell Lowell* (1966); Frank Otto Gatell, *John Gorham Palfrey and the New England Conscience* (1963); Hans L. Trefousse, *Benjamin Franklin Wade: Radical Republican from Ohio* (1963); and Roy F. Nichols, *Franklin Pierce* (1931). Studies of every facet of Abraham Lincoln's career abound. Two scholarly and engagingly written biographies are Benjamin P. Thomas, *Abraham Lincoln: A Biography* (1952), and Stephen B. Oates, *With Malice Toward None: The Life of Abraham Lincoln* (1977). Mark E. Neely, Jr., *The Abraham Lincoln Encyclopedia* (1982), is an immensely helpful reference.

CHAPTER 1

The structure of American politics at mid-century is carefully described by Richard P. McCormick in *The Second American Party System: Party Formation in the Jacksonian Era* (1966). Richard Hofstadter's elegant *The Idea of a Party System: The Rise of Legitimate Opposition in the United States, 1780–1840* (1969) traces Americans' growing acceptance of the beneficence, as well as necessity, of a party system. Joel Silbey, *The Shrine of Party: Congressional Voting Behavior, 1841–1852* (1967), and especially Thomas Alexander, *Sectional Stress and Party Strength: A Study of Roll-Call Voting Patterns in the United States House of Representatives, 1836–1860* (1967), make plain the mounting influence of sectional, as opposed to party, loyalties in shaping political behavior after 1845. William E. Gienapp, "'Politics Seem to Enter into Everything': Political Culture in the North, 1840–1860," in Stephen E. Maizlish and John J. Kushma et al., eds., *Essays on American Antebellum Politics, 1840–1860* (1982), 14–69, demonstrates widespread voter interest and participation in antebellum political campaigns. See also Jean Baker, *Affairs of Party: The Political Culture of Northern Democrats in the Mid-Nineteenth Century* (1983); Ronald P. Formisano, *The Birth of Mass Political Parties: Michigan, 1827–1861* (1971) and *The Transformation of Political Culture: Massachusetts Parties, 1790s–1840s* (1983); and Daniel Walker Howe, *The Political Culture of American Whigs* (1979). Ralph W. Wooster's *The People in Power: Courthouse and Statehouse in the Lower South* (1969) and *Politicians, Planters, and Plain Folk: Courthouse and Statehouse in the Upper South, 1850–1860* (1975) exhibit the substantial role of nonslaveholders and small slaveholders in Southern governments.

Two good surveys of the pre–Civil War economy are Stuart Bruchey, *The Roots of American Economic Growth, 1607–1861* (1965), and Douglass C. North, *The Economic Growth of the United States, 1790–1860* (1961). Paul W. Gates, *The Farmer's Age: Agriculture, 1815–1860* (1960), is the standard work on the topic, but it should be supplemented by Lewis C. Gray's classic *History of Agriculture in the Southern United States to 1860*, 2 vols. (1933). Various aspects of the South's slave-based economy are explored in Eugene D. Genovese, *The Political Economy of Slavery: Studies in the Economy & Society of the Slave South* (1965); Robert R. Russel, *Economic Aspects of Southern Sectionalism, 1840–1861* (1960), and, brilliantly, in Gavin Wright, *The Political Economy of the Cotton South: Households, Markets, and Wealth in the Nineteenth Century* (1978), as well as in the studies of slavery mentioned later in this section. John McCardell, *The Idea of a Southern Nation: Southern Nationalists and Southern Nationalism, 1830–1860* (1979), describes the ill-fated attempts of Southern nationalists to stimulate manufacturing in the slave states. George R. Taylor, *The Transportation Revolution, 1815–1860* (1951), not only exhaustively covers that subject but offers a brief survey of industrial beginnings as well. Zane L. Miller, *The Urbanization of Modern America: A Brief History* (1973), contains a succinct account of the changing urban landscape in the nineteenth century. Richard Wade, *The Urban Frontier: Pioneer Life in Early Pittsburgh, Cincinnati, Lexington, Louisville, and St. Louis* (1959), notes that Western cities often acted as spearheads of settlement, and Daniel Boorstin explains in *The Americans: The National Experience* (1965) how such communities left their imprint on the surrounding countryside. Economic and other statistics are conveniently gathered in United States Bureau of the Census, *Historical Statistics of the United States, 1789–1945* (1949), and Donald B. Dodd and Wynette S. Dodd, eds., *Historical Statistics of the South* (1973).

The starting point for an analysis of American culture and society in the prewar decades is Alexis de Tocqueville's masterful *Democracy in America,* 2 vols., Phillips Bradley, ed. (1945). Three superb anthologies of contemporary statements by and about Americans are George Probst, ed., *The Happy Republic: A Reader in Tocqueville's America* (1962); David B. Davis, ed., *Antebellum American Culture: An Interpretive Anthology* (1979); and David Grimsted, ed., *Notions of the Americans, 1820–1860* (1970). I am indebted to Grimsted for both the concept and examples of the "confidence-dread" syndrome discernible in the lives of antebellum Americans. See also his *Melodrama Unveiled: American Theater and Culture, 1800–1850* (1968). For evidence of social inequality among Americans, see Douglas T. Miller, *Jacksonian Aristocracy: Class and Democracy in New York, 1830–1860* (1967); Lee Soltow, *Men and Wealth in the United States, 1850–1870* (1975); Edward Pessen, *Riches, Class, and Power Before the Civil War* (1973) and "The Egalitarian Myth and American Social Reality: Wealth, Mobility, and Equality in the 'Era of the Common Man,'" *American Historical Review* 76 (1971): 989–1034.

The past quarter-century has witnessed a flood of excellent studies of Southern slavery and its defenders. A particularly helpful guide to this literature is Peter Kolchin, "American Historians and Antebellum Southern Slavery," in William Cooper, Jr., et al., eds., *A Master's Due* (1986), 87–111. Two especially provocative works, Stanley Elkins, *Slavery: A Problem in American Institutional and Intellectual Life,* 2d ed. (1968), and Robert W. Fogel and Stanley L. Engerman, *Time on the Cross: The Economics of American Negro Slavery* (1974), the former contending that the Old South's uniquely "closed" slave system so stunted the personality development of slaves as to make an infantile

"Sambo" the dominant plantation type, and the latter insisting that slaves enjoyed "material conditions . . . [which] compared favorably with those of free industrial workers" and were "on average . . . harder working and more efficient" than white farm workers, have drawn salvo upon salvo of rebuttal. See, for example, Ann J. Lane, *The Debate Over* Slavery: *Stanley Elkins and His Critics* (1971); Herbert G. Gutman, *Slavery and the Numbers Game: A Critique of* Time on the Cross (1975); and Paul A. David et al., *Reckoning with Slavery: A Critical Study in the Quantitative History of American Negro Slavery* (1976).

Perhaps the best general accounts of slavery in the Old South are Kenneth M. Stampp, *The Peculiar Institution: Slavery in the Ante-Bellum South* (1961), and Eugene D. Genovese, *Roll, Jordan, Roll: The World the Slaves Made* (1974), the latter a sophisticated Marxian analysis that stresses the reciprocity of master-slave relationships. Among the most helpful documentary collections are Willie Lee Rose, ed., *A Documentary History of Slavery in North America* (1976); Robert S. Starobin, ed., *Blacks in Bondage: Letters of American Slaves* (1974); and especially George P. Rawick, ed., *The American Slave: A Composite Autobiography,* 41 vols. (1972–79), a collection consisting mainly of interviews with former slaves compiled by the Federal Writers' Project in the 1930s. Eugene D. Genovese, *The Political Economy of Slavery* and *The World the Slaveholders Made* (1974), and James Oakes, *The Ruling Race: A History of American Slaveholders* (1982), offer strikingly different views of the nature of white involvement in the slave system. On the South's defense of slavery, see William S. Jenkins, *Pro-Slavery Thought in the Old South* (1935); Drew Gilpin Faust, ed., *The Ideology of Slavery: Proslavery Thought in the Antebellum South, 1830–1860* (1981); Clement Eaton, *The Freedom-of-Thought Struggle in the Old South,* rev. ed. (1964); Charles G. Sellers, Jr., "The Travail of Slavery," in Sellers, Jr., ed., *The Southerner as American* (1960), 40–71; Ralph E. Morrow, "The Proslavery Argument Revisited," *Mississippi Valley Historical Review* 48 (1961): 79–94; David Donald, "The Proslavery Argument Reconsidered," *Journal of Southern History* 37 (1971): 3–18; and William R. Taylor, "Toward a Definition of Orthodoxy," *Harvard Educational Review* 36 (1966): 412–26.

Since the mid-1970s historians have begun a fruitful examination of the slaves' own experience in bondage. Of special interest are John W. Blassingame, *The Slave Community: Plantation Life in the Antebellum South,* rev. ed. (1979); George P. Rawick, *From Sundown to Sunup: The Making of the Black Community* (1972); Leslie Howard Owen, *This Species of Property: Slave Life and Culture in the Old South* (1976); John B. Boles, *Black Southerners, 1619–1869* (1983); Herbert G. Gutman, *The Black Family in Slavery and Freedom, 1750–1925* (1976); Lawrence W. Levine, *Black Culture and Black Consciousness: Afro-American Folk Thought from Slavery to Freedom* (1977); Albert J. Raboteau, *Slave Religion: The "Invisible Institution" in the Antebellum South* (1978); and William L. Van Deburg, *The Slave Drivers: Black Agricultural Supervisors in the Antebellum South* (1979).

Richard C. Wade, *Slavery in the Cities: The South, 1820–1860* (1964), and

Robert S. Starobin, *Industrial Slavery in the Old South* (1970), reveal slavery's vitality in nonagricultural settings. The problem of slave resistance is best explained in Eugene D. Genovese, *From Rebellion to Revolution: Afro-American Slave Revolts in the Making of the Modern World* (1979), a book enriched by its comparative analysis of slave uprisings in many parts of the Americas. Other comparative studies that illuminate the distinctive features of Southern slavery are Carl N. Degler, *Neither Black Nor White: Slavery and Race Relations in Brazil and the United States* (1971); H. Hoetink, *Slavery and Race Relations in the Americas: Comparative Notes on Their Nature and Nexus* (1973); Herbert S. Klein, *Slavery in the Americas: A Comparative Study of Virginia and Cuba* (1967); Laura Foner and Eugene D. Genovese, eds., *Slavery in the New World: A Reader in Comparative History* (1969); and Robin Winks, ed., *Slavery: A Comparative Perspective* (1972). One distinguishing feature of race relations in North America has been the simple two-caste system which degraded free Negroes nearly as much as slaves. The precarious world of free blacks in the Old South is perceptively described in Ira Berlin, *Slaves Without Masters: The Free Negro in the Antebellum South* (1974), and, with special intimacy, in Michael P. Johnson and James L. Roark, *Black Masters: A Free Family of Color in the Old South* (1984). See also Johnson and Roark, *No Chariot Let Down: Charleston's Free People of Color on the Eve of the Civil War* (1984).

The literature on the antislavery movement is nearly as extensive as that on slavery itself. Two first-rate surveys are Merton L. Dillon, *The Abolitionists: The Growth of a Dissenting Minority* (1974), and James B. Stewart, *Holy Warriors: The Abolitionists and American Slavery* (1976). Gilbert H. Barnes's pioneering *The Antislavery Impulse, 1830–1844* (1933) is still worth reading, despite its decidedly anti-Garrisonian bias. As an antidote, see Aileen Kraditor, *Means and Ends in American Abolitionism: Garrison and His Critics on Strategy and Tactics, 1834–1850* (1969). Other valuable antislavery studies include Lewis Perry, *Radical Abolitionism: Anarchy and the Government of God in Antislavery Thought* (1973); Lawrence J. Friedman, *Gregarious Saints: Self and Community in American Abolitionism, 1830–1870* (1982); Russel B. Nye, *Fettered Freedom: Civil Liberties and the Slavery Controversy, 1830–1860* (1949); Peter Walker, *Moral Choices: Memory, Desire, and Imagination in Nineteenth Century American Abolition* (1978); Martin Duberman, ed., *The Antislavery Vanguard: New Essays on the Abolitionists* (1965); Lewis Perry and Michael Fellman, eds., *Antislavery Reconsidered: New Perspectives on the Abolitionists* (1979); David B. Davis, *The Problem of Slavery in Western Culture* (1966) and *The Problem of Slavery in the Age of Revolution, 1770–1823* (1975); and Ronald G. Walters, *The Antislavery Appeal: American Abolitionism After 1830* (1976).

The often difficult role of blacks in the liberation of their race is delineated in Benjamin Quarles, *Black Abolitionists* (1969); Jane H. Pease and William H. Pease, *They Who Would Be Free: Blacks' Search for Freedom, 1830–1861* (1974); and R. J. M. Blackett, *Building an Antislavery Wall: Black Americans in the Atlantic Abolitionist Movement, 1830–1860* (1983). On women abolitionists, see Blanche G. Hersh, *The Slavery of Sex: Feminist Abolitionists in America*

(1979). Betty Fladeland, *Men and Brothers: Anglo-American Cooperation* (1972), skillfully depicts the connections between American and British abolitionists; Richard H. Sewell, *Ballots for Freedom: Antislavery Politics in the United States, 1837–1860* (1976), and Alan M. Kraut, ed., *Crusaders and Compromisers: Essays on the Relationship of the Antislavery Struggle to the Antebellum Party System* (1983), explore abolition's political dimension. In examining antislavery's enemies, Leonard L. Richard's *"Gentlemen of Property and Standing": Anti-Abolition Mobs in Jacksonian America* (1970) inevitably sheds light on the abolitionists themselves.

Of the many excellent biographies of abolitionists, the following rate special attention: Bertram Wyatt-Brown, *Lewis Tappan and the Evangelical War Against Slavery* (1969); James B. Stewart, *Wendell Phillips: Liberty's Hero* (1986); Gerda Lerner, *The Grimké Sisters from South Carolina: Rebels Against Slavery* (1967); Tilden G. Edelstein, *Strange Enthusiasm: A Life of Thomas Wentworth Higginson* (1968); Walter M. Merrill, *Against Wind and Tide: A Biography of Wm. Lloyd Garrison* (1963); John L. Thomas, *The Liberator: William Lloyd Garrison* (1963); and Robert Abzug, *Passionate Liberator: Theodore Dwight Weld and the Dilemma of Reform* (1980).

CHAPTER 2

By far the best general history of the sectional crisis following the Mexican War is David M. Potter, *The Impending Crisis, 1848–1861* (1976), a book chock-full of arresting insights. For "revisionist" interpretations blaming irresponsible extremists, North and South, for stirring up an artificial crisis leading to a needless war, see Avery O. Craven, *The Coming of the Civil War* (1942) and *The Growth of Southern Nationalism, 1848–1861* (1953).

The standard work on the Wilmot Proviso, Chaplain W. Morrison, *Democratic Politics and Sectionalism: The Wilmot Proviso Controversy* (1967), emphasizes the racist component in free soil thought, as does Eugene H. Berwanger, *The Frontier Against Slavery: Western Anti-Negro Prejudice and the Slavery Extension Controversy* (1967). Different views are expressed in Eric Foner, "The Wilmot Proviso Revisited," *Journal of American History* 56 (1969): 262–79, which stresses the resentment of many Northern Democrats at Southern dictation of party policy, and in Richard H. Sewell, "Slavery, Race, and the Free Soil Party, 1848–1854," in Alan Kraut, ed., *Crusaders and Compromisers* (1983), 101–24, which finds a genuine antislavery impulse behind the free soil movement. The most careful and thoroughgoing dissection of the whole territorial issue may be found in Don E. Fehrenbacher, *The Dred Scott Case: Its Significance in American Law and Politics* (1978), especially chapters 4–6. See also chapter 2, "The Wilmot Proviso and the Mid-Century Crisis," in Don Fehrenbacher, *The South in Three Sectional Crises* (1980). Splits in the major parties that made possible the formation of the Free Soil party are examined in Herbert D. A. Donovan, *The Barnburners* (1925); Kinley Brauer, *Cotton versus Conscience: Massachusetts Whig Politics and Southwestern Expansion, 1843–1848* (1967); and Thomas H. O'Connor, *Lords of the Loom: Cotton*

Whigs and the Coming of the Civil War (1968). Joseph G. Rayback, *Free Soil: The Election of 1848* (1970), and Frederick J. Blue, *The Free Soilers: Third Party Politics, 1848–54* (1973), look closely at the party itself. William J. Cooper, Jr., *The South and the Politics of Slavery, 1828–1856* (1978), offers a detailed and perceptive account of Southern reactions to the territorial question, as does Michael F. Holt, *The Political Crisis of the 1850s* (1978), a stimulating book stressing Southern fears for republicanism.

The legislative history of the Compromise of 1850 is well told in Holman Hamilton, *Prologue to Conflict: The Crisis and Compromise of 1850* (1964), though students may also wish to consult such biographical studies as Irving H. Bartlett, *Daniel Webster and the Trial of American Nationalism, 1843–1852* (1972); Holman Hamilton, *Zachary Taylor: Soldier in the White House* (1951); William N. Chambers, *Old Bullion Benton: Senator from the New West* (1956); Richard H. Sewell, *John P. Hale and the Politics of Abolition* (1965); Charles M. Wiltse, *John C. Calhoun: Sectionalist, 1840–1850* (1951); Robert J. Rayback, *Millard Fillmore: Biography of a President* (1959); and Glyndon G. Van Deusen, *The Life of Henry Clay* (1937); as well as the lives of Seward, Douglas, Stevens, and Jefferson Davis, cited earlier.

Larry Gara, *The Liberty Line: The Legend of the Underground Railroad* (1961); Stanley W. Campbell, *The Slave Catchers: Enforcement of the Fugitive Slave Law, 1850–1860* (1970); and Thomas D. Morris, *Free Men All: The Personal Liberty Laws of the North, 1780–1861* (1974), treat the myth and reality of resistance to the Fugitive Slave Act. Thelma Jennings, *The Nashville Convention: Southern Movement for Unity, 1848–1851* (1980), and John Barnwell, *Love of Order: South Carolina's First Secession Crisis* (1982), probe the failed attempts of Southern radicals to disrupt the Union in 1850–51.

CHAPTER 3

Helpful surveys of immigration to the United States include Maldwyn Allen Jones, *American Immigration* (1960); Leonard Dinnerstein, Roger L. Nichols, and David M. Reimers, *Natives and Strangers: Ethnic Groups and the Building of America* (1979); and Thomas Archdeacon, *Becoming American: An Ethnic History* (1983). Oscar Handlin, *Boston's Immigrants: A Study in Acculturation,* rev. ed. (1959), is a cogent case history of the immigrant experience in one nativist stronghold. See also Robert Ernst, *Immigrant Life in New York City, 1825–1863* (1949). Although outdated, Ray A. Billington, *The Protestant Crusade: A Study of the Origins of American Nativism, 1800–1860* (1938), remains the standard work on nativists and nativism. It should be supplemented, however, with Jean H. Baker's excellent *Ambivalent Americans: The Know-Nothing Party in Maryland* (1977) and W. Darrell Overdyke, *The Know-Nothing Party in the South* (1950).

The power of nativism as a political force and the extent of its influence in shaping the Republican party is a matter of dispute among historians. The strongest claims for the primacy of nativism and related ethno-cultural concerns in the political realignment of the 1850s appear in Michael F. Holt, *Forging a Majority: The Formation of the Republican Party in Pittsburgh, 1848–1860* (1969) and "The Politics of Impatience: The Origins of Know Nothingism," *Journal of American History* 60 (1973): 309–31; Joel Silbey, *The Transformation of American Politics* (1967) and "The Surge of Republican Power: Partisan Antipathy, American Social Conflict, and the Coming of the Civil War," in Stephen E. Maizlish and John J. Kushma, eds., *Essays on American Antebellum Politics* (1982), 199–229; Ronald P. Formisano, *The Birth of Mass Political Parties* (1971); Robert Kelley, *The Cultural Pattern of American Politics: The First Century* (1979); and Paul Kleppner, *The Third Electoral System, 1853–1892* (1979). My own more skeptical view of nativism's political staying power is shared by Eric Foner, *Free Soil, Free Labor, Free Men: The Ideology of the Republican Party before the Civil War* (1970); Stephen E. Maizlish, *The Triumph of Sectionalism: The Transformation of Ohio Politics, 1844–1856* (1983) and "The Meaning of Nativism and the Crisis of the Union: The Know-Nothing Movement in the Antebellum North," in Maizlish and Kushma, eds., *Essays on American Antebellum Politics*, 166–98; and Dale Baum, "Know-Nothingism and the Republican Majority in Massachusetts: The Political Realignment of the 1850s," *Journal of American History* 64 (1978): 959–86 and *The Civil War Party System: The Case of Massachusetts, 1848–1876* (1984). William E. Gienapp gives more or less equal weight to nativism and antislavery in accounting for the Republican party's rise to power. See his "Nativism and the Creation of a Republican Majority in the North before the Civil War," *Journal of American History* 72 (1985): 529–59, and *The Origins of the Republican Party, 1852–1856* (1987).

Roy F. Nichols, "The Kansas-Nebraska Act: A Century of Historiography," *Mississippi Valley Historical Review* 43 (1956): 187–212, critically assesses much of the literature on that fateful measure. The best recent accounts of Douglas's bill may be found in Robert W. Johannsen, *Stephen A. Douglas* (1973); Gerald W. Wolff, *The Kansas-Nebraska Bill: Party, Section, and the Coming of the Civil War* (1977); David Potter, *Impending Crisis* (1976); and Don Fehrenbacher, *The Dred Scott Case* (1978). The troubles in Kansas are clearly portrayed in Alice Nichols, *Bleeding Kansas* (1954), and James A. Rawley, *Race and Politics: "Bleeding Kansas" and the Coming of the Civil War* (1969), a book that overstates Republican racism. William E. Gienapp, "The Crime Against Sumner: The Caning of Charles Sumner and the Rise of the Republican Party," *Civil War History* 25 (1979): 218–45, shows how Preston Brooks's assault gave credence to reports of proslavery violence in Kansas.

Gienapp's monumental *The Origins of the Republican Party, 1852–1856* (1987) is now the definitive work on that topic, but serious students should also consult Eric Foner's discerning *Free Soil, Free Labor, Free Men* (1970); Ruhl J. Bartlett, *John C. Frémont and the Republican Party* (1930); Jeter Isely, *Horace Greeley and the Republican Party, 1853–1861* (1947); Michael F. Holt, *The Political Crisis of the 1850s* (1978); and Richard H. Sewell, *Ballots for Freedom* (1976). William B. Hesseltine and Rex G. Fisher, eds., *Trimmers, Trucklers &*

Temporizers: Notes of Murat Halstead from the Political Conventions of 1856 (1961), contains the colorful reportage of one of the North's shrewdest journalists.

CHAPTER 4

Stanley I. Kutler's documentary collection *The Dred Scott Decision: Law or Politics?* (1967) nicely supplements Don E. Fehrenbacher's masterful *The Dred Scott Case* (1978). In addition to the works on "Bleeding Kansas" already mentioned, those interested in the early history of that territory should refer to James C. Malin, *John Brown and the Legend of Fifty-Six* (1942); Samuel A. Johnson, *The Battle Cry of Freedom: The New England Emigrant Aid Society in the Kansas Crusade* (1954); and Don E. Fehrenbacher, "Kansas, Republicanism, and the Crisis of the Union," chapter 3 of his *The South and Three Sectional Crises* (1980).

The fragmentation of the Democratic party is scrupulously detailed in Roy F. Nichols, *The Disruption of American Democracy* (1948); Michael F. Holt, *The Political Crisis of the 1850s* (1978); and David Potter, *The Impending Crisis* (1976). Both Harry V. Jaffa, *Crisis of the House Divided: An Interpretation of the Lincoln-Douglas Debates* (1959), and Don E. Fehrenbacher, *Prelude to Greatness: Lincoln in the 1850s* (1962), are essential to an understanding of Lincoln's attempts to give his party a distinct identity after the resolution of the Lecompton crisis. John Brown's violent exploits in Kansas and at Harpers Ferry are thoroughly examined in Oswald G. Villard, *John Brown: A Biography Fifty Years After* (1910), and Stephen B. Oates, *To Purge This Land with Blood: A Biography of John Brown* (1970). Oates offers a nicely balanced assessment of Brown's alleged insanity, the subject also of a Freudian analysis by James W. Davidson and Mark H. Lytle, "The Madness of John Brown," in their *After the Fact: The Art of Historical Detection,* rev. ed., 2 vols. (1986). Brown and the meaning of the Harpers Ferry raid are also the topics of trenchant essays by C. Vann Woodward, "John Brown's Private War," in his *The Burden of Southern History* (1960), and Bertram Wyatt-Brown, "John Brown's Antinomian War," in his *Yankee Saints and Southern Sinners* (1985). Benjamin Quarles depicts Brown's relationship with Afro-Americans in *Allies for Freedom: Blacks and John Brown* (1974). Louis Ruchames, ed., *John Brown: The Making of a Revolutionary* (1969), and Richard Scheidenhelm, ed., *The Response to John Brown* (1972), provide collections of documents helpful in understanding Brown's mind and the public's reaction to his bloody deeds.

A modern, comprehensive, book-length treatment of the secession movement is much needed. The last such study was Dwight L. Dumond, *The Secession Movement, 1860–1861* (1931). An interesting short analysis which stresses the South's conviction that slavery had to expand to survive is William L. Barney, *The Road to Secession: A New Perspective on the Old South* (1972). At present, the course of secession may best be understood by consulting biographies of prominent fire-eaters (see especially the lives of Hammond, Quitman, Rhett, Ruffin, and Wise listed previously) and histories of disunionism in individual states. Among the best state studies are Steven A. Channing, *Crisis of Fear: Secession in South Carolina* (1970); William L. Barney, *The Secession Impulse: Alabama and Mississippi in 1860* (1974); J. Mills Thornton, *Power and Politics in a Slave Society: Alabama, 1800–1860* (1978); Michael P. Johnson, *Toward a Patriarchal Republic: The Secession of Georgia* (1977); and Walter L. Buenger, *Secession and Union in Texas* (1984). William J. Evitts, *A Matter of Allegiances: Maryland from 1850 to 1861* (1974), accounts for the decision of one border slave state not to secede. Ralph A. Wooster, *The Secession Conventions of the South* (1962), examines the political, social, and economic characteristics of secession delegates. Seymour M. Lipset, "The Emergence of the One-Party South—The Election of 1860," in Lipset, *Political Man: The Social Basis of Politics* (1960), and Peyton McCrary, Clark Miller, and Dale Baum, "Class and Party in the Secession Crisis: Voting Behavior in the Deep South," *Journal of Interdisciplinary History* 8 (1978): 429-57, analyze the elections that chose these delegates. Bertram Wyatt-Brown's essay "Honor and Secession" in his *Yankee Saints and Southern Sinners* (1985) argues persuasively that a deeply rooted sense of honor shaped the South's response to the crisis of the 1850s. A sophisticated evaluation of the economic motives of Southern disunionists may be found in Gavin Wright, *The Political Economy of the Cotton South* (1978), especially chapter 5, "On Making Sense of Cotton, Slavery, and the Civil War."

David M. Potter, *Lincoln and His Party in the Secession Crisis* (1942), and Kenneth M. Stampp, *And the War Came: The North and the Secession Crisis, 1860-1861* (1950), are both distinguished studies of the Northern response to disunion. Robert G. Gunderson, *Old Gentlemen's Convention: The Washington Peace Conference of 1861* (1961), and Jesse L. Keene, *The Peace Convention of 1861* (1961), chronicle the failure of compromise efforts, and Richard N. Current, *Lincoln and the First Shot* (1963), traces the steps leading to Fort Sumter.

CHAPTER 5

Initial reactions to the onset of war may be found in Henry Steele Commager, ed., *The Blue and the Gray: The Story of the Civil War as Told by Participants,* 2 vols. (1950); George W. Smith and Charles Judah, eds., *Life in the North During the Civil War* (1966); and William H. Russell, *My Diary North and South,* Fletcher Pratt, ed. (1954). Joel Silbey, *A Respectable Minority: The Democratic Party in the Civil War Era, 1860-1868* (1977), depicts the qualified support Northern Democrats gave to the war effort; Damon Wells, *Stephen Douglas: The Last Years, 1857-1861* (1971), gives an accurate portrayal of Douglas's "Union-saving" labors after the shots on Fort Sumter. The hopes and fears of Northern thinkers are described perceptively in George Fredrickson, *The Inner Civil War: Northern Intellectuals and the Crisis of the Union* (1965). The South's early enthusiasm for the war, and its subsequent disillusionment, is nicely captured in Bell I. Wiley, *The Road to Appomattox* (1956). See also

E. Merton Coulter, *The Confederate States of America, 1861–1865* (1950), and Allan Nevins, *The Improvised War, 1861–1862,* vol. 5 of *Ordeal of the Union* (1959).

The standard monographs on conscription are Albert B. Moore, *Conscription and Conflict in the Confederacy* (1924), and Eugene C. Murdock, *Patriotism Limited: The Civil War Draft and Bounty System* (1967) and *One Million Men: The Civil War Draft in the North* (1971). The social and political divisiveness of the Confederate draft laws is thoughtfully discussed in Paul Escott, *After Secession: Jefferson Davis and the Failure of Confederate Nationalism* (1978).

The following works contribute significantly to an understanding of Union and Confederate grand strategy: Russell F. Weigley, *The American Way of War: A History of United States Military Strategy and Policy* (1973); Richard E. Beringer et al., *Why the South Lost the Civil War* (1986); Grady McWhiney, "Who Whipped Whom?" in McWhiney, *Southerners and Other Americans* (1973); James M. McPherson, "Lincoln and the Strategy of Unconditional Surrender," Fortenbaugh Memorial Lecture, Gettysburg College, 1974; Herman Hattaway and Archer Jones, "Lincoln as Military Strategist," *Civil War History* 26 (1980): 293–303; and especially Hattaway and Jones's learned and stimulating *How the North Won: A Military History of the Civil War* (1983).

David P. Crook presents an excellent overview of Civil War diplomacy in *The North, the South, and the Powers, 1861–1865* (1974), and, more succinctly, in *Diplomacy During the Civil War* (1975). Still valuable are earlier studies by Ephraim D. Adams, *Great Britain and the American Civil War,* 2 vols. (1925), and Donaldson Jordan and Edwin J. Pratt, *Europe and the American Civil War* (1931). Frank L. Owsley, *King Cotton Diplomacy: Foreign Relations of the Confederate States of America,* 2d ed. (1959), remains the fullest account of the South's bid for European assistance. Frank J. Merli, *Great Britain and the Confederate Navy* (1970), details the purchase of Rebel vessels abroad. French sympathy for the Confederacy is thoroughly explained in Lynn M. Case and Warren F. Spencer, *The United States and France: Civil War Diplomacy* (1970). Norman Ferris offers a balanced discussion of the North's first diplomatic maneuvers in *Desperate Diplomacy: William H. Seward's Foreign Policy, 1861* (1976) and *The Trent Affair: A Diplomatic Crisis* (1977). Jay Monaghan, *Diplomat in Carpet Slippers: Abraham Lincoln Deals with Foreign Affairs* (1945), somewhat inflates President Lincoln's role in shaping the Union's foreign policy; the biographies of Charles Francis Adams, William H. Seward, and Charles Sumner (cited earlier), as well as James G. Randall and Richard N. Current, *Lincoln the President,* 4 vols. (1945–55), provide helpful correctives. Norman Graebner furnishes a shrewd analysis of "Northern Diplomacy and European Neutrality" in David Donald, ed., *Why the North Won the Civil War* (1960).

CHAPTER 6

We greatly need a detailed modern study of life in the North during the Civil War. Pending its appearance, students seeking general accounts of Northern economic, social, and cultural developments should consult Emerson D. Fite, *Social and Industrial Conditions in the North During the Civil War* (1910); Arthur C. Cole, *The Irrepressible Conflict, 1850–1865* (1934); Allan Nevins, *The War for the Union,* vols. 5–8 of *Ordeal of the Union* (1959–1971); George W. Smith and Charles Judah, eds., *Life in the North During the Civil War* (1966); and Maury Klein, "The North at War," in William C. Davis, ed. *Shadows of the Storm,* vol. 1 of *The Image of War* (1981). Histories of various Northern states during the war years also provide useful information. The best of these is Richard N. Current, *The Civil War Era, 1848–1873,* vol. 2 of *The History of Wisconsin* (1976).

The Civil War's impact on the Northern economy, a subject of lively controversy among historians, is debated by the contributors to Ralph Andreano, ed., *The Economic Impact of the American Civil War,* 2d ed. (1967). See also Stanley Engerman, "The Economic Impact of the Civil War," *Explorations in Economic History* 3 (1966): 176–99, and Frederick Merk's still-useful *Economic History of Wisconsin During the Civil War Decade* (1916). Developments on Northern farms are discussed in Paul W. Gates, *Agriculture and the Civil War* (1965); Richard H. Sewell, "Michigan Farmers and the Civil War," *Michigan History* 44 (1960): 353–74; and Wayne D. Rasmussen, "The Civil War: A Catalyst of Agricultural Revolution," *Agricultural History* 39 (1965): 187–96. Although he is more concerned with politics than economics, David Montgomery, *Beyond Equality: Labor and the Radical Republicans, 1862–1872* (1967), has much to say about the Northern labor movement during the Civil War.

James M. McPherson splices illuminating documents with perceptive commentary about the experiences of Afro-Americans in *The Negro's Civil War: How American Negroes Felt and Acted During the War for the Union* (1967). The third volume of Philip S. Foner, ed., *The Life and Writings of Frederick Douglass,* 4 vols. (1952), shows how the North's preeminent black leader responded to wartime events. The meaning of the war for women is the subject of Mary E. Massey, *Bonnet Brigades* (1966).

Joel Silbey demonstrates the vitality of a loyal opposition in *A Respectable Minority: The Democratic Party in the Civil War Era, 1860–1868* (1977). Northern disloyalty is the subject of several able studies by Frank L. Klement, among them, *The Copperheads in the Middle West* (1960), *The Limits of Dissent: Clement L. Vallandigham & the Civil War* (1970), and *Dark Lanterns: Secret Political Societies, Conspiracies, and Treason Trials in the Civil War* (1984). See also Wood Gray, *The Hidden Civil War: The Story of the Copperheads* (1942). Lincoln's record in dealing with such disloyalty is variously appraised in James G. Randall, *Constitutional Problems Under Lincoln,* rev. ed. (1951); Harold M. Hyman, *Era of the Oath: Northern Loyalty Tests During the Civil War and Reconstruction* (1954); and (most critically) Dean Sprague, *Freedom Under Lincoln* (1965).

Civilian life in the Confederate South is vividly described in Charles W. Ramsdell, *Behind the Lines in the Southern Confederacy* (1944); Bell I. Wiley, *The Plain People of the Confederacy* (1943); and Charles P. Roland, "The

South at War," in William C. Davis, ed., *The Embattled Confederacy,* vol. 3 of *The Image of War* (1982). Paul D. Escott, *After Secession: Jefferson Davis and the Failure of Confederate Nationalism* (1978), thoughtfully assesses the sources of popular disaffection; see, especially, chapter 4, "The Quiet Rebellion of the Common People." Richard E. Beringer et al., *Why the South Lost the Civil War* (1986), exaggerating, I think, the economic, political, and military vitality of the Confederacy after 1863, concludes that it "succumbed to internal rather than external causes," especially guilt over slavery and an underdeveloped sense of Southern nationalism. This argument was first advanced by Kenneth M. Stampp, "The Southern Road to Appomattox," in *The Imperiled Union* (1980).

For Confederate efforts to cope with wartime shortages, see Mary E. Massey, *Ersatz in the Confederacy* (1952). Emory M. Thomas emphasizes the South's transformation "from a state rights confederation into a centralized, national state" in *The Confederacy as a Revolutionary Experience* (1971). The adjustments and sacrifices made by Southern women are outlined in Francis B. Simkins and James W. Patton, *The Women of the Confederacy* (1936); Bell I. Wiley, *Confederate Women* (1975); and Mary Massey, *Bonnet Brigades* (1966). The problems of the Confederate political system are discerningly examined by David Potter, "Jefferson Davis and the Political Factors in Confederate Defeat," in David Donald, ed., *Why the North Won the Civil War* (1960), and Eric L. McKitrick, "Party Politics and the Union and Confederate War Efforts," in William N. Chambers and Walter D. Burnham, eds., *The American Party Systems* (1967). The thesis that the Confederacy "died of state rights," argued most forcefully in Frank L. Owsley, *State Rights in the Confederacy* (1925), is turned on its head in Richard Beringer et al., *Why the South Lost the Civil War* (1986). See especially Appendix 1, "The Politics of Local Defense: Owsley's State-Rights Thesis."

James L. Roark, *Masters Without Slaves: Southern Planters in the Civil War and Reconstruction* (1977), offers ample evidence that the planters' paramount concern for plantation slavery at times impeded the struggle for independence, a position corroborated by Stanley Lebergott, "Why the South Lost: Commercial Purpose in the Confederacy, 1861–1865," *Journal of American History* 70 (1983): 58–74. The wartime experience of Southern slaves may be gleaned from Bell I. Wiley's dated but still useful *Southern Negroes, 1861–1865* (1938); Leon F. Litwack, *Been in the Storm So Long: The Aftermath of Slavery* (1979); and Ira Berlin et al., eds., *Freedom: A Documentary History of Emancipation,* 5 series projected (1982–). For the controversy over black soldiers, see Robert F. Durden, *The Gray and the Black: The Confederate Debate on Emancipation* (1972).

Georgia Lee Tatum, *Disloyalty in the Confederacy* (1934), remains the basic work on that subject. A fascinating case study of loyalty and treason in Appalachian North Carolina is Phillip S. Paludan, *Victims: A True Story of the Civil War* (1981). Ella Lonn, *Desertion During the Civil War* (1928), is also worthwhile.

CHAPTER 7

There are any number of absorbing, well-written narratives of the battles and campaigns of the Civil War. Among the liveliest and best informed are the many books of Bruce Catton, notably *The Centennial History of the Civil War,* 3 vols. (1961–65), and his marvelous trilogy on the Army of the Potomac, *Mr. Lincoln's Army* (1951), *Glory Road* (1952), and *A Stillness at Appomattox* (1953). Equally colorful and well grounded is Shelby Foote, *The Civil War: A Narrative,* 3 vols. (1958–74), a work distinguished by its Southern perspective and balanced treatment of both the Eastern and Western theaters. A superb single-volume military history is Herman Hattaway and Archer Jones, *How the North Won* (1983). Narrower, more technical, but still immensely useful is Matthew F. Steele, *American Campaigns* (1951). T. Harry Williams, *The History of American Wars from 1745 to 1918* (1981), and Allan R. Millet and Peter Maslowski, *For the Common Defense: A Military History of the United States of America* (1984), not only provide instructive chapters on the Civil War but help to place it in a broader context.

Russell F. Weigley, *The American Way of War* (1973), contains masterful chapters on both Union and Confederate strategy. Other noteworthy strategic and tactical studies include Frank E. Vandiver, *Rebel Brass* (1956); Archer Jones, *Confederate Strategy from Shiloh to Vicksburg* (1961); Thomas L. Connelly and Archer Jones, *The Politics of Command: Factions and Ideas in Confederate Strategy* (1973); Michael C. C. Adams, *Our Masters the Rebels: A Speculation on Union Military Failure in the East, 1861–1865* (1978); and Grady McWhiney and Perry D. Jamieson, *Attack and Die: Civil War Military Tactics and the Southern Heritage* (1982). J. F. C. Fuller, a British historian, scrutinizes the top Union and Confederate commanders in *Grant & Lee: A Study in Personality and Generalship* (1957) and finds Grant the more adept at modern warfare.

Abraham Lincoln's quest for capable army commanders is well treated in Kenneth P. Williams, *Lincoln Finds a General: A Military Study of the Civil War,* 5 vols. (1949–59), and T. Harry Williams, *Lincoln and His Generals* (1952). The best account of Grant is the trilogy begun by Lloyd Lewis in *Captain Sam Grant* (1950) and completed by Bruce Catton in *Grant Moves South* (1960) and *Grant Takes Command* (1969). William S. McFeely's prize-winning *Grant: A Biography* (1981) gives short shrift to Grant's military exploits. There is no fully satisfactory biography of the brilliant and complicated William T. Sherman, but Lloyd Lewis, *Sherman: Fighting Prophet* (1932), paints a flattering portrait, whereas John B. Walters, *Merchant of Terror: General Sherman and Total War* (1973), offers a decidedly hostile appraisal. Perceptive sketches of both Grant and Sherman may be found in Edmund Wilson, *Patriotic Gore: Studies in the Literature of the American Civil War* (1962). Other worthwhile biographies of Federal commanders are Stephen E. Ambrose, *Halleck: Lincoln's Chief of Staff* (1962); Warren W. Hassler, *George B. McClellan: The Man Who Saved the Union* (1957); Freeman Cleaves, *Rock of Chickamauga: The Life of*

General George H. Thomas (1948) and *Meade of Gettysburg* (1960); Richard O'Connor, *Sheridan the Inevitable* (1953); and William M. Lamers, *The Edge of Glory: A Biography of William S. Rosecrans, U.S.A.* (1961).

A grand, absorbing, and sympathetic life of the greatest Confederate general is Douglas S. Freeman, *R. E. Lee: A Biography,* 4 vols. (1934–35). For a more critical assessment of Lee and the legend that grew up around him, see Thomas L. Connelly, *The Marble Man: Robert E. Lee and His Image in American Society* (1977). Douglas S. Freeman, *Lee's Lieutenants: A Study in Command,* 3 vols. (1943–44), follows the actions of those who fought under Lee. See also Frank E. Vandiver, *Mighty Stonewall* (1957); Donald B. Sanger and Thomas R. Hay, *James Longstreet* (1952); T. Harry Williams, *P. G. T. Beauregard: Napoleon in Gray* (1954); Grady McWhiney, *Braxton Bragg and Confederate Defeat* (1969); Gilbert E. Govan and James W. Livingood, *A Different Valor: The Story of General Joseph E. Johnston, C.S.A.* (1956); Charles P. Roland, *Albert Sidney Johnston, Soldier of Three Republics* (1964); Emory M. Thomas, *Bold Dragoon: The Life of J. E. B. Stuart* (1986); and James I. Robertson, Jr., *General A. P. Hill: The Story of a Confederate Warrior* (1987).

Firsthand accounts of the war are available in a raft of published soldiers' diaries and journals and in the memoirs of prominent fighting men. By far the best of the latter are Ulysses S. Grant, *Personal Memoirs of U. S. Grant,* 2 vols. (1885), and William T. Sherman, *Memoirs of Gen. W. T. Sherman,* 4th ed., 2 vols. (1892). Also revealing are George B. McClellan, *McClellan's Own Story* (1887); Philip H. Sheridan, *Personal Memoirs of P. H. Sheridan,* 2 vols. (1888); and Robert E. Lee, Jr., ed., *Recollections and Letters of General Robert E. Lee* (1904). Robert U. Johnson and Clarence C. Buell, eds., *Battles and Leaders of the Civil War,* 4 vols. (1887–88), contains essays on military engagements by Union and Confederate officers who fought in them. Those interested in wartime documents should consult the *Official Records of the Union and Confederate Navies in the War of the Rebellion,* 30 vols. (1894–1922), and *War of the Rebellion: Compilation of the Official Records of the Union and Confederate Armies,* 128 vols. (1880–1901). For casualty figures, see Thomas L. Livermore, *Numbers and Losses in the Civil War in America,* 2d ed. (1901).

Bell I. Wiley's *The Life of Johnny Reb: The Common Soldier of the Confederacy* (1943) and *The Life of Billy Yank: The Common Soldier of the Union* (1952) colorfully describe the experiences of those in the ranks. Because Wiley pays greatest attention to Eastern armies, these volumes should be supplemented with Joseph T. Glatthaar, *The March to the Sea and Beyond: Sherman's Troops in the Savannah and Carolina Campaigns* (1985). See also Bell I. Wiley, *They Who Fought Here* (1959); Richard Wheeler, ed., *Voices of the Civil War* (1976); and Henry Steele Commager, ed., *The Blue and the Gray* (1950). The circumstances of war are also graphically revealed in William C. Davis, ed., *The Image of War,* 6 vols. (1981–1984), a magnificent compilation of more than 4,000 Civil War photographs.

CHAPTER 8

Abolitionist pressure for emancipation is detailed in James M. McPherson, *The Struggle for Equality: Abolitionists and the Negro in the Civil War and Reconstruction* (1964). For growing receptivity to such pressure in Congress, see Hans L. Trefousse, *The Radical Republicans: Lincoln's Vanguard for Racial Justice* (1968); Allan G. Bogue, *The Earnest Men: Republicans of the Civil War Senate* (1981); Herman Belz, *A New Birth of Freedom: The Republican Party and Freedmen's Rights, 1861 to 1866* (1976) and *Emancipation and Equal Rights: Politics and Constitutionalism in the Civil War Era* (1978); Louis S. Gerteis, "Salmon P. Chase, Radicalism, and the Politics of Emancipation," *Journal of American History* 60 (1973): 42–62; and biographies of Republican congressmen, cited earlier.

Two excellent articles on Abraham Lincoln's racial attitudes are Don E. Fehrenbacher, "Only His Stepchildren: Lincoln and the Negro," *Civil War History* 20 (1974): 293–310, and George M. Fredrickson, "A Man but Not a Brother: Abraham Lincoln and Racial Equality," *Journal of Southern History* 41 (1975): 39–58. Lincoln's rapidly developing emancipation program receives favorable treatment in Benjamin Quarles, *Lincoln and the Negro* (1962), and LaWanda Cox, *Lincoln and Black Freedom: A Study in Presidential Leadership* (1981). John Hope Franklin, *The Emancipation Proclamation* (1963), offers a short scholarly history of that document. Contemporary responses to it are examined in Mark Neely, "The Emancipation Proclamation as an Act of Foreign Policy: A Myth Dispelled," *Lincoln Lore,* No. 1759, September 1984; V. Jacque Voegeli, *Free but Not Equal: The Midwest and the Negro During the Civil War* (1967); Forrest G. Wood, *Black Scare: The Racist Response to Emancipation and Reconstruction* (1968); and Joel Silbey, *A Respectable Minority* (1977). Thomas Wentworth Higginson's account of the celebration at Beaufort, South Carolina, is in *Army Life in a Black Regiment,* Howard N. Meyer, ed. (1962). The slaves' own contributions to emancipation are richly revealed in Ira Berlin et al., eds., *The Destruction of Slavery,* series 1, vol. 1 of *Freedom: a Documentary History of Emancipation,* (1985).

For the North's recruitment of black soldiers and their experience in the Civil War, see Dudley T. Cornish, *The Sable Arm: Negro Troops in the Union Army, 1861–1865* (1966); James M. McPherson, *The Negro's Civil War* (1967); Leon Litwack, *Been in the Storm So Long* (1979); and especially Ira Berlin et al., eds., *The Black Military Experience,* series 2 of *Freedom: A Documentary History of Emancipation, 1861–1867* (1982). Wartime experiments in free black labor are critically examined in Willie Lee Rose, *Rehearsal for Reconstruction: The Port Royal Experiment* (1964); Louis S. Gerteis, *From Contraband to Freedman: Federal Policy Toward Southern Blacks, 1861–1865* (1973); William F. Messner, *Freedmen and the Ideology of Free Labor: Louisiana, 1862–1865* (1978); and Janet S. Hermann, *The Pursuit of a Dream* (1981). James G. Randall and Richard N. Current discuss the genesis of the Thirteenth Amendment in *Lincoln the President: The Last Full Measure* (1955).

CHAPTER 9

Herman Belz, *Reconstructing the Union: Theory and Policy During the Civil War* (1969), is an admirable, comprehensive account of wartime Reconstruction. See also William B. Hesseltine, *Lincoln's Plan of Reconstruction* (1960), which argues that Reconstruction was the "basic issue of the Civil War." LaWanda Cox, *Lincoln and Black Freedom* (1981), is a splendid study that uses Louisiana as a case study of Lincoln's Reconstruction policy. Peyton McCrary comes to somewhat different conclusions in *Abraham Lincoln and Reconstruction: The Louisiana Experiment* (1978). James Roark illuminates the effect of wartime experiences upon Southern race relations in *Masters Without Slaves* (1977). Also insightful, though sometimes wrong-headed, is W. J. Cash's classic, *The Mind of the South* (1941).

Index

Abolitionists: censure Kossuth, 37;
criticize Lincoln's Reconstruction
policies, 188; and land reform,
182–84; praise John Brown, 70; tactics
and strategy of, 17–20; and wartime
emancipation, 164–65
Adams, Charles F., 29, 52, 96
Adams, Henry, 99
Adams, John Quincy, 20–21
Agriculture: before the Civil War, 5–7;
in Confederacy, 115–16; of North
during the Civil War, 98, 105–6
Aiken, William, 50
Alcorn, James L., 120
American Anti-Slavery Society, 19–20
American Colonization Society, 18–19.
See also Colonization
"Anaconda Plan," 93
Anderson, Robert, 83, 159
Antietam, battle of, 97, 141–42, 168
Antislavery movement, 17–21, 85
Appomattox Court House, Lee's
surrender at, 159
Armour, Philip D., 104
Army, Confederate: battles and cam-
paigns of, 131–59; casualties of, 127;
departmental command system of,
128, 131; recruitment of, 86–88;
strategy of, 90–93, 128, 131, 138, 146,
148; weapons of, 90–91, 126–27
Army, United States: battles and campaigns of, 131–59; black soldiers in,
164, 173–80; casualties of, 92–93, 127;
before Civil War, 3; Civil War
strategy of, 93–94, 133–34, 139–40,
142–43, 146, 148–49; command system
of, 128; and freedmen, 181; wartime

recruitment of, 84, 133; weapons of,
90–91, 126–27
Ashe, William S., 118
Atchison, David R., 42, 44, 62
Atlanta campaign, 157–58

Baker, Edward, 162
Ball's Bluff, battle of, 87, 135, 162
Bancroft, George, 63
Banks, Nathaniel P., 136; captures Port
Hudson, 153; elected Speaker, 50; and
Reconstruction in Louisiana, 188; and
Red River campaign, 156, 179
Barksdale, William, 67
Barton, Clara, 110
Beauregard, Pierre G. T., 120, 148;
claims victory at Shiloh, 150; exploits
geographical knowledge, 91–92; at
first battle of Bull Run, 131–32;
strategic ideas of, 128
Beecher, Charles, 38
Beecher, Henry Ward, 159, 183
Bell, John, 33, 36, 45, 75–76
Benezet, Anthony, 17
Benjamin, Judah P., 99
Benton, Thomas H., 42; and Com-
promise of 1850, 32, 34; and 1856
election, 52, 54; on slavery in the
territories, 26; spurns Southern
Address, 31
Bentonville, battle of, 159
Bingham, Kinsley S., 49
Binney, Horace, 84
Birney, James G., 19
Blacks: changing attitude of Southern
whites toward, 194–95; in Con-
federacy, 120–22, 194; as "con-

44–48; and nativism, 41; and slavery in the territories, 26–27, 32–33; and Southern Address, 31
Whiting, William, 184
Whitney, Eli, 6
Whittier, John G., 76, 85
Wick, William, 26
Wigfall, Louis T., 120
Wilderness, battle of, 126–27, 156
Wilkes, Charles, 96–97
Wilmot, David: joins Republican party, 48–49; and Republican convention of 1856, 52; and slavery in the territories, 24–26
Wilmot Proviso, 24–26, 31

Wilson, Henry, 65–66
Wilson's Creek, battle of, 87
Winder, John H., 117
Winthrop, Robert C., 27, 33
Wise, Henry, 53, 71, 92
Women: during the Civil War, 107, 109–10, 115, 123; at mid-century, 10–11
Wood, Fernando, 85, 112
Woolman, John, 17

Yancey, William L., 29, 71, 74, 78
Yates, Richard, 150
Yorktown, siege of, 137